FOREWORD BY BILL JOHNS

Renaissance Kids

OLIVIA SHUPE

© copyright 2013 Renaissance Kids by Olivia Shupe First Edition
www.RaisingTomorrowsLeaders.net

Cover & Interior Design and Formatting : Lorraine Box PropheticArt@sbcglobal.net
Editing : Julie Mustard, Lorraine Box, Brigit Ritchie, Charis Scofield

ISBN: 13:978-1481021135
ISBN: 10:1481021133

Acknowledgements

Without the combined contribution and encouragement of friends, family and mentors this book never would have been possible. I want to express my deepest gratitude and appreciation to each of you!

My Heavenly Father, thank you for working all things together for good in my life. Thank you for sending me encouragement at just the right time and making sure I didn't give up or give in. Thank you for your Presence and for teaching me, loving me, and blessing me with such a special family and so many wonderful friends. I love you, God.

My husband, Jeff, thank you for believing in me more than I have believed in myself. Thank you for exhorting me to risk, stretch, and follow all the nudgings of the Holy Spirit. Your wisdom, sacrificial lifestyle, and dedication to our family are what make our family what it is.

My four children, Anna, Wesley, Christian, and Joshua, thank you for being the best kids any mom could wish for. I've observed your vision, passion for life, and love for others firsthand. I've watched your struggles to overcome and your joy in discovering your gifts and talents. I've seen you seek the Lord and then share Him with your friends. Thanks for being patient and eating lots of fast food as I finished this book! I'm thankful beyond words to have such special children.

Diane Peterson, who when I called you from an infra-red sauna (no use wasting time right?) and asked what you thought of me writing a book replied, "Yes, I love it—I think you should do it! " You have the gift of encouragement! I appreciate all your prayer and support!

Dr. John and Leeba Curlin, you are my second family. It was watching your home life over the years that planted this vision in my heart. Many of the principles and themes herein reveal the fingerprints of your influence. Dr. Curlin, thank you for treating me like a daughter. For spending hours on the phone praying, listening, mentoring me, and even reading a book I inquired about *just* to give me your thoughts. Your understanding of neuroscience, inner healing, and what-really-works in parenting provided great insight and direction for much of this material. Leeba, thank you for reading my chapters before they were completed, and imparting positive feedback and encouragement. Your parenting wisdom was also incredibly valuable! When I think of what it means to be a Godly mom and wife, I think of you. Thank you both for your prayers and dedication. Thank you for serving so many in the Kingdom.

Dad and Mom, thanks Dad for listening to me and believing in me. Mom, thanks for encouraging me to seek God in His fullness and for getting excited about "every chapter." I'm so grateful that you've always inspired me to go for my dreams.

Caryn Southerland, thanks for being the most encouraging and loyal friend anyone could wish for. Everyone who has a friend like you is rich indeed. Thanks for your ideas and encouragement throughout this writing journey.

Brigit Ritchie, thanks for reading and editing many of my chapters. Thanks for offering your perceptive insights and consistent encouragement. Your sharp mind and intuitive wisdom provided me with ample ideas to improve and clarify the manuscript.

Robert Sutherland, thanks for exhorting me to finish this project even when you read it in raw form. Your writing and editorial expertise helped me envision with more clarity what I needed to. You helped me understand the *value* in this project. Thanks for spending time coaching me in organizing my writing as well as exhorting me toward excellence and integrity.

Charis Scofield, thanks for taking time out of your busy family life to work on editing. Thanks for providing feedback regarding content as well as details. Your contribution was so helpful!

Lorraine Box, I'm thankful for your extraordinary gift of empowering and casting vision. You helped me *see* the possibilities as well. You have provided both emotional support and practical help. Your ideas were just what I needed to push forward. Thanks for having "big belief" in this project and me! And thanks for creating all the beautiful graphics and design for the book! I love them!

Wendy Tang, thanks for being an incredible friend and partner in ministry. You are a woman of rare quality and depth. You've stood by me, spurred me on, and sacrificially served with me for years. Thanks for editing and giving me your sage advice. Thanks for pouring into so many moms through teaching, example, and always taking time for the one.

Karen Johnson, thanks for being one of the first moms to review my chapters. You always shared how much they impacted your life and it made me want to finish! Thanks!

Larry and Laura Randolph, thanks for being such awesome friends! Larry, thanks for teaching on the "Renaissance Era" and how it prophetically parallels our times. God used your message to inspire me with the title of this book! You truly are a "quintessential Renaissance Man!" Laura, you are a precious and treasured friend! Thanks for reflecting God's love and wisdom to so many in your sphere of influence.

My favorite pastor, Bill Johnson, thanks for leading the way in book-writing at Bethel!! Thanks for encouraging and believing in me and *so* many others. Without seeing even one chapter, you shared you felt that God had great plans for this project. Having "faith" in what God is doing in and through people is what you *do* for many in the Kingdom. I'm so thankful for you!

Kim Shaw, thanks for helping and encouraging me. Thanks so much for teaching "writing" to children each week at my home. You have a gift for bringing out the writer in everyone!

Julie Mustard, thanks for being a top-rate editor. You have a true gift for seeing the overall picture and also attending to details. You have been wonderful to work with!

To all the dedicated moms who have faithfully attended the "Raising Tomorrow's Leaders" class—You are such an inspiration to me. I am grateful for all the encouraging emails and prayers. Thanks for sharing your testimonies of breakthrough as well as your trials and challenges. Thanks for continually asking, "When's the book coming out?" You guys are amazing!

Endorsements

Quoting the author, "Children change and grow when parents change and grow" is a perfect theme for this book! This creative, encouraging, and inspirational book explores the awesome things God has planned for your family! *Renaissance Kids* is a great reminder that we should surround ourselves with other parents, other spiritual encouragers. Don't do it alone! Use this tool that can lead your children through the trials of today and keep them emotionally and spiritually healthy! If you want to save your family or just bring them closer together, take the time to read this book!"

Joe White
President, Kanakuk Kamps
Author of sixteen parenting books

Renaissance Kids gives rare insights for parenting that bleed through all the pages of this book. Skillfully written! Greatly inspiring, and packed with Godly principles that can shape the character and destiny of an emerging generation. Laura and I LOVE THIS BOOK! Olivia's dedication to pursue God's ways in relating to life and family has always captured our hearts! This book clearly portrays a wealth of experience and the (challenging yet rewarding) years of raising children who possess a sense of their individual purpose in life.

Larry Randolph
Conference Speaker
Author *User Friendly Prophecy*, and *Original Breath*

Olivia Shupe's book, *Renaissance Kids*, is a treasure map that illuminates the way to raise the next generation. The truths revealed in this book will bring hope and direction to parents who are trying to navigate the often challenging and sometimes frustrating waters of parenting. If you long to impart to your children a love for learning and a passion for God, this book is for you! I highly recommend it.

Kris Vallotton
Senior Associate Leader, Bethel Church, Redding, California
Co-Founder, Bethel School of Supernatural Ministry
Author of nine books, including *The Supernatural Ways of Royalty* and *Spirit Wars*

I feel honored by Olivia's acknowledgment of our longstanding friendship since she was a teenager. I greatly enjoyed our conversations regarding many of the subjects included in *Renaissance Kids*, but I did not realize until I read her book that it would address the multiple areas of understanding required for today's serious, proactive, and Godly parent. In my medical training I was taught to learn the fundamentals, which would enable you to adjust to future changes. For this reason I recommend this book as a source of parenting fundamentals that will equip you for present and future parenting challenges!

Dr. John Curlin MD ACOG
Host of American Family Radio

Renaissance Kids offers real wisdom and insights for the parenting journey. It's not a book about theories! I've watched first hand how Olivia (and husband, Jeff) raised their children. The one thing that strikes me about Olivia's parenting concepts is that she is very Intentional about her role as a parent. She really listens to God about what He says about her children.

As a business consultant who specializes in helping senior executives achieve their goals, while maintaining their integrity, I have found a fundamental similarity in our approaches. I treat every executive as a unique person with a unique God-given purpose and destiny. I use no "cookie cutter" tools. Olivia advocates the same approach in raising children. Each one is unique and requires a "customized" intentional plan for them to be all that God desires. I believe Olivia, in this book, has captured the essence of how God wants us to fulfill our role as the developer of His kids!

Mike Frank
President, Frank Consulting, CEO, TheOnRamp
Author, *Prosperity with Purpose: An Executive's Search for Significance*

As parents we want a step-by-step road map to direct us through the chaos of current issues in parenting. Instead Olivia gives us a compass for the wild expedition! Each chapter is a springboard for thought and discussion to explore the pathways and possibilities. The chapters altogether aim true north! *Renaissance Kids* is a passionate challenge wrapped in hope and comfort!

Anne Stock
Charles & Anne Stock, Senior Pastors
Life Center, Harrisburg, Pennsyvania

Contents

How to Get the Most out of this Book

First, for anyone who can, I would encourage you to not only read this material, but also to work through it in a small group. We gain the deepest understanding from new information by engaging in dialogue and then taking time to work through what we are personally learning. Answering questions at the end of each chapter and/or discussing them in small groups is a great place to start. The journey of parenting was never meant to be travelled alone.

A Few Small Groups Tips

- If you plan to lead or be a part of a small group, it would be beneficial to spend time implementing the *Sharing Spiritual Journeys* component. Please see the end of this book for more information about *Sharing Spiritual Journeys* and Small Group dynamics.

- Schedule a weekly or bi-monthly time to meet in your small groups.

- Visit my website www.RaisingTomorrowsLeaders.net for additional articles as well as recommended DVDs to read or watch as a group. In the future the website will have more materials available for small group leaders.

- At the end of this book you will find a listing of resources and appendices with additional information.

Foreword

*R*enaissance Kids is filled with uncommon brilliance, and it couldn't come at a better time. To say the family is under attack is a great understatement. Yet if you're looking for a book to help your family survive in perilous times, you may be disappointed. This book does not carry one ounce of survival mentality. It's not that you won't receive that kind of help; it's just that this book aims much higher. *Renaissance Kids* is about raising up a transformational generation by equipping parents to tap into the heart of God and release children who become the answer to society's cries for help. This truly is about raising renaissance kids.

I love Olivia Shupe's approach to the book. She is not preachy, nor is she a know-it-all. Instead, the author presents a journey, one that is both compelling and inviting. She models a lifestyle of excellence and great wisdom, encouraging her children to become all that God meant them to be. This also happens to be what the world around them needs the most. Olivia combines biblical truth and insights from her own journey of parenting four children. Unusually well read, she offers wisdom gleaned from various studies to equip parents to raise powerful, strong children who know and love God, are secure in their identity, and have vision and the tools needed to change the world. Reading this book will inspire you and give you a fresh vision for who your children can become.

Olivia navigates through many tough topics, looking at how to parent in a way that protects children now, yet also sets them up for a future of successfully facing the challenges that the world brings them. Her insight into the way children develop sheds light on what makes different approaches appropriate and effective. I especially love how she cultivates a God-centered family that encourages children to grow their own relationship with God. She gives parents courage to take a stand that is radically different from the secular approach, yet looks at how to navigate this path without swinging to extremes that harm relationships or hurt their children's ability to succeed later in life.

The author shows no timidity in the subjects she covers, which makes this book extremely contemporary. She tackles issues like education, social media, and television without compromise, yet with grace and much wisdom she shows the effects of these areas on children. In *Renaissance Kids*, the reader is equipped to raise up children to be radical lovers of God and bring the Kingdom to the world in which we live. Parents are trained not to react in fear, but to respond to God's purposes. The key to it all is that the Holy Spirit is present to help at every step.

Godly parenting is not just about the children, but also about the life parents live. This book shows how this simple concept affects children and addresses the importance of cultivating a life of good example for your children.

Ultimately, the book goes beyond basic child development, into the realm of raising children to be powerful leaders. It is also a fantastic tool to see families brought together, equipped, and set up to change the world around them today, in the next generation, and in many generations to come.

Bill Johnson
Senior Leader, Bethel Church, Redding, California
Author, *When Heaven Invades Earth* and *Hosting the Presence*

Introduction

*Do you want the world to change your children,
or are you willing to do what it takes for your children
to change the world?*

— Julie Ferwerda

It is no doubt that we live in some of the most intense yet exciting times in history. A new generation is coming forth who will lead our nation and the world into the future. You can almost hear the trumpet call summoning the forthcoming Churchills, Wilberforces, Michelangelos, and George Washingtons of our day. Global change, whether for good or evil, is imminent and rapidly surging.

If you are reading this, you already desire to create a successful family. You already aspire to raise a child that will make a difference, a child who might even change the world. In all likelihood, you realize that successful families don't just happen. They are a result of focus, time, good old-fashioned determination, and most of all sacrifice on the part of the parent. As parents, we can't just know what to do; we have to be willing to actually do it.

As certain forces have come into play, the world as we know it, will never be the same. Times are faster, more complicated, and more extreme. Society as a whole no longer undergirds family values which forces parents and children to face obstacles and temptations unheard of in prior generations. To adjust to our rapidly changing world we, as parents, have to be willing to *face* what our children *face*!

I believe parenthood is one of the highest callings in life. If you interview any seasoned adult or grandparent, they will tell you their greatest regret or deepest fulfillment had to do with how they handled the role of "being a parent." There is no pain like the pain of a lost or broken relationship. There is no regret like the regret of misguided energy or lost time. The comforts of financial success, occupational accolades, personal triumphs, or engrossing hobbies hold no significance when they can't be shared with the next generation. No earthly gain is worth losing your children or any part of what they could have become. Many parents would do anything to start over, anything to turn back time.

On the other hand, few things compare to seeing your children grow up to be emotionally healthy and spiritually strong "agents of change" to the world around them. If we succeed at nothing else, our lives will most likely be rich and full. We can learn from those who have gone before us how to capture fully the season of parenting—knowing that the family is the cornerstone of a healthy society. God made family first, next came the church, and then all of our professions and hobbies. A healthy family leads to a healthy church.

It's important to view your children as people, as future leaders, not just kids—children who will be adults in a few short years. You have the opportunity to help shape their character and worldview. The world is in desperate need of more leaders—leaders who are whole. Not every child will become a world-renowned leader or legendary trailblazer, but all kids have the propensity to become a leader to someone. The next generation includes those whom some would consider an *average* kid, the kid who won't necessarily be the next president or Olympic champion but who never-the-less will affect change in his or her personal sphere of influence.

Having said that, I don't believe there are *average* kids. Average by today's standardized testing maybe—but average meaning void of special gifts and talents, I don't think so! I believe all kids have amazing gifting and potential; it just may not be packaged the way we expect. Raising a kid who makes a difference is not about being a perfect parent or having kids with extra-special talents or super high IQ's. Parenting at its core, is all about helping kids *discover* and *become* the people God created them to be.

I believe we are in a season when the Lord is extending the challenge to every parent to raise the bar, dream bigger, and expect more! Don't give into the world's low expectations for your children or the common forecasts likening the teenage years to the "great tribulation." Our end game is not that our kids "make it into heaven"—our end game is that our children fulfill their destiny in God and place in history.

A Little Background

After spending our first years of marriage in youth ministry working with preteens, teens, and parents, my husband and I transitioned into having children of our own. We had our four children very close together, and I remember feeling like we always had "one more than we could handle." Can anyone relate to this feeling? Reminds me of Elizabeth Elliot's grandmother's response regarding her eight children when others asked, *how she did it?* She quickly retorted, "If one can take all your time, then eight can't take much more." Amen to that!

A few short years after our daughter was born, we embarked on a new chapter of our lives as missionaries in Romania. While we lived in Romania, we took in several orphans alongside our biological and adopted children. For several years, we had seven to eight children under our roof. My wings seemed like they were clipped a little more with each additional child. Sometimes it felt like the walls were closing in on me and temptation to join the feminist movement or maybe even run away had occasional appeal.

Thanks to the healing of Jesus, the power of the Holy Spirit, and the influence of Godly mentors, I have increasingly learned to genuinely enjoy my children and my role as a parent. Each of us has to overcome the unhealed places in our soul, society's pressure to strive and perform outside our home, and the ultra feminist propaganda that says, "So, what do you do?"

So Why Another Parenting Book?

While debating internally whether to write yet another parenting book, one of the biggest obstacles for me personally was the knowledge that parenting material is glutting our market as never before. The Barna Group reported that more than 75,000 parenting books are presently available for purchase. After spending the last decade reading piles of parenting material myself (some of it good, other material... hmmm maybe it's better not to comment), I have to agree with a recent author who avidly warns new parents, "Don't trust the experts. Especially parenting experts!" Reading all the conflicting and contrasting advice and opinions can leave a parent... well, pretty confused and disillusioned. What experts say one decade, you can be sure they'll be saying the opposite, the next. I couldn't help but laugh at one author and mom who expressed— "Today with all the information out there by parenting experts on how to raise kids, maybe we should just forget about a college fund and invest our money in a *therapy fund* instead."

While probably not the wisest course of action, most parents, *parent* according to the latest cultural trends which sad to say change about as often as—well you know—trends do. So while I'm not a big advocate of following trendy parenting theories devised by Ivy League experts whose own children are no picture of health and stability, I do believe there are universal truths and Biblical principles that can lead to extreme success when applied to family life.

It has been my goal to find those truths and principles, which are proven over time to foster greatness and emotional health in families and individuals and make those available to you the reader. The insights, examples, and principles in this book are a result of dialoguing with and interviewing successful parents and grandparents, uncovering parenting principles mined from parents of Olympians and other historical figures, analyzing biographies for effective family patterns, and conducting research on various topics such as neuroscience, emotional healing, and leadership.

This material is further designed to be an interactive study guide to be worked through alone or even better—in small groups. Many parents struggle to parent successfully due to their personal lack of success or breakthrough. This is one reason *working through* this material is so profitable. The truths presented have the potential to change not only children, but more importantly, their parents. Why is this crucial? Because children change and grow when parents change and grow. It's that simple.

In addition to equipping and encouraging parents, it's my genuine aspiration to bring HOPE to parents regardless of their current situation. There are no "normal or perfect families" out there. I was amused when I recently read, "Normal is a setting on the dryer. Other than that, there isn't any normal!"[1] Every family has issues. Our families are all in different places. A handful of families are already strong but want to get stronger. Some families are looking for help, but only in specific areas. Other families are just hanging in there. So whether you experience a vibrant and healthy home life or are a struggling single parent... whether you are on the brink of divorce or financial disaster... or battling sickness and physical disease, HOPE is what God wants to give you. I love what Stephen Covey (motivational speaker and best-selling author) says about families, "Good families—even great families—are off track 90% of the time!" The point he is trying to make is this—it's not being perfectly on track that produces great families; it's having a sense of destination and aiming for it that matters most. When we put our best energy into the things that matter most in life, our efforts will always bear fruit. When we're trying to live what we believe, struggling and even striving to move in the right direction, our children will usually accept our values and move toward our principles.

This is the perfect spot for a disclaimer. First, I don't consider myself one of those parenting experts. (As I've said, I'm not even sure those exist.) Second, my husband and I are still in the thick of parenting ourselves, so in every way we are all in this together. Our family is not perfect, actually *far* from it. We face the same temptations, challenges, and joys so common to *parenting*. Ultimately, we have the same hope that our children will walk with God and fear that they won't, that all parents share.

I like what Dani Johnson says in her book *Grooming the Next Generation for Success*:

> "Our generation needs to rise up and declare, 'Hands off! Not my seed, and not on my watch! We will raise a remnant that will succeed and change the future.' This great nation, the 'land of the free and the home of the brave' was established by a few, by a remnant, by a seed, and that's what it will take to change the course and direction of the next generation and our nation. If we stand together, this generation's course can be corrected and their destinies fulfilled beyond our wildest imaginations."[2]

If a remnant can start our nation, then certainly a remnant can change it as well.

Consider the power of the remnant as explained by Dani. The difference lies in the distinction between two populations—the 2% and the 98%. Statistics show that the vast majority of the population (98%) reach the end of their lives not having accomplished their life's goals, while 2% do. Why? Because only a small remnant will do what it takes to succeed. In parenting, business, marriage, and sports you can see this phenomenon repeatedly. Only the "2%" are willing to pay the price to achieve something more than status quo, and paying the price is what sets them apart.

If you are prepared to do what it takes to give your child a better chance of succeeding in life, it will be worth the effort. Not only that, but as a believer and follower of Christ, you are called by God to live differently, to live set apart, and to go the extra mile. This often entails living counter-culturally, and as disconcerting as this might feel—consider the alternative. If you do what everyone else does, you'll get the same results that everyone does.

As parents we are commissioned to partner with God in raising up this next generation. This may feel like an impossible task when we consider the issues some of us face.

But without God's intervention and help none of us can truly thrive as a family. We need Him to intervene in our imperfect family dynamics. We all require various levels of breakthrough that can only come when God is part of our equation. Thankfully restoration is God's specialty; taking impossible, messy situations and making something beautiful is where our Father excels most!

What if They Turn Out Bad?

So what if your kids turn out bad? Whose responsibility is the end result? It's really hard for parents to accept or believe this, but our children are ultimately God's responsibility. As a parent we can only do *our best* with our personal capacity and acquired tools, and we will often fall short of what we know our children need. Yes, we will certainly have much greater odds of our children loving God and living a life of greatness if we model this, but in spite of all our efforts and sacrifice, they are individuals who must choose for themselves. Each of us has to decide whether to live a life of rebellion or devotion to God—a life of impact or a life of mediocrity. The power to choose is God's greatest gift to mankind, and He will never take that away. There are no guarantees that our children won't make mistakes, even big ones. Yet, the good news for every praying parent is that the Lord is very skilled at bringing our children back to Him when they veer off course. He is the master of arranging unparalleled situations to turn hearts toward home and toward Him. The Bible provides parents much hope that if we *train* a child in the way he should go, in the end he will walk in those ways (Proverbs 22:6). The ideal place to begin as a parent is with the choice to trust the Lord with our children, which ultimately means putting them in His hands.

The Lord spoke these words to me recently, "When parents don't trust me with their children, they assume that they love their children more than I do." If you think about it, it doesn't even make sense to surmise that we could possibly love our children more than God. He loves our children far more than we can humanly fathom.

God is magnificently and fully working on our behalf and on behalf of our children. All we can do is our best—nothing more—nothing less. There is no such thing as perfect parents—or perfect parenting, only parents who have determined that raising the next generation will hold the same priority as it does in the Father heart of God. As my pastor Bill Johnson likes to quote, "The light that shines the farthest shines the brightest at home." Let your light shine, but let it shine FIRST at home.

Why the Title Renaissance Kids?

The Renaissance Era was an era of tremendous reform, reconstruction, and innovation. It was known for vast learning and far-reaching educational reform. It was an era bursting with creativity and artistic ingenuity.

Communication increased rapidly during this time period. Much like the Internet today, the printing press spread throughout Europe allowing information to be disseminated as never before in history. Information became accessible to everyone. Exploration boomed (Everyone was sending someone somewhere.) and the map of the world neared completion by the end of Renaissance—paralleling the present spread of the gospel that has reached almost every corner of the globe. Advances in science ignited great progress in astronomy, geography, chemistry, physics, mathematics, and engineering much like today as scientific advances are once again attaining unparalleled levels.

The Renaissance period experienced revolutions, as well as social and political upheaval, and yet it was a time of transition for good. It was a time of turmoil and conflict as well as a time of promise and progress. I believe much of what is to come will fall to our children's generation—it will be up to them to reflect God's Kingdom in a world of divergent forces. It will be their mission to reveal His promise and His presence in a rapidly changing world, which will look very different from the one we parents grew up in! As in all of history God will raise up His remnant of "Kids" to accomplish His will upon the earth. We as parents have the awesome privilege of partnering with Him to see His incredible plans and purposes come to pass through the next generation!

Note to the Reader

Please note that I have pulled from many different sources while writing this book. I have used secular sources as well as parenting materials that some may consider controversial. There are a wide range of voices out there regarding parenting philosophies. Because I quote a particular ministry or author doesn't mean I endorse or agree with everything they teach or adhere to. I believe it's helpful to sift through assorted ideas while gleaning the truth that each may carry. No ministry or person has the "corner" on all truth. So please endeavor to keep an open heart and mind as you read through this book—there are lots of wonderful parenting nuggets to come!

Throughout this material I will sometimes refer to the surveys conducted by Barna

Group, which was founded by George Barna, a world-renowned researcher. Barna Group is considered one of the most respected statistics groups of the 21st century. After conducting a series of in-depth surveys as well as thousands of interviews with young adults and their parents, the research was compiled in the book *Revolutionary Parenting*. In this book, children who grew up to be successful, spiritually mature adults are referred to as "spiritual champions." When I reference "spiritual champions" throughout my material, this is the study to which I am referring. For a summary of the main similarities found among successful families please see the appendix in the back—it's worth the read!

ENDNOTES

[1] Julie Hiramine, *Guardians of Purity* (2012, Lake Mary, FL), 99.

[2] Dani Johnson, *Grooming the Next Generation for Success* (2009, Destiny Image), 50.

CHAPTER ONE

Relational Parenting

Relationship Is Everything to a Child

When relationships are good and the boundaries of Godly disciplines are intact, there is no limit to the influence of the Christian home.

— Bill Johnson

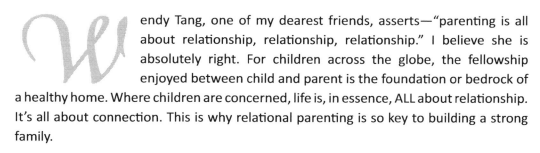 endy Tang, one of my dearest friends, asserts—"parenting is all about relationship, relationship, relationship." I believe she is absolutely right. For children across the globe, the fellowship enjoyed between child and parent is the foundation or bedrock of a healthy home. Where children are concerned, life is, in essence, ALL about relationship. It's all about connection. This is why relational parenting is so key to building a strong family.

Think about it—adults can substitute plenty of outlets when relational connections are weak. A mom can lose herself in friends, TV, shopping, or surfing the Internet; a dad can find identity in work, sports, or hobbies. Relationships are only part of an adult's world, but they are everything to a child! When relationships are weak, turbulent, or absent in the world of children, they often feel emotionally lost and abandoned.

This is why family break-up is so devastating to children. Some of you may remember the blockbuster film about divorce, "Kramer vs. Kramer." Although for many this movie is "before your time." It was the first movie produced that focused on the emotional tragedy of divorce. The entire story line depicted the intense emotional pain and suffering that occurs in families who experience this. More specifically, it zeroed in on the pain a child endured as he watched his family detach and divide. I still distinctly recall seeing that movie as a young girl and thinking there was probably nothing worse in the world than having your family break up. "How do children even survive that?" I painfully wondered as I reflected on the movie. Today, the most popular movies depict drug use, trafficking, and violence which of course are terrible for anyone to be exposed to. My point is that society is so familiar with fractured families, that we've become desensitized to the effect it has on children—we've lost site of how vital strong and unified family relationships are to the emotional needs of children.

While divorce has become common for children to experience (Presently in California between 68-82% of marriages end in divorce.), it's still just as overwhelming to them as when it was less common. Family separation often *seems* easier in the short run, but what many don't realize is that in many cases (not all) it's far more *difficult* and *painful* in the long run to *break up* a relationship than to *heal it*. When kids are involved this becomes even truer. I realize that talking about the tragedy of divorce is walking on sensitive waters, since most of us have experienced its effects in one realm or another. However, I believe as parents we need to recognize and reflect on how it impacts our children. For those of us who have experienced divorce, the last thing I want to do is stir up feelings of condemnation. Sometimes divorce is impossible to avoid, and we need remember that God can restore and heal *any* situation. We can trust Him to revive and reconcile the broken places of our lives, as doing this is one of His great specialties!

Unity Between Dad and Mom

Speaking of relational parenting—when it comes to family turmoil, children can take inconsistent parenting styles much better than "tension and constant conflict" between Dad and Mom. Unity in the marriage is much more key to producing stable kids than consistent standards for every behavior and habit. The greatest thing you can do *for* your children is *love* and *enjoy* your spouse; doing this creates incredible confidence in your children. Children get their sense of security from the way they see their parents treat each other. When kids see Dad and Mom laughing together or enjoying each other's company, they feel safe. They feel secure.

In other words, it's more important to get along than it is to make sure Dad doesn't feed the kids more sugar than Mom would. Presenting a united front really does produce the best results, but parents who are *not* in *strife* are even more important. If Dad and Mom are united and joyful, you can rest assured you are more than halfway to nurturing "happy, secure kids." But if Dad and Mom are in constant tension, you can drive home all the principles and standards you want and still have only minimal influence with your kids. When conflict and strife run high, children's hearing runs low. Positive guidance will only be as productive as the strength of the relationship between Dad and Mom. You can't have a higher quality family life than the state of your marriage. While family is the foundation of society, the *marriage* is the foundation of the family.

When children know they are loved and that their parents love each other—they are resilient and secure. Loved children know who they are. Loved children become secure adults who can later love their children as well!

Attract Your Kids

To be a relational parent, we have to attract our kids. We are, first and foremost, *models* to our children. What our children *see in us* and *feel from us* is what really determines the depth of influence we carry in their lives. The best way to attract our kids is by being both a parent and a friend. Doing things with your children that they enjoy, showing interest in what interests them, listening to their concerns, and respecting their ideas are all ways we attract and build strong bonds with our kids. As parents we start with the advantage that God put inside each of our children the desire to please and win the approval of their parents. But in the long run, they won't emulate someone they don't trust and admire. The trust you want to see when they are older is established when they are young. Children will seek to be like the person who attracts them the most.

If our lives attract our children, we will most likely never have a rebellious child (at least not one who rebels for long). Yet, if we fail to foster bonds of mutual respect and honor, it often bears negative fruit in later years. When our children's primary reason for obedience stems from fear or control, that obedience will last as long as the consequences remain severe enough to deter their rebellion. Obedience gained by fear or control only *seems* to work during formative years. The transition from children who obey out of fear, to those who oppose and rebel against their parents occurs during the preteen and teen years. "If you have lost the child's heart, then the child will have lost the heart to please you. If the child is not in agreement to pull with you, it is vain to try to harness him to your rules. Your influence will not exceed the limits of your fellowship."[1] As a parent, you can't teach or train beyond the strength of your relationship with your child. Being well connected to your kids is the best long-term safeguard against your children making negative choices or falling into destructive behaviors.

Relational Parenting Means Parenting from Love not Fear

During his incredible teaching about love and fear, Mark Hamby relates the following story involving a close family friend. This friend's family loved having guests over to encounter their unique family pet. The scenario always went something like this: visitors would arrive and take a seat in the living room. Within moments the family pet, a skunk, would waddle into the room and sit down in the midst of everyone. The guests would immediately fluster and panic! What if he sprays? Can't skunks blind you with their fumes? We might stink for years—they worried!

The family comforted the guests assuring them that this skunk had lived amid their loving family for years and never, ever sprayed—not even once. The visitors were incredulous. How could this be? After spending a lovely evening with the family, and their novel family pet, the guests were offered the secret to their success. "The reason our pet skunk has never sprayed is because—PERFECT LOVE CASTS OUT ALL FEAR!" (1 John 4:18). And if you have the guts to try out a skunk for a family pet, make sure you've got a lot of love flowing in your home—and please send me your stories... I'd love to hear.

So now that you've heard a real-life story of how much more powerful love is than fear let's take a look at the science that validates this phenomenon. Fascinating new brain science is being discovered about the emotions of love and fear. The science reveals that every type of emotion literally has only two roots—LOVE or FEAR. All other emotions flow from these two primary emotions. Scientists have researched the anatomy and physiology of love and fear right down to a molecular, genetic and epigenetic level. "They have found a deep system in the brain concerned with positive love emotions and negative fear emotions. They have discovered that these two systems cannot coexist, rather at any one conscious moment, we will be operating in one or the other for each cluster of thoughts we think." Not only that, but take a look at what they have discovered about *fear*. "Fear is actually a distorted love circuit. We were created for love and all that goes with it, but we have learned to fear."[2] Thus, every place we have fear, we should have love. God created our emotional circuits to flow with love.

One of the most encouraging findings in neuroscience is the powerful transformation that occurs in the brain when we *choose* to operate in love. As we relate to each other out of love, "the brain releases a chemical called oxytocin, which literally melts away the negative toxic thought clusters so that rewiring of new non-toxic circuits can happen. This chemical also flows when we trust, bond, and reach out to others. Love literally wipes out fear!"[3] Wow! It's actually been scientifically proven that love is more powerful than fear. When we *choose* to love, God in his magnificent wisdom blesses our minds (brains). While fear is powerful, and can have devastating effects on our emotional health, love is much more powerful.

As relationships based on love are the heartbeat of Heaven, relationships fueled by fear are the foremost strategy of the enemy. As much as love casts out fear, fear also casts out love. You can exaggerate the fear or severity of God, but you can never exaggerate the love of God. God's love is the most powerful and motivating force in the universe!

Relational Parenting Means Enjoying Your Kids

What spells love to a child? Joe White, founder of Kanakuk Kamps, sums it up like this, "Children spell love, T-I-M-E, not quantity, not quality, but both." Almost nothing communicates the value you place on your children more than giving them your time. Children especially love one-on-one time with their parents. This is when children will often share the things on their hearts that might not be shared in larger family settings. Children tend to be more vulnerable when not everyone is listening, as well as more willing to receive input. Meaningful one-on-one time often deposits in the emotional bank account of a child in a way that naturally produces long-term trust and security.

Quantity of time is not the only ingredient that makes these connections meaningful. As I've said earlier, children must feel that you *admire* and *enjoy* them. If your children know that you authentically take pleasure in what they like and who they are, they will stop at nothing to please you! Recently, my son Joshua constructed a town out of Legos, with fences, horse stalls, homes, bridges, and all that goes with a "cowboy town." In the midst of his construction, I was endeavoring to finish a chapter in this book, but I stopped to interact over the different parts of his Western wonder. While there remains room for improvement, I'm growing in the area of "playing with my kids!" I expressed my admiration at Joshua's skill, creativity, and attention to detail and immediately took pictures to send to Grandma. (Grandmas always have time to praise and admire what our children do or make.) Josh grew three inches taller when I read him Grandma's praises and tributes toward his stunning creation. In fact, it was enough to send him back for several more hours of rigorous work on his expanding Western empire. Enjoyed children become secure children who form strong and healthy attachments to their parents and siblings.

After interviewing numerous seasoned parents, I would go so far as to say that "enjoying your children and your role as a parent" is probably the single most important component to good parenting. One woman recently told me that her grandparents shared with her that if they could change one thing as a family, they would have "laughed more." Yes, just plain old "laughed more." Not trained more, educated more, or spent more money on their kids, but "laughed more" as a family. Laughter is God's great tension releaser. It's a producer of endorphins that releases a sense of pleasure and relief from pain. Healthy humor reflects the light-hearted nature of God. So for all you imperfect parents out there, just make sure that "enjoying your kids and laughing together" is at the top of your list.

Even as adults, we gravitate toward those who really enjoy our company and value who we are. When we sense people enjoy us, we often respond in kind. The family relationships we endure out of duty bear little if no meaningful connections. Have you ever noticed that you can't deeply connect with someone unless you enjoy and value them? Jesus could not do miracles in his own hometown. Why? In his own town, He was not valued. No one saw who He was. Sometimes it is hardest to recognize the special and unique gifting of those who are closest to us. For the developing soul of a child, any lack of validation is detrimental. Remember that most adults have the world figured out (at least enough to function), but to a child everything is new. Their minds are still developing and they oftentimes wonder, "Am I valuable?" "Am I funny?" "Do you like me?" "Am I smart?" "Am I capable?" "Am I special?"

The opposite of enjoyed children are tolerated and neglected children. These kinds of kids usually become insecure, withdrawn, and detached. Detached children emanate from detached parents who can't relate to their children's emotional needs. Parents who are constantly lost in their adult world or who have no grid for their children's varying emotions, won't reach the deepest places in their hearts. Sadly, neglected children will, at best, be a product of the culture around them—and we all know that's pretty scary. It is common to hear parents say, "I can't wait until the kids go back to school." "These kids are driving me crazy." Even grandparents share how wonderful it is to be able to "send the kids home." While some of these comments are made with partial jest —what adults often miss is that children usually take these comments to heart.

Please don't beat yourself up if you struggle with occasional absent-mindedness, as every parent gets preoccupied at times. Our kids won't end up in lifelong therapy just because we space out once in a while, or we aren't available to compliment their every doodle. Though, in the name of trying to connect to your child, be cautious of culture's pop psychology and humanistic propaganda. Love to children isn't shallow or superficial as portrayed in most Hallmark commercials. Young kids bond emotionally through "doing life together" in a fun and meaningful way; interacting *as* they go along. The Bible doesn't say, "Sit down and have one-hour counseling sessions training and teaching your children." Rather, the Bible teaches parents to instruct their children as they *go about life*. "Teach them to your children, talking about them when you sit at home and when you walk along the road, when you lie down and when you get up" (Deuteronomy 11:19).

A few years ago, when our family went to Blackholm-Whistler for a ski vacation, we momentarily debated whether to take our five year old along. The rest of us could all ski and board, and we mistakenly thought maybe our Caboose, Joshua Caleb, would not pick up skiing well enough to enjoy the trip.

"Maybe he would have more fun with Grandma?" we reasoned. Or maybe we were really thinking he might slow us down on the slopes? Thank goodness that was no more than a passing thought. It's a huge cringe factor for me just thinking about "leaving him behind." To this day, Joshua remembers it as one of his favorite Shupe family adventures.

After arriving at Whistler, we signed him up for ski school. The first morning of ski school, we walked him to join the other one hundred children from around the world entering the assembly line of future skiers. Josh received his number strapped to his jacket back and was assured of much adventure and fun to come—though doubt lay etched across his small face. The rest of us took off to ski with just a tinge of doubt ourselves.

At lunch Jeff and I decided to check in on Joshua. We headed over to the lodge packed with a few hundred beginning Olympians eating hot dogs and chips. Surely Josh was having the time of his life! I peaked around the corner and soon spotted Joshua. Downcast and deflated he sat, slowly eating the hot dog before him. As he looked over and noticed me, instantly the tears started flowing. Another surprise—Joshua HATED ski school. We exhorted Josh to finish out the day, and we would allow him to try skiing with us the next morning. No more ski school? Now, this was real incentive!

The next day Josh learned to ski in record-breaking speed. By the end of the afternoon, he was flying down slopes, jumping everything in sight, and all the while bragging to anyone within earshot! Sailing past adults he was heard yelling, "Hey Mister, I just took sixty jumps." Of course, the fish just keeps getting bigger! Joshua is very social and outgoing, but to him there is nothing like hanging with the family. And yes, Dad gave up finding some of the best black runs in North America to watch Joshua take his "sixty jumps" on beginner green slopes. But really, what competes with bonding with your children through the thrill of adventure? Don't underestimate the value young children place on connecting with the family and being a part of whatever they are doing.

Think Like a Child

"Jesus knew the kingdom was hidden in small things and little children" (Matthew 18:3).

Ever wonder why Jesus kept talking about the importance of being childlike? It's obvious in Scripture that Jesus was just crazy about kids. It's not hard to figure out why if you spend a little time thinking about it. Children overflow with curiosities and loves. They are expectant and full of faith. They are always eager to learn. They're inquisitive, unassuming, and ready to take risks or try new things. They trust without a lot of explanation. They are honest and frightfully forthright. They live in the moment and find awe in even the smallest wonders. What means nothing to us as adults, often means the world to them. Everything is new and exciting in the world of a child.

Think back to what you loved as a child... catching fire flies in jars and making your own night light, sneaking through the woods as you made up your own version of cowboys and Indians, frequenting the local stream to pan for gold, spying on a sibling with a homemade spy glass, trying to cook recipes which only you would appreciate...These are just a few things I remember.

Or maybe you had an infatuation with chickens? Around third or fourth grade, I remember gathering all the chickens I could find from our neighbor's farm and dragging them into our house. After hauling them two at a time, one under each arm, I must have collected close to ten chickens. The next challenge—getting them all on the counters at the same time. After several attempts, I finally had them all lined up in a row on the kitchen counter. I quickly grabbed some Life cereal and threw it into the air to see if the chickens could really fly.

Bummer, their large, fluffy wings just didn't seem to work. No flying resulted from my brilliant and innovative experiment. But I did end up with a head full of lice and a REALLY messy kitchen. I'll leave the kitchen to your imagination. Doesn't it say something about foolishness being bound up in the heart of a child? Or maybe I should just call it good old-fashioned curiosity!

Laughing as your kids dance, act, or perform their latest gig... giggling at their no-punch-line jokes (Those seem to peak in fourth grade.)... beaming as your kids try new feats on their bikes or skateboards... standing in amazement as they exhibit no fear in catching local bugs and crawly critters... turning out all the lights to play tickle tag... riding around on Dad's back for bull rides... lighting up when your child comes home... create those "you are really enjoyed" memories and bonding for small children.

Studies have now proven that just *smiling* at your baby on a regular basis creates pathways of love and connection in a baby's brain. Spending time hiking, swimming, reading, playing soccer, Legos, dolls, or engaging in their made-up games creates the real fellowship that 'throwing them a little bit of token time so you can go out with your real friends' will never do. Let your kids be your best friends, favorite comedians, greatest adventurers, and closest confidants. As your children develop, you *are* their world. Be a part of their life, and they will always want to be a part of yours!

God Cares About What We Care About

It's important to not just teach your kids *about* God but to also help them get to *know* Him. You do this by modeling a vibrant relationship with your Heavenly Father but also by sharing and talking to God together about your dreams and desires. Part of how children learn about their Heavenly Father is by watching Him work in their lives.

When our daughter Anna was about six years old, we were headed to Carmel, California. The weather forecast was 100% rain in Carmel. Upon hearing the foreboding forecast Anna disappointingly said, "But I want it to be sunny when we are there!" I remember lying beside her as we were going to sleep and saying, "Well, if it matters to you, it matters to God!" Pondering the implication of what I had just told her, she gasped. "Wow, Mom!" What else is a mom supposed to say? Before bed, we decided to talk to God about Anna's desire and see if He could help change the weather in Carmel, California—at least for just a day.

The next day as we were approaching the coastline of Carmel, there was no sun, only dark clouds and rain. Then all at once as we came closer, we literally saw the rain clouds parting as the sun pushed its way through the grey horizon. Anna was amazed and squealed with delight. The kids played all day in the sand and sun. In the late afternoon, as we were driving out of Carmel we saw the weather patterns shift, and rain began to pour once again.

Anna learned that God is good *and* that He can do anything! She also learned that the weatherman isn't always right. Experiencing first hand God's heart toward her desires and thoughts made a significant impression on Anna, which of course doesn't always mean she will get what she wants! Remember, God wants to bless us more than we want to be blessed, but many times He gives us what we need at the time, or what's best for us, not what we want.

Relational Parenting Involves Adventure

Children love adventure. In fact, most children would quickly agree with Helen Keller who said, "Life is either a daring adventure, or nothing!" Make it your family goal to build a storehouse of good memories and fellowship through adventure. For some families, this looks like collecting bugs and looking at them under microscopes or visiting scientific museums. For others, building homemade zip lines and life-size wooden castles spells adventure. Other families prefer board games or cards.

For our family, nothing competes with skiing and snow boarding. None of us will forget the vacation when my husband, Jeff, decided to teach Christian who was six at the time, to snowboard. All was going well until on Christian's second day, Jeff decided he was ready to board a black slope (the most difficult kind for you non-skiers). Christian, who loves a challenge, gave it a try. He did awesome, well almost awesome.

As dusk came and went at the resort, Jeff and Christian were still not down! At 8PM Mom vaguely spotted Christian coming down the mountain riding in a big yellow snow cat while Dad followed along behind. Christian was having a ball in that oversized Tonka truck—this was true adventure. Wow, Dad's ideas can lead to anything!

Another unforgettable and funny memory involving our children occurred when Wesley was in second grade. Jeff had taken our little guys camping and brought along an eight-year-old friend named Colton. In the middle of the night, Colton needed to go potty so he unzipped the tent, went nearby, and did his business. When Colton attempted to re-enter the tent, Jeff was beginning to wake but was still in a partial dream state. As Colton entered, Jeff wearily looked up and saw a shadowy figure jumping into the tent on all fours. He was sure he was seeing a full-scale Pit Bull trying to invade their habitat.

Seeing *Braveheart* and *Gladiator* plenty of times, Jeff knew exactly what to do. He quickly grabbed a sleeping bag, threw it over the Pit Bull's face (Colton) and grabbed its neck shoving its face toward the entrance yelling, "Get out of here DOG!" Finally, little Colton whimpered from under the sleeping bag, "But I don't want to go, Mr. Shupe!" Oh boy, wrong Pit Bull! Jeff apologized profusely to poor Colton, who took it all in stride, and offered his parents payment for any future counseling bills.

Relational Parenting Involves Discipline and Training

Parents often buy into the misguided notion that really relational parents don't discipline or train their children very much. Those who hold this view believe modeling and love alone are sufficient to create great kids—as long as Dad and Mom model good character, eventually the kids will adopt the same values. These parents feel that loving their children is sufficient to produce great kids. They espouse no need for teaching and training because if as parents they constantly communicate unconditional love, it will cover a multitude of sins. In essence, love is the answer to everything. This line of thinking is a misunderstanding of love; it's an incomplete definition of what true love encompasses.

While modeling the right values and behavior is probably the *most* important component in training, it is not enough. One of the most *non-relational* things you can do as a parent is not discipline and not train. Parents who are so afraid of losing connection that they don't train, guide, or discipline their children end up producing insecure, confused children. Josh McDowell says, "Rules without relationship = rebellion while relationship without rules = confusion."[4] This is a powerful truth. Children's brains are literally wired for authority and structure. Increasing discoveries in neuroscience are undergirding the importance of discipline and structure in children's lives. Structure and clear boundaries in the home environment create security and help children's brains develop and mature in a healthy way. Furthermore, studies show that children raised with overly-permissive parents usually turn out worse than children whose parents are a little too authoritative. When parents don't discipline or train their kids in a wholesome way, children feel *unloved* not *loved*.

Concluding Thoughts

Remember that your children are adults in the making. Faster than you can imagine, your children will transition from a newborn baby into a full-scale adult. Ask any grandparent, and they will warn you how fast your children will grow up! As the saying goes—time waits for no one!

This first chapter contains some very simple but foundational principles for creating a strong, successful family. As I'm approaching the finish line of this manuscript my first child has just reached adulthood, and my three others are not far behind. I can relate to most people who feel there's a gap between what matters most to them and the way they live their daily lives. As I've personally reflected on my children's former years, I wish I had understood on a deeper level the privilege and gift of *enjoying* my kids. I wish I had been more intentional. Partly due to my own past, I was sometimes guilty of being one of those parents who was there but not "there." I did the best I could during those first years, and yet today I feel convinced with much greater urgency—that I don't have time for things that don't matter. We are never too old to make adjustments or to capture fully the season we are in. I'm excited about the present… about the future. I want to spend more time on those things that are most important to me—people. First my family and then the relationships that God has brought across my path. I encourage you, my fellow parents, to do the same and may God grant you great joy and blessing as you *enjoy* your children!

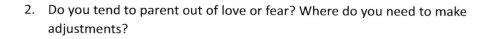

Discussion and Discovery

1. Are there any mindsets regarding parenting that you feel need adjusting in your own life? What are they?

2. Do you tend to parent out of love or fear? Where do you need to make adjustments?

3. Why is relationship "EVERYTHING" to a child?

4. How do children interpret love? What can you do to foster stronger ties with your children? Do you enjoy your children? What steps can you take to enjoy them more?

5. Why is not training non-relational?

ENDNOTES

[1] *To Train Up A Child* (1994, Pleasantville, TN).

[2] Dr. Caroline Leaf, *The Gift in You* (2009, United States of America), 143.

[3] C.B. Pert, *Molecules of Emotion, Why You Feel The Way You Feel* (Simon and Schuster, UK).

[4] Josh McDowell and Dick Day, *How to Be a Hero to Your Kids* (Nashville: Thomas Nelson, 1993), 28.

CHAPTER TWO

Relational Parenting Involves Good Communication

Building Strong Relationships Through Healthy Communication

"What we have here is a failure to communicate!"

—Cool Hand Luke

Sometimes because of our own woundedness and past, we communicate things we don't intend and cause our children to feel emotions that are not in line with productive communication. It's easy to presume that fruitful communication has occurred, when in reality our tone and demeanor are communicating something entirely different than we imagine. I've been guilty of this many times.

Somewhere between 60-90% of communication is non-verbal. Our eyes, expressions, body posture, and tone of voice speak much louder than any of the sounds coming from our lips. From the moment babies enter the world, they are interpreting our communication from our non-verbal cues—from our voice tones, our touch, and our facial expressions. That is why something as simple as "smiling at your baby" has such a positive effect on a baby's developing mind. As a baby takes in the joyful expression staring down at them, their brains are literally wiring connections for experiencing joy later in life. They *hear* from your smile, "I am enjoyed and loved."

How we communicate with our non-verbal clues often leaves others feeling either good or bad. Poet Maya Angelou quipped, "I've learned that people will forget what you said, people will forget what you did, but people will never forget how you made them feel."[1]

Have you ever been in a meeting with an authority who is supposed to be encouraging you and when you leave his or her presence, the feeling you walk away with couldn't be further from encouragement? In contrast, have you ever experienced a leader telling you something incredibly hard and clearly correctional, and yet you felt loved, secure, and empowered after leaving his or her presence? How we communicate can empower or dis-empower those we love most, particularly when it comes to parenting.

"Barna surveys among young adults pointed to verbal abuse as one of the most serious mistakes made by parents. A surprisingly large number of baby busters criticized their parents for saying things that were permanently hurtful."[2] One of the reasons parents converse in ways that hurt their children is because they often lack confidence that their children really hear them. In an effort to drive their points home, they speak too harshly and fear fuels their words. What parents need to remain conscious of is children, especially young children, take words to heart at a much deeper level than they imagine.

Once I had made a comment to my son who was home schooling at the time about being lazy with regard to his reading (with most likely some heightened emotion). Without realizing how harsh my words were coming off to his young mind, I had attempted to correct him by using the word "lazy." Bad choice! It didn't sound harsh at the time and he didn't seem upset. A month later, he was talking to a home-schooling mom and suggested a book her son might like. Then he proceeded to tell her that he needed to read more because he was a lazy reader. Yikes, as I overheard him from a nearby room telling her about his "laziness," I could tell he was ashamed of himself. My words had "stuck" with him, and he had received them in a much heavier way than what I had intended. I felt horrible hearing him share his feelings. Note to self, "Communication often comes off much harsher than intended. Don't come off so strong next time and definitely choose better words."

Even more crucial, children are better able to grasp what you are saying when you say it in a relaxed, peaceful way. When tension exists young children often tune out the words being spoken. While a challenge for many parents—the adage *soft tones, soft words,* is a powerful tool for cultivating good communication.

Failure to establish wholesome communication can stem from underlying negative emotions and wounds that need to be dealt with; but for many of us healthy communication habits can be cultivated and developed. One of the most foundational principles for good communication is taught by Stephen Covey, "Nothing is more validating and affirming than feeling understood. And the moment a person begins feeling understood, that person becomes far more open to influence and change. Empathy is to the heart what air is to the body."[3] Seek to understand before you seek to influence.

Learning to ask questions and understand another person's perspective and feelings is the beginning of good communication and especially important when relating to teens and preteens. You can listen to someone to *counter* what they are saying, or you can listen to *understand*. Most people listen to talk; they don't listen to *understand*. The word, understand, means to "stand among" or to "stand with." Stephen Covey also offers this example in his book, "A short time ago a father shared with me the experience of punishing his young son who kept disobeying him by constantly going around the corner. Each time he did so, the father would punish him and tell him not to go around the corner again. But the little boy kept doing it. Finally, after one such punishment, this boy looked at his father with tear-filled eyes and said, "What does *corner* mean, Daddy?"[4]

Misunderstanding is at the heart of much family pain. Families can perform and be highly functional without real understanding; but meaningful and rewarding family life has *understanding* as a cornerstone. This doesn't mean there's no conflict. What it means is that family members regularly take time to try to understand each other.

It's amazing how much grace our children will extend to us if they see that we are at least *trying* to understand. One of the deepest hungers in the human heart is to be understood. Small children have so much to say and heaps of emotions to sort through. Teens and preteens are undergoing great change and emotional challenges as they transition into adults—they often need the most understanding. If you will listen and attune to your children when they are young and throughout the teen years, they will listen to you later as well. King Solomon prayed for an understanding heart. Why? Because he knew that understanding brings wisdom. If we will seek understanding, the Lord will give us the wisdom we need to develop strong, meaningful relationships.

Communicate About Emotions

A few months ago while away at a retreat, I asked a seasoned parenting teacher and counselor what he considered to be one of the weakest areas for today's parents. His answer—"their ability to understand and deal with emotions." This came as kind of a surprise to me (probably because I am definitely one of those parents), but the more I've reflected and researched, the more I have found this to be true. When it comes to our kids, helping them cultivate the ability to understand and deal with their emotions is probably one of the most significant ways we can help them grow.

In his book, *The Anatomy of the Soul,* Curt Thompson states, "Emotion is the very energy around which the brain organizes itself. It is the means by which we experience and connect with God, others, and ourselves in the most basic way possible."[5] Many Scriptures reveal that God feels joy, pain, delight, anger, grief, compassion, and numerous other emotions in response to us. In the very beginning of history, we see one of the first examples of God's emotions in response to humankind. "The Lord regretted that he had made human beings on the earth, and his heart was deeply troubled"(Genesis 6:6). While suggesting that God has emotions, I am in no way suggesting that His nature is anything less than immutable and self-sufficient. Nor am I advocating that He is dependent on humans in any way. Rather, I am underscoring what Curt Thompson asserts, that emotion is much more important and vital to God than many of us realize. God is very interested in relating to us through our varying emotional states.[6]

Perhaps you grew up in a home where either your emotions were unattended to, or maybe they were attended to, but in an overwhelming and stressful way. If you were raised in a family where emotions and feelings were seen as weak, or unimportant—a home where emotions were dismissed, then you may have learned to *not pay attention to your emotions.* You may have concluded that *feelings don't matter,* and lived accordingly. As a result, you probably struggle understanding and perceiving your own emotions, and in turn struggle to make sense of your child's varying emotions and inner conflicts. Or perhaps you grew up in a home that was emotionally charged—but in a negative way. A home where anxiety, fear, anger, depression, or enmeshment caused you to either shut down (becoming a locked-up or detached adult), or to express yourself in similar negative patterns which will ultimately become overwhelming to your own children. Regardless of your personal past, the best place to start is with yourself.

While there is much more to be said on this subject, if your past home experience was lacking in emotional understanding, the most useful thing you can do as a parent is begin paying attention to your own emotions and allow God to take you from a place of insecurity to security; from a place of anxiety and confusion to a place of peace and trust. Attaining a revelation of God's deep joy and attunement toward us is a process well worth the effort. Journaling about your emotions and then listening and engaging with the Lord, or joining a small group and telling your story are both wonderful places to start. A helpful tool that will profoundly impact your understanding and provide many *"aha"* moments on this topic would be reading the book, *Anatomy of the Soul,* by Curt Thompson.

Back to our kids—when we are mindful and perceptive of our children's needs and emotions and are flexible in how we respond to them, we are allowing them to grow into healthy adults; adults who will be aware of a God who cares about them; adults who don't just know *about God* but who *know Him in an intimate way.* Implementing new patterns of communication usually takes some adjustment. Consider Curt Thompson's insightful questions, "For instance, do you attune to your child's emotions, or do you act only in response to your own as you react to your child's behavior? When your son mouths off after a hard day at school, do you immediately ground him for disrespecting you? Or do you not only correct him for his sassiness but also invite him to talk about what he's feeling about his struggles at school?" His point—life is fundamentally about emotion so we can't disregard emotion as we relate to and train our children. Further, he warns this about emotion, "If you do not attune to it, you will eventually respond to it anyway, but in forms of thought, feeling, and behavior that bring you closer to shame than glory."[7]

A Few Tips

In place of always asking our children what they *think*, particularly when they are upset or overwhelmed, it would be helpful if we learned to ask them what they *feel*. While this might be obvious for some of us, it is not the time to focus on rules and right behavior when a child is overwhelmed by emotion. Instead, asking "feeling questions" helps children and teens identify what is going on inside of them. For instance, when your child expresses anger, they may really feel fear but not realize this. Since anger is a secondary emotion often fueled by fear and anxiety, helping your child identify root feelings will give them the ability to process life in a more attuned way. By *attuned* I mean attuned to what they are really feeling. Feelings of inadequacy, fear, rejection, being misunderstood by others, loneliness, joy, hope, trust, and love are important emotions to acknowledge and understand.

If children can *identify* painful emotions, it will be much easier for them to attune to God and let Him help them with their emotions. In contrast, when parents deny emotions, children develop detached, denial-based systems of dealing with life. They may grow into high-functioning individuals who are, at the same time, relationally handicapped or stuck. People who are outwardly triumphant, while inwardly defeated. These kinds of children often become adults who operate with high control patterns where rules replace relationship or perhaps adults who live detached and impaired from developing deeper relationships.

For clarity's sake, I'm not advocating the cultivation of overly-sensitive kids. Similar to children who suffer from lack of attunement, we've all seen children who become emotionally weak and fragile due to the over-involvement and enmeshment of their parents. If you obsess about your child's every emotion and treat them as if every discomfort could possibly crush them, before long, you'll have a very insecure and overly-sensitive child. You know the sort... the kid in kindergarten who cries every day about each and every perceived insult or wrong; the kind of kid who gets his or her feelings hurt over the slightest issue and runs for help. These kids are usually either totally neglected at home (a truly sad scenario which I'm not making light of) and are using this as a way to get attention, or more likely, they have parents who are unconsciously cultivating this kind of fragility by obsessing over every emotion and potentially hurtful incident.

Overall, kids come out better when parents attune to them but also perceive when to help their children "let things go." For the mom who fixates on each scraped knee or hurt feeling, a good question to explore would be —*why* she feels the need to hover or obsess about her children. Discovering and examining the answer to this unhealthy form of control and fear is where the possibility for breakthrough in the parent/child relationship begins.

It's wonderful to see kids who are so secure that they don't really take much notice of childish insults... the kind of kid who when he falls down and gets a little scrape, jumps back up and keeps on playing. Come to think of it, overly-sensitive adults aren't that fun either.

Children learn how to feel by *feeling understood*, and children learn the skills of showing empathy by receiving empathy. We need to help our children embrace emotions rather than denying them, but we need to do this in a balanced way. So keep in mind that while children need to process life through feelings and emotions to be healthy, they also need to process life through logic and reasoning. So attune to their emotions, but don't get so touchy-feely that you chuck their *left brains* out the door.

Good Communication Involves Confrontation and Conflict Resolution

As one person aptly concluded, "The problem with the communication is the illusion that it has occurred." Good communication avoids misunderstandings, confusion, and drama by contending for clarity and openness. No family or marriage has perfect communication; the most important ingredient is to communicate regularly and purpose to engage your children and family at a heart level.

When empathy and emotional connection are in place, other necessary communication can occur. Some parents are afraid to communicate clearly and ask the hard questions. Good communication involves confrontation. When parents are afraid to confront their children, children end up making mistakes that good communication or enough communication could have prevented.

Family friends who recently asked their grown children what they felt they could have done better or differently during the teen years got this response… "Even though you communicated a lot with us, we wish you had asked us more hard questions." Even the uncomfortable communication is necessary and highly beneficial. Looking back these kids knew they needed more of the communication that parents often dread. Part of equipping our kids is not being afraid to ask the difficult questions.

Learning how to resolve conflict and work through misunderstanding is also important. Conflict is present in all healthy relationships as no two people agree all the time; each of us has areas that are sensitive. It's important to teach our children how to work through conflict rather than avoiding or handling it in an emotionally harmful way. When we help our kids develop good communication skills, we are setting them up for success. You can give your child the best education, send them to an Ivy-league college, and still not prepare them for relational success. Your child may have been a straight-A student, top-notch athlete and gifted musician and yet lack the skills to handle pressure that often taxes a family or marriage relationally. Having been valedictorian won't save a person's marriage. A gifted young executive who doesn't know how to resolve conflict at home or genuinely attune to someone else's emotions could end up with a failed family life. Teaching relational skills and conflict resolution gives your kids much greater odds of having success where it matters most—at home.

We're All Pretty Tender

After decades of getting to be around all kinds of leaders, I've observed this—when you get behind the curtain of people's lives, everyone is tender. Personally, I don't know any person or leader who doesn't desire to be understood and loved. Even the people we perceive as the strongest are created with the same emotional desires and needs. As Stephen Covey says, "All people are sensitive and very, very tender."

Some have learned to protect themselves from getting hurt and being vulnerable by acting tough, indifferent, or highly independent; but behind these masks we, as humans, want to feel safe, understood, and unconditionally loved. Experts in the field of marriage and family agree that creating a caring, relational, and encouraging environment at home is more important than almost everything else put together. In order to parent relationally, we have to cultivate the kind of culture in our home that is conducive to meeting the innate needs we each have: to be understood, to belong, and to be loved. May God grant us parents the grace and wisdom to create home environments that truly emanate a relational Kingdom culture.

Discussion and Discovery

1. What are some things you can do as a parent to improve your communication?

2. Is confrontation a part of your communication with your children? What impacted you most about this section?

3. Share about some of the ways you struggle to communicate about emotions with your children?

4. Do you struggle understanding your own emotions? Do you relate to God in and through your emotions?

5. How were emotions dealt with in your personal family background? What things would you like to implement with your own children? What changes would you like to see?

ENDNOTES

[1] Kevin Hall, *Aspire, Discovering Your Purpose Through the Power of Words,* (2009, Bookwise Publishing), 135.

[2] George Barna, *Revolutionary Parenting* (2007, Tyndale House Publishers, Inc.), 85.

[3] Kevin Hall, Aspire, Discovering Your Purpose Through the Power of Words, (2009, Bookwise Publishing), 156.

[4] Stephen Covey, *The 7 Habits of Highly Effective Families* (1997, Golden Books), 206.

[5] Curt Thompson, M.D., *Anatomy of the Soul* (2007, Tyndale Publishers), 90.

[6] Curt Thompson, M.D., *Anatomy of the Soul* (2007, Tyndale Publishers), 90.

[7] Curt Thompson, M.D., *Anatomy of the Soul* (2007, Tyndale Publishers), 104.

Excellence vs Performance Parenting

Inspiring Your Children To Excellence
Without Damaging Their Identity

Life in God is not about our push or our performance,
it is about His presence.

— Larry Randolph

Over the years I've thought and wondered a lot about the difference between encouraging excellence in children and producing "performance kids." As parents, it is easy to be "too soft" or "too hard" on our children. Most parents aspire to keep a healthy balance between the two, although no parent is ever perfectly balanced. After watching many parents and observing the lack of initiative in a lot of young people today, it seems that in our fear of *parenting performance kids* or *wounding our children*, we often don't push our kids enough. Some of us are so afraid of the "driven-parent syndrome," that we unwittingly cultivate underachievers who lack initiative and the ability to persevere. Sadly, we all know children who are driven to perform deriving their self-worth from what they do instead of who they are. Nonetheless, I come across many more children who are dissatisfied and despondent due to their lack of accomplishment and work ethic.

Motivating our children begins with understanding the difference between the *performanc*e mindset and the *excellence* mindset. The performance mindset is driven from an unhealthy need to perform for self-worth and self-acceptance. When people operate from a performance mentality, they *need* to *succeed* for personal significance. In contrast, people with an excellence mindset derive their sense of self-worth from who they *are* not what they *do*. Performing well should never be connected to self-worth. Bill Johnson explains, "Excellence is the high standard set for personal achievement because of who we are in God, and who God is in us. A spirit of excellence is about a great attitude, not great ability. It is not the same as perfectionism. Perfectionism is the cruel counterfeit of excellence."[1] Perfectionism is the mother of the performance mentality.

Religion is performance-based. The core difference in "religion" and "genuine Christianity" can be summed up like this: Religion is based on what *we do* for God and Christianity is based on what *He has done* for us. Religion works *for love*, while Christianity works *from love and relationship. It is the religious mindset that demands perfection and causes people to perform; it celebrates perfection instead of progress.*

While the root of performance stems from a religious mindset and childhood wounds, *excellence* stems from a Kingdom mentality and an identity rooted in Christ. This is an important mindset to examine within yourself as a parent first. When parents struggle with performing "for love," instead of "from love," it is crucial that they get free themselves. This is the best thing they can *do* for their children in this area. Childhood wounds often foster performance mindsets because they damage our ability to form healthy relationships and blind us from our God-given need for authentic relationship. Those who operate from a performance mentality can commonly trace it back to wounds from their own parents who may not have been able to communicate love through deep connection and intimacy. Because Mom or Dad could not process pain well or feel love, the children grew up without someone who really *enjoyed them*.

The opposite response to performance parenting occurs when children appropriate a sense of powerlessness, often manifesting in underachieving. In many instances, underachievers are individuals who feel if they can't do things perfectly or well enough—why try at all? So whether children adopt an "I won't try at all" or an "I have to do it perfectly mindset," each stem from a performance mindset. Both feelings of inadequacy and perfectionistic striving emanate from performance wounds. We've all encountered over-achieving kids who can't accomplish enough and conversely, children who are terrified to try things because of overbearing and demanding parents. Anxiety and fear paralyze excellence and effort, while striving and unhealthy ambition steal peace and joy.

Possible Evidence of a Performance Mentality Include...

- Tendency to be overly responsible about everyone and everything.
- Struggle to relax and enjoy relationships (Perfectionists have little down time.)
- Lack of ability to laugh easily, get jokes, or enjoy humor.
- An inability to receive criticism or handle failure.
- Difficulty handling confrontation, receiving it as an assault on self-worth.
- Never feel they are doing *well enough.*
- Judges, or is critical of self and others.
- Struggles with guilt.
- Task oriented – which is characterized by lists, stress, and anxiety.
- Struggles to appreciate the simple things in life.
- Difficulty trusting – always have to figure out solutions on their own.
- Often feel they have to "protect themselves" which sometimes leads to excessive boundaries.
- Continually compare themselves to others rather than simply *doing their best.*

Traits of Performance Parents

- Performance parents have a hard time perceiving what is age-appropriate. The performance parent will get angry when a child does something wrong as a result of simple childishness.
- Performance parents tend to point out what is *wrong* more often than what is *right.*
- Performance parents tend to focus on image. They want to look like they have it all together and are afraid of being vulnerable and transparent.

- Performance parents are *ungrateful* because nothing is ever good enough.

- Performance parents have a high need to *control* situations and people around them.

- Performance parents often overreact because of emotions going on inside of themselves.

- Performance parents have *irrational or unrealistic* expectations for themselves and their children.

- Performance parents tend to reward performance not effort. Example…"You can have a new bike if you make straight As for a year." Giving rewards for accomplishing things is healthy and motivating; however, rewards should be tied to *effort* not perfection. It's also important that children not be required to *earn* everything they get. When everything that is important to a child has to be *earned,* it sends the message that *works* are more important than relationship.

Excellence Mentality

- Excellence flows out of rest and peace not anxiety; it is the by-product of a heart and soul at rest.

- Excellence flows when individuals understand their unique design and personal gifting. Part of breaking performance is discovering your unique and divine design. Trying to be someone you are not often results in a high level of striving and performance.

- Excellence flows from being attuned and connected to Jesus.

- Excellence flows when people feel loved by God, when they experience God's love for themselves

- Excellence flows from partnering with the Holy Spirit.

- Excellence is the result of feeling secure and connected in community.

- Excellence emanates from a place of abundance, whereas performance begins from a place of lack.

Performance patterns are usually a defense or a way of coping with the deeper emotions of feeling inadequate or not measuring up. Healing from a performance mentality results from experiencing the reality and depth of the Father Heart of God and learning to live relationally which takes practice for those accustomed to operating from a task-oriented mindset. Once parents deal with the issues that block relationship, healing becomes possible. Repentance from not trusting the Lord is often a starting point for getting free from performance patterns. When you choose to sincerely trust the Lord instead of your own understanding, it opens up the way for healing. Healing happens when the Lord sets you free in your ability to let Him love you! You can't *work* your way out of a performance mentality; you have to *experience* your way out. You must experience God for yourselves along with the healing that comes from living relationally.

What happens when you experience the presence of God? You aren't worried, anxious, or task oriented; you don't need to see immediate solutions because trust prevails! In the same way, as you become free from performance, relational connection is augmented, and you feel lessening levels of anxiety and stress. Another result of living relationally and not in task is *clarity*. When you are no longer in charge of your universe and bearing the weight of all that goes on around you, clarity and peace increase in your life. When you are living relationally, the need to "have it all figured out" loses its power, and the ability to hear solutions from the Lord and community around you increases. On the other hand, those who live a works-oriented or performance lifestyle often experience confusion and mental striving. John Paul Jackson teaches that peace is the potting soil of all revelation. In other words, when you are in a place of peace, you can hear God!

Dr. John Curlin says this, "The Western culture values performance over relationship, and it is a major reason why we have the problems we do. When parents struggle with performance, they substitute task and performance for relationship. God created us to live in relationship, not TASK. In fact when you are *in relationship,* you can get exponentially more done, not less." [2]

Learning to trust God and live relationally fosters freedom from living in task. True excellence and God-fueled productivity stem from passion for God and desire to bring Him glory as well as from relational connection to those around us. Excellence goes above and beyond but flows from an abundant heart and is motivated by healthy passion!

Parenting that produces excellence begins with the health of the parents. So whether you struggle with a performance mentality or not, be careful not to instill in your children that they must perform to be accepted. Make sure you exercise your authority but do it in a relational way. Teach your children to celebrate progress and effort not perfection.

Part of My Story!

Don't be discouraged if you see signs of performance in your own life because we are all works in progress. Until recent years, I struggled a lot with a performance mentality.

I grew up with an unhealthy amount of stress and pressure around me. My insecurities and lack of deep relational connection resulted in a task-oriented lifestyle. While some children respond to pressure with denial or by detaching from those around them, I took on an overly responsible and intense mindset toward life. As is common with any deception, I assumed everyone felt stressed and driven.

While I did like adventure, I could never quite relax or enjoy life fully. In fact, when the Toronto Blessing (a Christian movement in which some believers were overcome by a manifestation of laughter) was breaking forth in the early 90s, I remember intensely warning a fellow believer not to have anything to do with it. I heard about people laughing and experiencing God in weird ways and was sure it could not be God. God was way too serious and worried about the state of the world to be making people laugh. I actually remember saying something to this effect in 1994, "Do you seriously think God is laughing in the Heavens right now?" I have a huge cringe factor just thinking about how religious (for lack of a better term) I used to be. Wow! My view of God was sadly, way off-center.

We often imagine that God is "like us." If we are uptight and worried, He must be the same way. I did not understand that God is truly in a good mood and wanting to spread His joy! He is actually sovereign enough to see and feel the pain in the world and yet remain full of love and joy. He longs for His children to experience His joy, His peace, and His presence on a continual basis.

Healthy parents love to tickle their kids and then watch them laugh. Watching their children experience pleasure brings them pleasure. Our *Father* feels this same way about HIS children, except He is a much better Father than we could ever aspire to be. Jesus taught that we must become like "children" to enter and experience the Kingdom. Healthy children are not uptight, worried, or somber. Healthy children laugh a lot, receive easily, and are in awe of the world around them. Studies now show that small children laugh on average hundreds of times each day, while adults often laugh less than a dozen times a day!

A few years after my very first encounter with the Holy Spirit, I was walking and praying – something I've always loved to do, when the thought suddenly entered my mind, "How come I've never asked God if I could laugh? That might be fun!" By this time I was used to seeing "Crazy Charismatics" laughing and rolling around on the floor jubilantly experiencing a touch of the Holy Spirit. Looking that ridiculous didn't really appeal to my sense of dignity, and the idea of being out of control was even less appealing. Suddenly, the Holy Spirit planted the following idea in my mind, "Drunk people don't worry about what they look like." A heavenly light bulb went off for me, "If I got authentically touched by God, the last thing I'd be worrying about was what everyone else thought." I prayed right then and there, "If this is you God, I think I'd like to laugh instead of always crying when I'm touched by you." (For those of you who need to see this laughter/drunk in the Holy Spirit experience modeled in Scripture, see Acts 2:15, *"These men are not drunk, as you suppose...."* They were not drunk on natural wine but rather intoxicated with the Holy Spirit. (See also Ephesians 5:18.)

The same weekend I utttered that prayer, my family and I were headed to a conference in Harrisburg, Pennsylvania. Looking back, I now realize the Holy Spirit set-up taking place in my mind and heart. The first night of the conference, during ministry time I went up for prayer because I was hungry for more of God. Hundreds of people were lined up at the front as prayer servants were coming through ministering to them. Some people were standing quietly experiencing the peace of Heaven, others were weeping, while others were shaking. Each person's experience was unique to what God was doing in them.

When the prayer servants got to me a lady said, "Come Holy Spirit," as she laid her hands on my head. I immediately fell to the ground laughing hysterically. I laughed and laughed and could not stop laughing. It was as if I'd just seen the funniest movie ever coupled with a feeling of deep joy from Heaven. I laughed so hard that my five-year-old daughter came running over and was staring incredulously down at me. A nearby lady assured her that all was "okay" and that I was being touched by the Holy Spirit. Anna didn't mind as she probably concluded, "My Mom may be a lot more fun after this!" Anyway, I enjoyed myself immensely. The more I laughed the more God seemed to be pulling the overly serious roots and uptightness from my life.

The church often imagines Jesus as predominantly sorrowful and serious; however, the Scriptures reveal that Jesus was "full of joy" and "acquainted with sorrow" not full of sorrow and acquainted with joy. Wow! Jesus' predominant mood is one of light-heartedness. Joy is the aroma and culture of Heaven and a fruit of the Holy Spirit!

God touching His people through laughter is an awesome thing. Growing studies indicate that laughter brings emotional, as well as physical healing. Doctors have written articles after observing that their patients literally got better after laughing. The idea that serious people get more done is just NOT true. People who laugh tend to be more creative and more productive. Fortune 500 companies now look for executives who have a good sense of humor knowing that humor, laughter, and joy causes people to work together better and accelerates productivity. Authentic laughter and joy is healing and healthy.

Charismatics laughing to look spiritual is just another form of performance—another way of looking for love and acceptance. Let God touch you with His joy, but don't work it up.

Experiencing the joy of Heaven is instrumental in uprooting the performance mentality, but a person doesn't need to roll around or laugh during ministry time to experience God's joy. This personal experience I had was only a small part of my journey toward healing and not a formula for anyone else. As you grow in your own personal healing, you will experience a deep joy and peace that is with you all the time.

Be Transparent and Vulnerable

An important key to getting free from *performance* is living in a transparent and vulnerable way. A performance mindset is often tied to keeping up a front which stems from the feeling (lie) that your worth and identity would be threatened if people really knew you. What's exciting is that when you choose transparency, the need to perform along with false shame and hidden guilt begin to lose their emotional grip in your life. In addition, you will discover how emotionally freeing it feels to be honest and open. You can't *feel* relational unless you are being transparent. Living in the truth is much more than not telling lies; living in the truth means being open. "If you are not honest with others, you'll deceive yourself, and if you are not honest with yourself, you won't be able to be honest with others." [3] Honesty and transparency go hand in hand. You can't have one without the other.

Think about it, transparent people are much more endearing and attractive than those who are aggressively striving to appear as if they have it all together. Larry Randolph says it best, "All things in Heaven and Earth are attracted to authenticity. It's being genuine that makes you believable and puts people at ease with who you are." In contrast, performance and aggressive striving are a turn off to others. Who wants to be vulnerable with a perfect person anyway?

Choosing transparency also means coming out of darkness and into the light. Once a person chooses to bring issues (and everyone has them) into the light, breakthrough and healing are possible. This is because satan legally uses things we hide against us, which often manifests in internal torment and anxiety. Bringing the issues in our life into the light is not about God shaming or punishing us, as that is against His very nature. It is about us feeling the freedom, acceptance, and support from the body of Christ as we live in a transparent way. Naturally, it's not wise to tell everyone everything, as that would prove more damaging than prudent. The point is finding a small group, or some close friends with whom you can live a transparent and authentic lifestyle.

Live in Community

Long-term performance patterns cause people to live independent of others. Independence and isolationism are really forms of pride and survival. Pride builds walls to protect itself from the influence of others. This attitude appears *strong* but is really *weak* and *afraid*. "Having it all together" is a defense against letting others into your world—a protection from getting hurt. In reality, no one has it all together; the Godliest and most influential people have personal weaknesses and areas of struggle. The good news is—there is no limit to how God can use believers who are comfortable with being a *work in progress*—believers who live dependent on Him and interdependent with a community of believers around them. I love what Larry Randolph says about being a *work in progress*, "When God created your destiny, He factored your mistakes and blunders into the equation."

The power of community and connection is presently being restored to the church in an unprecedented way. We are designed to live in community, and thus there is a level of freedom that simply cannot be attained outside of connection to community. Many of our personal strongholds simply won't be overcome without the help of others. Living relationally is deeper than joining a small group structure or spending time with other human beings.

Living this way is saying to those around you...

> *I am not untouchable*
>
> *I need you, and I want your input*
>
> *I want to know you and be known by you*
>
> *I trust that you can see things that I can not.*

Jack Frost in his powerful messages on coming out of darkness and into light says that "intimacy" in relationships is really all about... IN-TO-ME-SEE. It's hard to describe transparency better than that. When you choose transparency, others around you will follow suit. As I have personally learned to be more transparent, I've experienced a much deeper joy and relational connection with friends and family! Be vulnerable and transparent! It's scary at first, but it's worth it!

Healthy Competition

Having a family of athletes, we are pretty known for loving good, healthy competition. My husband often jokingly tells his soccer teams, "We're out here to have fun and WIN!" Some people in their fear of becoming a performance parent or putting too much pressure on their kids have a misguided fear of healthy competition. Yet, competition and stretching experiences are healthy for children. Why is that? Because personal growth is always a degree or two beyond our comfort zone. Like Dr. John Curlin wisely encouraged, "Competitiveness is GOOD if it is not tied to your identity." In other words, wanting to win is healthy unless your identity and self-worth depend on winning.

Any thriving athlete loves winning and has to deal with the disappointment of losing. It is even more important that kids learn to feel good about themselves when they have done their best, even if they don't win. Children instinctively know when they have pushed and stretched themselves to the limit, and they FEEL good. Doing their very best is much more important and fulfilling than winning. Unfortunately rather than doing their best, some of the most gifted athletes are just "getting by." Winning without effort never brings the satisfaction that "giving it your all" does. Winning does not equal excellence as the real winners and losers are not revealed by the results on the scoreboard. In the long run, it is attitude and effort that produce the real winners in the game of life! Show me a kid who puts in 100% and has a great attitude, and I'll show you someone who is going somewhere good in life.

Once, my husband Jeff was giving our son, Wesley, an intense pep talk on the side of the soccer field. Watching as an outsider, I'm sure he looked just like a "performance parent." But after decades of coaching soccer, Jeff knew that Wesley was not playing even close to his potential. Wesley is a gifted athlete, and since he is also a natural leader, most of the teammates tend to play as hard as he does. After this fervent exhortation from his father, Wes took his dad's hard words to heart and played the second half of his game with a new zeal. After the game, Wesley was so proud of himself that he excitedly wanted to discuss every play on the three-hour drive home from the tournament.

It is not uncommon for children and even adults to live unaware of their potential. Stretching ourselves toward greatness often takes exhortation from coaches, parents and mentors. Thomas Edison once said, "If we all did the things we are really capable of doing, we would literally astound ourselves." It is impossible to reach peak potential without pushing, and extending ourselves beyond our perceived limits.

Children feel joy and satisfaction when they do their best! The joy is not in the winning but in the "doing their best." Exhorting your kids to do their best in a healthy way is NOT performance parenting! The real winners in life are those who give life their all!

Encourage Effort
But Don't Resort to False Praise

Praise given from a performance mindset is unhealthy because it connects how a kid performs to his or her value. Kids who are truly extraordinarily gifted sometimes become insecure and question their value apart from their gifts. When these kids are praised too much for their talent, they start finding their identity in their gifts or talents and not in their work ethic. Furthermore, studies now indicate that many *overly* praised (praise that often comes with pressure) children develop insecurities and feel extreme pressure whether real or imagined to live up to their parents' teachers', and coaches' expectations.

False praise is equally unproductive. In an effort to build confidence in their kids, well-meaning parents often resort to false praise. The problem is false praise actually makes kids more insecure not less. Parents attempting to follow the latest trends are offering so much "positive affirmation" that their words have become meaningless in the ears of their children.

For instance, when you tell a kid who is mediocre at something that he is amazing and gifted, it is counterproductive because children intuitively know what you are saying is not true. Not too long ago, I made this mistake with my son, Christian. He is probably our hardest worker and almost never wants to quit anything. He works very hard at the sport of soccer. After losing a game at the beginning of the season, and playing *ok*ay, I endeavored to encourage him. I said, "Christian, you played great!" Glaring and frustrated Christian said, "Don't tell me that, Mom! That is NOT true!" and then added, "I played terrible, I kicked that ball just like a wady!" (lady). Point taken Christian, I won't try that again! Note to self—*false praise never works*.

Encourage kids for their effort, but don't resort to false praise. A spirit of excellence is about great attitude and great effort, not great ability. "You worked hard out there. I am so proud of you!" "You are getting better and better at the piano!" "All your hard work is paying off, isn't it?" On the other hand, when your kids do amazing or put in lots of effort, don't be sparing with the encouragement. Some people actually pride themselves in being slow to give compliments. Don't withhold encouragement — children need lots of it! Praised children are happy children! Build your kids up, but focus on the effort not the outcome!

Encouraging what's "right" increases ability. "One of the best hitting instructors in baseball is Reggie Smith, who hit over 400 home runs as a switch hitter, reported, 'When I see a kid swinging, I find what they're doing right not what they're doing wrong. And I increase what they're doing right to the point where they're so positive, that if there's negative in their swing, they eventually will listen to me and then correct it.'"[4]

For more information on the negative effects of false praise look up, *How Not to Talk to Your Kids* by Po Bronson, published February 12, 2007.

Be Excellent, but not in Everything!

Most people have heard the saying, "If something is worth doing, it is worth doing well." This is one of those half-truths that many of us have unquestioningly believed for generations. I am a firm believer in developing your *gifts*, not your *weaknesses* which entails putting your best energy toward areas of giftedness. Yet, this obviously doesn't negate the need to take care of responsibilities in areas where we are not naturally talented. What I mean is that we shouldn't spend the majority of our time trying to accomplish *greatness* where there is little or no innate ability. *Developing your weaknesses* can be one of the biggest time wasters you'll ever engage in. All good athletic and business coaches exhort their clients to find their natural God-given talents and develop those; in fact, one of the best ways to get free from performance is find what you were designed by God to do and focus on it. Have you ever heard of an Olympic athlete spending 10 hours a day trying to be the next Rhodes scholar?

Our daughter, Anna, is very musical and artistic; however, she is required to learn math and science as a part of her overall education. While math and science are important, if Anna spent all her time trying to get As in these subjects, she would literally have no time left to develop her gifts. She might be able to make an A in math, but it would take ten times the effort than for someone who is gifted in that way. So yes, Anna applies herself in math, but I do not expect As in this subject from her.

Coincidentally, in the business arena many of the A students end up working for the C students who have acquired better relational and leadership skills. In the world of business "emotional intelligence and leadership skills" pay much higher dividends than having a high school or college diploma laced with As. This is partly due to the fact that success in the marketplace is substantially more tied to the whole person rather than performance in academic realms. This should be a big encouragement for all the entrepreneurs and natural leaders out there who aren't necessarily straight-A students.

So while it's important to teach your children to do their best, be careful not to fall into pushing them to cultivate their weaknesses. Find their strengths and focus your best energy on those!

Martha or Mary?

Lastly, many of you have heard more than enough illustrations on being a Martha or a Mary to last you a lifetime. I'd like to end this section with an excerpt from Bill Johnson's book, *Dreaming With God*. Martha was a textbook example of a woman struggling with a "performance mindset." She operated from a task mentality and expected everyone else to do the same. Martha, who probably came from a long line of micro-managers, was not satisfied to just be busy herself; she had to keep everyone else busy as well! Mary was not lazy or indifferent; she merely operated from a place of relationship and intimacy with Jesus *not* performance.

"Mary sought to please Jesus by being with Him while Martha tried to please Him through service. When Martha became jealous, she asked Jesus to tell Mary to help in the kitchen. Most servants want to degrade the role of friend to feel justified in their works-oriented approach to God. Jesus' response is important to remember: '*Mary has chosen the better part.*' Martha was making sandwiches that Jesus never ordered. Doing more for God is the method servants use to increase in favor. A friend has a different focus entirely. They enjoy the favor they have and use it to spend time with their friend.

"To say we need both Marys and Marthas is to miss the point entirely—it simply isn't true. I've heard it said that nothing would ever get done if we didn't have Marthas. That, too, is a lie. That teaching comes mostly from servants who are intimidated by the lifestyle of friends. Mary wasn't a non-worker; she just learned to serve from His presence, only making sandwiches that Jesus ordered. Working *from* His presence is better than working *for* His presence. Pastor Mike Bickle put it best when he said that *there are lovers and there are workers. And lovers get more work done than do workers!* A passionate lover will always outperform a good servant in pleasing Him." [5]

Discussion and Discovery

1. Do you personally struggle with a performance mentality as a parent? In what areas?

2. Think about your current relationship with the Lord. Do you feel connected to Jesus on a deep level?

3. Ask the Lord if there are things in your life that are blocking deeper relationship with Him. Is there anything you need to give up that may be hindering a deeper connection to His presence? Examples could be distraction, busy-ness, having to be in control or not trusting. Interact with Jesus and write down what you sense and hear.

4. Think about your prevailing parenting patterns. Do you feel you've been too hard on your children, or do you not expect enough? Are they under-challenged or over-pressured?

5. Do you feel you encourage true effort or struggle with resorting to false praise?

Optional Assignment

Ask the Lord to teach and show you the areas your children are called to be excellent in. This will be a process so be prepared to partner long-term with the Lord.

Spend time going over the preceding questions. Journal what you feel and sense the Lord is saying.

Endnotes

[1] Bill Johnson, *Dreaming with God* (2006, Shippensburg, PA), 46.

[2] Dr. John Curlin, quotes taken from phone interview (September 10, 2009).

[3] Barry Byrne, talk given at their residence, (November 21, 2009).

[4] Dewey Friedel, *Imagine That* (2006, Shippensburg, PA), 122.

[5] Bill Johnson, *Dreaming with God* (2006, Shippensburg, PA), 26.

CHAPTER FOUR

Raising Overcomers

*Teaching Your Children to Overcome in a Balanced
and Age-Appropriate Way*

*One of the best things you can do for your children's self-esteem
is NOT let them give up.*

Have you ever wondered how some people develop the character to overcome seemingly impossible obstacles while others can't seem to get victory in even the smallest circumstances? How do men and women of every age face overwhelming odds, tragic losses, and constant set backs while still pressing on without giving in or giving up? What do overcomers understand that others don't?

As human beings, regardless of our age or innate gifting, we are designed to continually stretch beyond our present abilities and comfort zones. Embracing emotional, physical, and spiritual challenges is foundational to personal growth. In life, no challenge equals no growth. We can never be fully satisfied unless we are advancing to new levels in one realm or another because we are created for growth. To become an overcomer you need something to overcome in the first place. Being a Christian and living as an overcomer are not the same thing, yet we are called by God to live in this way. *"He who overcomes will inherit all this and I will be his God and he will be my son"* Revelations 21:7.

Since we all begin our journey in different places with various gift mixes and personal circumstances, what constitutes overcoming for one person could be mere mediocrity for another. A person with a high level of gifting could perform far above the norm but still be living a mediocre lifestyle. A person with great constraints could perform below average, yet be constantly overcoming. In essence, overcoming is about breaking through the boundaries of our perceived limits. To overcome we have to face the impossible, the uncomfortable, the painful, the scary, the impractical, sometimes even the seemingly unattainable or unimaginable.

Living as an overcomer is not a one-time event. It's a lifestyle we embrace which often starts with mental obstacles. Mental overcoming means seeking truth where we may have previously embraced deception. When it comes to "overcoming," mental obstacles and emotional strongholds can often be some of the most difficult places to gain victory. While these are generally more challenging than physical obstacles, they usually bring the greatest rewards. Even in sports, high level athletic trainers focus on helping athletes overcome their mental constraints, which if not dealt with, can profoundly inhibit their performance. Breakthrough starts in the mind, with what we think and believe.

In an effort to keep us from significantly impacting the world around us, the devil regularly attempts to plant and cultivate a lie in our minds where the truth would do him the most harm. People who are terrified of speaking, may be avoiding their greatest area of gifting. Public speaking is ranked as the number one fear for many people. What would history have been like if some of the most anointed preachers and speakers had given in to this fear? What if they had chosen not to overcome their perceived limitations? If they had given in to fear, some of the greatest outpourings of God would never have occurred. Through struggle we exercise the muscles we need to reach our God-given potential. Life is all about overcoming.

Learning from Those Who Overcame

One of my favorite professors at Wheaton College used to regularly exhort his students to read biographies. Every day in class he'd scribble more titles on the board, quoting in his ancient mesmerizing voice, "If you want to get to know God, get to know the men who did!"

Reading about yesterday's leaders inspires young people to follow in the footsteps of those who have gone before them. In our family we sometimes assign biographies to our kids during summer vacation or read them out loud together. Not much competes with well-written biographies as each attests to the truth that all men and women who have achieved greatness did it through facing and overcoming seemingly insurmountable difficulties. A great biography is never boring!

One biography we've read as a family is about the life of Winston Churchill. Probably few men in recent centuries knew more about what it means to overcome than Sir Winston Churchill. It was his personal belief that no one could achieve greatness without a character forged through struggle.

Churchill's childhood was one of crushing disappointment accompanied by physical and mental trials. He was born a small and sickly child with a horrific lisp, was accident-prone, and a target of schoolmates. Verbal abuse and neglect characterized his home life. Isolated and physically inferior, Churchill fell drastically behind in school and was considered a mediocre student at best.

Churchill's father, Lord Randolph, never stopped talking of his disappointment over his disturbing and dull son. His father mocked him for never passing any examinations and being the "bottom of his class." Lord Randolph concluded Churchill would become a "wastrel of slovenly, shiftless habits."[1]

Partly because Churchill was considered an academic failure, his teachers never managed to inspire him with the passion for education necessary to progress intellectually. In spite of the lack of encouragement and support from authorities in his life, Churchill determined to educate himself and build his own reservoir.

While stationed at a British outpost in Bangalore, India and nearing his twenty-second birthday, Churchill began his journey into the oceans of higher learning by reading and studying approximately four to five hours a day in the sweltering heat of the Indian summers. Winston learned voraciously. He memorized entire books of quotes and lengthy poems. He read history, philosophy, poetry, and literature widely. Churchill studied the parliamentary debates, inserting his own views and ideas into the margins. This self-imposed practice would later prove foundational to his incredible debate skills.

Churchill's self-education benefitted him for life. Decades after Churchill's initial season of learning he could still recite poems verbatim. He became an extraordinarily educated man proving the point that you can bloom intellectually at any age and overcome almost any academic and intellectual challenge if you are willing to pay the price.

His life became a living testimony of the powerful statement that life either happens to you or you happen to life! Hopefully your child will not go through the intense struggles that Winston Churchill faced or have a father like Lord Randolph. But do let his life be a demonstration of the depth of character and resolve that can develop from even the toughest physical, emotional, and mental challenges. Greatness is almost always forged in the furnace of testing rather than the land of comfort and mediocrity.

Churchill Becomes an Orator

In spite of oppressive surroundings, Winston exercised an iron will to rise above bitterness and into greatness. He was brutally honest in assessing his own weaknesses and possessed an astounding ability to exert himself against his own nature—to push beyond his limitations. Churchill experienced first hand the quote, "The hounds of doom stand at the doors of destiny."[2]

Churchill, with his distinct lisp, was acutely aware of what he needed to overcome to be an orator. He was terrified of speaking in front of crowds but worked tirelessly using his incredible memory and his love for the English language to break through these personal strongholds. Churchill was known to spend as many as twelve hours preparing to give one speech.

During WWII his words were heard across the radio waves of Europe urging the people and soldiers to defeat Hitler and his regime whatever the cost. History heralds the fact that during the war against Hitler's evil command, God used Winston Churchill's words to inspire the people of Europe to press on and "never give in."

Churchill's lifelong dream of using "words" to change history has become reality as more of his words have been put into print than those of Charles Dickens or Sir Walter Scott. In his lifetime he wrote fifty books, published hundreds of articles, and gave thousands of speeches.

Early Years

Teach your kids how to overcome, but teach it in a balanced and age-appropriate way.

This may be stating the obvious but during the very early years in a child's life too much challenge and stress is unhealthy and often traumatic. Excessive stress and pressure create fear and anxiety which can literally shut down a young child's normal capacity to perform.

Some children experience so much pressure athletically or academically that the ability to "enjoy life" is stolen away by an overly demanding parent. These are the same kids that end up with anxiety attacks, uptight attitudes, and an overly serious outlook about life. These are the kids that fall apart if they make a "B," miss a basketball shot, or don't make the school play.

I met such a kid at a local soccer tournament. He had scored a brilliant goal, so I found him after the game and praised him for his amazing feat. Sadly, he was unable to receive the compliment and responded in distress, "But I missed a shot earlier." This young man was more focused on what he did wrong than what he did right. His unhealthy performance mentality stole his joy and victory.

Consider academics—formative years are no place for excessive pressure but the season to cultivate a love for learning. These early years are when overly demanding parents often do the most damage. During this period, lifelong paradigms about learning are forming in a child's brain. One study espouses that fear can inhibit up to 70% of our brainpower when it comes to learning. This means that while your child is sitting there overwhelmed, he may be performing at 30% of his intellectual capacity. Although many times spoken of in jest, painful learning experiences in kindergarten have left too many men and women with an entrenched dread of learning and a sense of academic powerlessness. Heavy academic pressure at young ages can destroy a child's natural love for learning.

Small Children:
Learning to Love Challenge and Overcoming

It is not as important what children *overcome* as it is for them to learn *how* to *overcome*. Children need a challenge like a plant needs water or a flower needs sun. Under-challenged children soon wither from boredom and the indifference that sets in when life is void of adventure and a place to grow. *How* children encounter challenge varies according to their age. The early years should be chiefly times of security and love where new challenges are met in a positive environment. It's best to enjoy *with* your children the challenges they encounter. You want your child to associate challenge with JOY and FUN.

As a parent, encouragement is the engine that must drive your training philosophy. The greater the foundation of love and encouragement in a child's life, the more positively and confidently they will embrace challenge later in life. To children the world is full of adventure and wonder. Each time a child accomplishes something new or breaks through a previous barrier they will internalize the habit of living as an overcomer. When a small child builds a high tower with blocks, figures out how to use a screwdriver, or masters a puzzle, and it's met by parents who brag on his accomplishments, that child is learning the joy of achieving and overcoming. Early challenges like learning to walk, getting dressed, building a castle, eating by themselves, or cleaning up their toys are all developmental feats that should regularly be met with encouragement. In contrast, when kids are habitually left alone with little positive feedback or adult attunement, or when they are constantly told they are too young or too small, they begin to lose their natural strength and passion.

"The 'can do' spirit is made from many little 'I did' experiences. A spirit of 'nothing can stop me' grows out of overcoming many little barriers. Build their confidence and boldness by arranging their environment so they can be an overcomer. Circumstances and environment are different for each one of us. Find the challenges in your environment and participate with your children in fabricating fun in a constructive and rewarding way."[3] Small children need to be doers and not observers. Unless you want a television for a lifelong babysitter, be as hands on as possible with your children. The main point is that early life experiences often determine a child's confidence toward challenge and growth in ways that stay with them.

Keep in mind that even during formative years a certain amount of pain accompanies growth. Teeth coming in for a baby has an unavoidable amount of pain involved and yet it is a regular part of life. Ultimately, God designed us to be able to grow through pain and testing while also experiencing a life filled with joy.

Overcoming Develops Internal Strength

As children grow older, it's vital that they continually be stretched. Children love and need adventure and challenge, and when this is missing, they often seek it in the wrong ways or worse maybe they won't seek it at all. With older children challenge is accompanied by more pain and discomfort than is healthy for small children. Children get stronger by overcoming stress and frustration. When a child gets frustrated at a difficult piano piece, sticking with it helps to develop internal strength. Perhaps a child is one of the weaker players on a sports team, pushing through and developing better skill makes a child strong in spirit. Internal strength comes from persisting in challenges until present limitations are overcome or skills are mastered.

If you think about it, the best coaches and teachers are tough and yet full of encouragement; they are challenging and optimistic. When children know their authorities believe in them and will do whatever it takes to help them reach their goals, they will often rise to great heights. Children and teens can take toughness when they discern it is for their best.

Recall your favorite sports movies. Would they hold your attention, if they contained touchy, feely coaches training apathetic players? Or if mediocre players went on to win great championships without painful or massive obstacles? No, because these kinds of movies would never satisfy the need inside of every human being for challenge and growth. Blockbuster films like *Gladiator, Braveheart, and Remember the Titans* contain these innate themes which touch the deep-seated desires in the heart of man to press toward victory and full potential.

Overcoming obstacles builds confidence and inner strength.

Staying Relational

Embracing pain and challenge must be accompanied by staying relationally connected to be truly effective. What do I mean by this? Well it's important for children and teens to be relationally connected to authorities in their lives. We are not created to triumph alone or struggle in isolation. Olympic athletes have close relationships with their coaches who help them achieve their goals. More people fail not because of lack of talent or capability, but because they try to achieve on their own what is only possible with the help of others. The Bible says, "One can put a thousand to flight but two can put ten thousand to flight" (Deuteronomy 32:30).

In much of Western culture, authority has a negative connotation, causing many to reject anything having to do with it. The world's permeating message of independence without accountability has left youth feeling disillusioned and purposeless. Unfortunately, the lack of true authority and relational connection has produced a generation of children who feel unloved and insecure. The culture around them tells them to live individual independent lives and to create their own destiny, but experimentation with these ideals has left them emotionally wanting at most.

"Children were not only created for relationship with God; they were created for relationship with other people. God always talks of people as people in relationship. The self-sufficient, self-made individualism of Western culture is foreign to Scripture. The goal of a person's life is not to be a healthy individual; the goal is to be a person living in community with other people who are living in community with God!"[4]

Look for Opportunities That Involve Challenge and Overcoming!

Not too long ago, some friends encouraged us saying, "Your kids would be amazing wrestlers." No one in our family had ever wrestled, and frankly I thought the sport was rather barbaric. Little did we know it would be so life transforming for our boys.

About this time my husband, Jeff, discovered that almost every significant president of the United States wrestled competitively. He then heard a story about a group of 4,000 men who trained to be Navy Seals, an elite commando unit. Only 300 out of the 4,000 men became Navy Seals. At the opening banquet, they asked how many of the 300 men had been wrestlers—ALL 300 stood up! Hearing these stories about wrestling sealed it for my husband. He signed up all three of our boys. What could better prepare them to become the next William Wallace right?

Wrestling has indeed proven to be incredibly tough both emotionally and physically. At wrestling tournaments I noticed that moms didn't rush over to care for their "wounded child" when he got a bloody nose or twisted an ankle. It seemed like no one really noticed or worried about minor injuries that would have a normal soccer team "taking a knee." I had never seen this breed of mom before. At the first tournament I comically thought to myself, "These are probably what the moms of gladiators were like during the Roman times."

Nothing builds confidence in children like accomplishing a feat or learning a skill they thought was impossible or out of reach.

All of our boys have loved and feared the challenge of wrestling. Each has shed tears during matches but learning to overcome the fear and pain on the mat has done wonders for their emotional development. The joy on their faces when they win against a difficult opponent is priceless.

One morning a couple of years ago, my boys and I showed up at 6:15 AM to weigh in before a tournament; my son, Josh, is a naturally gifted wrestler. The first tournament he ever participated in he beat the four-year record holder in Northern California. Josh's stellar beginning boasted great potential; however, Joshua got hurt at an away tournament the week before. Fear, as they say, will paralyze even the most gifted, and

Josh felt paralyzed. Right as we headed to the mat for his first match, he started bawling hysterically. He said, "I will NOT wrestle!"

Knowing my determined son and seeing that he was truly petrified, I too began to panic internally. I wanted to cry with him; instead, I was determined to let Josh see my utter confidence in his ability. I faked my indifference to his crying—knowing full well that one look of pity from me could end it all!

Since Jeff was not there, I decided to take Joshua to the coach and let him do the persuading. (It did occur to me that Josh probably would never have even cried with Dad.) The wrestling coaches in our district are incredibly tough but also encouraging! To my surprise, the coach offered Josh one dollar and an ice cream if he would wrestle in the tournament.

I stood by silently praying and making no eye contact with Joshua. Finally Joshua reluctantly agreed. As the match progressed, Josh was crying too hard to engage his opponent and was being thrown down over and over without much of a fight on his part. The battering continued several rounds. I felt like I was living out the strain and tension often depicted in modern day sports movies. Moments into the match, I anxiously thought, "This is more than I can bear!" The opposing wrestler was beating Joshua, 14 to 0. With only a few seconds left, something rose up in Joshua. Maybe he remembered the story of David and Goliath. Within several seconds he overpowered and pinned the other kid, winning the match.

Joshua was as surprised by the win as anyone. He chose courage over fear and got some unexpected results. The true definition of courage is being afraid but doing tough and scary things anyway. You can't have courage if you are not afraid in the first place. Or as someone once said, "Courage is fear that has said its prayers."

Alex and Brett Harris say, "The surefire way to build confidence and competence is to do hard things."[5]

Anna Overcomes

Our daughter, Anna, is very right brained. She has struggled with a sort of dyslexia that causes her to have headaches, dizziness, and reading difficulty (words moving on the page), which made all academics burdensome to say the least. The pressure she felt starting in kindergarten marked the beginning of years of academic struggle.

Not wanting Anna to have more pressure than she could handle, we decided to home school. This choice allowed us to focus on her art and music gifts while still overcoming the academic difficulties bit by bit.

Anna is now in eleventh grade, and school is still not easy, but she continues "taking on" high school at a local preparatory school. Her perseverance and the experience of overcoming academic challenge over a prolonged period has become her internal reward, not the results themselves. It's not the kids who have it hard that we should be concerned about, it's the ones that everything comes easy to who often struggle later in life. As parents, we must resist the temptation to rescue children from all challenges because many of them are perfect opportunities to create strength and endurance in our children.

Hindrances to Overcoming

Too Much Comfort

"Real warriors are tough. They know how to endure hardness as good soldiers of Jesus" (II Timothy 2:3). "If training is easy, then the player is weak" was the maxim of author Graham Cooke's rugby coach.[6]

We are all accustomed to comfort in various forms. We like comfortable cars, comfortable homes, comfortable clothes and even comfort food. Comfort in and of itself is not bad; comfort used for refreshing and regenerating is healthy. It is when comfort gets in the way of overcoming or dulls our ability to take on challenge that it becomes a problem. To attain our personal dreams and achieve significant goals, we usually have to go beyond our comfort zone. In other words to be an overcomer, "We have to be willing to do what is uncomfortable until it becomes comfortable."[7]

There is a lot of truth in the all too familiar statement: *no pain, no gain!* It's the idea that victory goes to the one who is willing to do what his or her opponent will not. Almost nothing of significance ever happens without going beyond what is comfortable and convenient. Life is meant to be full of joy but not easy or comfortable.

Our society as a whole focuses on comfort and pleasure in a way that is alien to most foreign cultures or even previous generations in our own country. Whole corporations and multi-million dollar marketing plans revolve around sparing our kids from any and all discomfort. Discomfort whether it be emotional, physical, spiritual, or financial is to be avoided at all costs. And costs? Well, the marketing gurus are counting on plenty of that. The amount of comfort marketers are pushing on parents is ludicrous. Consider the following advertisement targeting comfort-obsessed parents.

"Baby knee pads. Yes, knee pads. Exactly what you'd want your nine-month-old to wear if he were drafted into the NFL. Except that these pads – 'the cushiest, comfiest knee pads ever,' according to One Step Ahead catalog—are for crawling. 'These medical-grade neoprene knee guards give little crawlers unparalleled protection, while slip-proof traction beads guard against skidding.' Skidding? Like your baby is going to round the corner so fast, we'll see sparks shooting out of her Huggies! What kind of fools do they take us for? Knees were made for crawling. So were kids! Yes, look what one mom wrote on the One Step Ahead website, under the baby knee pads product review: 'Sometimes my daughter has problems going from carpeting to the wood and marble floors. It helps her with the traction from spinning out. Unfortunately, she did not like the feel on her legs and refused to wear them.'"[8] Does this sound like obsession with comfort to anyone else? As hilarious as I personally found this, far too many parents are *way* too serious about avoiding discomfort.

Back to reality—as young people experience pain and stretching with loving parents alongside them, they are enabled to handle more and more challenge without panicking or losing trust. Too much comfort has the opposite effect of what parents intend in that it often makes children fragile, even fearful. Just as an unused muscle becomes weak, a deficit of testing and discomfort leaves a child unprepared for inevitable challenges later in life. We get stronger *through* challenge and pain not by avoiding them.

Quoting Graham Cooke again, "Under real pressure we fold or we focus."[9] Spiritual overcomers have internally trained themselves to focus and trust in Jesus. Trusting Jesus is just another religious cliché if we have nothing to trust Him for. Scripture doesn't promise a life of ease but rather that in all things Jesus is with us. We can fully trust in His power and goodness. People who arrange their lives in such a way as to keep life comfortable and safe may not experience much pain, but they will also never experience the deep joy that comes from engaging pain while staying relational and trusting Jesus. There is incredible opportunity to grow closer to God and others if we don't run from discomfort or challenge. The more any of us experiences the "God is with us lesson," the deeper we grow in God. When we are willing to embrace discomfort, we can be "comforted" with the comfort of God that our soul really needs.

Fostering a Fragile Child

Emotional paradigms are important to address because children are learning at young ages how to handle pain and discomfort from their family's attitudes. Parents would be astonished how much their children are looking to them and reacting according to how they see their parents respond to situations. Children imbue most of how they will respond to life's pain and circumstances by watching their parents.

We already talked a little bit about parents who foster over sensitivity in their children by obsessing too much about their emotions. When parents buy into the trendy parenting philosophies that consider children overly fragile, they tend to contribute to this by treating them as if their self-esteem is constantly on the brink. One harsh word or a little too much stress and snap, little Johnny may need therapy for years.

The truth is for the secure child, this couldn't be further from the truth. Children who *feel* loved are hard to hurt in a devastating way, predominantly because they know who they are. When difficult things happen, their sense of security remains in place. If your child knows you love them, you can assume emotional strength not fragility.

Have you ever seen an excessively nurturing mom say to a child, "Are your feelings hurt?" And a child who was actually not feeling in the least bit hurt upon hearing her mom's invitation begins to think, "Yes, hmm maybe I am hurt," as her smile fades to self-pity. Unintentionally, this mom is actually cultivating and inviting self-pity and over sensitivity into her child's life. If a parent is overly sensitive about their children, the fruit will be "overly sensitive" children.

These examples are in no way given to excuse parents from being attuned to the feelings of their children. When a child is truly hurt or afraid, a parent can help make sense of a situation in a way that strengthens and deepens the emotional health of the child. Being either *too harsh* or *too nurturing* has proven to have negative effects on kids and yet there is no perfect formula for balance in this area. Parents must trust Jesus to show them when and how to respond to their children in a manner that will help them grow toward a healthy adulthood.

The Victim Trap
We either become victors or victims—we can't be both. One of the greatest hindrances to overcoming is a victim mentality. A victim mentality is one of the most crippling life paradigms and is passed on from parents to children. Children are ultimately a reflection of their parents; thus the invitation is first to us as parents. When children witness us overcoming emotional, physical, spiritual, or financial obstacles, they will follow suit. Our breakthroughs, small and big, will ultimately become a blessing to our children and others in our sphere of influence. Like the familiar saying in the church goes, our personal breakthrough becomes a corporate blessing. Denise Rainey, founder of Family Life Ministries, says, "It's the righteous man who lives for the next generation."[10]

Home is not the only place children learn these attitudes. A victim mindset is pervading our society, media, schools, and government. This paradigm of thinking results from a pervasive belief: entitlement. With entitlement comes the *you owe me attitude* and a *culture of blame*. The entitlement mentality expects without producing or contributing and blames rather than taking responsibility.

There is hope for any situation, even those who have survived the most horrific trauma, but there is really no hope for the victim. Why? People deal with pain in various ways. But as one wise counselor observed, no matter how intense or how minimal the pain in someone's life—those with a victim mentality, almost never change and never heal. A person can overcome the most atrocious life circumstances with the right attitude, while that same person can live completely defeated by even the smallest hardship if he or she adopts a victim mentality. It's true that it is not what happens to people in life that makes them who they are but how they respond. Better said, it's not the intensity of the trial or hardship that determines our destiny; it's our attitude and our response that dictate our long-term success.

The greatest gift each of us is born with is the power to choose. Our choices determine our destiny much more than either our genes or the environment around us. Culture and genetic make-up certainly impact us, but they do not determine the life we will live—we do.

By emphasizing the freedom and power of choice to our children, we help them understand *their* potential and *their* responsibility. Understanding the *power of choice* fosters accountability. There is no room for excuses if we are responsible for our attitude and our actions. Successful business coaches report that the #1 reason for long-term failure in a person's life is excuse making; not bad circumstances, lack of talent, or too many hard knocks in life but plain old excuse making.

Victims make excuses and blame, while successful people set goals, take personal responsibility, and follow through. Victims focus on the problems; successful people focus on solutions particularly their personal role in the solution. I once heard a great definition of an entrepreneur—an entrepreneur is a person who finds solutions for problems. Successful people are solution finders; victims on the other hand can take even the best solution and turn it back into a problem.

A successful person is a person who has formed the lifelong habit of doing things that failures won't do.
A successful person regularly does what others won't.

When your child doesn't make a favored sports team, you can foster an overcoming attitude or a losing attitude depending on your response. When our son recently got cut from a travelling soccer team, we encouraged him to try a different sport and helped him see that there is probably a better fit for his gift mix than soccer. Presently, he is still trying various sports like basketball, track, and wrestling. He is yet to discover his sports niche, but he is learning a lot in the process. Hard things are much greater opportunities for growth than easy and comfortable situations. Failure and discomfort are foundational to lifelong success. I guess that's why they call "failure" the new success. You've got to be able to fail to handle success.

Back to where we started... Few men had more reason to feel like a victim than Winston Churchill, and yet because of his mindset, he refused to blame, accuse or feel sorry for himself. He even determined to honor his abusive father long after his death. Churchill gave himself so entirely to making a difference and serving his beloved country that blaming his parents, former teachers, or harsh upbringing did not occur to him. Churchill's mindset allowed him to become one of the greatest inspirations and contributors of all time.

You can't be an overcomer and a victim at the same time.

The Distraction Trap
Another reason people find it hard to overcome obstacles or develop their gifts is because they allow too much distraction and not enough focus. To overcome or break through, you have to focus. The latest brain science substantiates that our brains are specifically wired for focus and depth of thought. We get good at things and overcome weaknesses by sustained focus. Moreover, our brains actually go into a toxic state when we have too many choices and too much information coming at us at one time.

In spite of this growing knowledge about how we are designed to function, our society is increasingly becoming an ADD culture where we are actually conditioned *not* to focus. It has become "trendy" to multi-task—texting, typing on the computer, and eating all the while listening to the latest tunes is vogue, but is it healthy? Is it helpful? The latest brain science says, "No." In reality when we lose the ability to focus, to go deep, to pay attention for extended periods of time, we also lose the opportunity for optimal development.

We have already seen that Churchill overcame his speech impediment and learning deficits by long periods of focus and concentration. Would this be the case if he hadn't been willing to spend twelve hours practicing a single speech? Or what if he had decided it was too uncomfortable to spend four to five hours a day educating himself in the sweltering heat in India? Consider Olympic athletes who spend hours a day practicing specific skills. Or surgeons who spend years preparing to perform risky surgeries. Reaching peak potential is the result of consistent focus and in-depth attention.

The past is dotted with amazing stories of breakthroughs which changed the landscape of history for generations. Before 1953, it was considered physically impossible to break the four-minute mile. Psychologists claimed that mentally and physically it could not be done. However, Roger Banister, an Englishman, would prove the psychologists wrong. After extensive mental and physical training, along with encouragement from mentors, Roger broke the four-minute mile in 1953.

Six weeks later, John Laddy broke Banister's record. Within two years, 30 men had broken the four-minute mile. One man's breakthrough and determination opened the way for many others to do the same! So go ahead, determine with God's help to live as an overcomer and remember you are never too old to stretch farther, take on new challenges, or plow new territory. Little eyes and little ears are watching!

Discussion and Discovery
---

1. As a parent, what area(s) in your personal life do you feel you still need to overcome?

2. What is the Lord asking you to give up or do so you can be victorious in this area(s)?

3. In what areas do you struggle with a victim mentality? Are you willing to give up any accusation, blaming, and entitlement so you can come into alignment with a Kingdom mentality?

4. In your parenting patterns, are there any ways you may be contributing to your children being fragile, or areas where you are making life too comfortable for their optimal development? How can you make adjustments?

5. In what areas would you like to see your children overcome? Write those down and then ask the Lord how you can partner with Him to foster their development.

6. Are your relational connections strong with your children? Where do they need to be strengthened? In what ways do you need to be more intentional about encouragement or casting vision?

Optional Assignment

Spend some time listening to Jesus and interacting with the Holy Spirit over the subject of overcoming. Listen and then commit in your mind and heart to trust and obey the Lord as He directs and guides. Write down what you are sensing and feeling.

ENDNOTES

[1] Stephen Mansfield, *Never Given In* (Elkton, MD: Highland Books, 1995).

[2] Quote from Kris Vallotton

[3] NGJ Magazine, article, *Training Children to be Strong in Spirit.* Sept-Oct 2011

[4] Paul David Tripp, *Age of Opportunity* (Philipsburg, New Jersey, P& R Publishing, 1997), 44.

[5] Alex & Brett Harris, *Do Hard Things* (Colorado Springs, CO,: Multnomah Books: 2008).

[6] Graham Cooke, *Qualities of a Spiritual Warrior* (Brilliant Book House, 2008), 119.

[7] Kevin Hall, *Aspire, Discovering Your Purpose Through the Power of Words,* (2009, Bookwise Publishing),195WE.

[8] Lenore Skenazy, *Free Range Kids* (San Francisco, CA, Jossey-Bass, 2009), 33.

[9] Graham Cooke, *Qualities of a Spiritual Warrior* (Brilliant Book House, 2008), 76.

[10] Dennis Rainey, from a keynote address at Cry of the Orphan Summit, Ft. Lauderdale, FL. May 1-3, 2008.

CHAPTER FIVE

Finding the God-Zone in Your Children

Where Personal Passion and Natural Aptitude Meet

Set yourself earnestly to discover what you are made to do,
and then give yourself passionately to doing it.

— Martin Luther King Jr.

Christians are too often known for what they don't do, instead of what they do. As one middle-aged woman recalled asking her mother as a child, "Mother, I know what we are against, but what are we actually for?" It's unfortunate that when the world thinks of Christians and the church, often the first things that come to their minds is what we are "against."

As believers, we are called to live from Heaven to earth, not earth to Heaven. This means conveying the creativity, passion, and solutions of Heaven to those around us. Believers should lead the way in creativity and innovation. We should be known for great exploits and awesome accomplishments. Yet most of the church remains largely irrelevant to the world around us, and rather than leading the inventive realms, it's known as the church that "changeth not." Larry Randolph expresses it well, "Although diversity may be the most difficult thing for the Western Church to embrace, it's perhaps the most dangerous thing to ignore."[1]

> *Christianity was never meant to be known by its disciplines.*
> *It's to be known by its passion.*

> — Bill Johnson

While it is true that God never waivers or changes in His character, it would be impossible to overlook His creativity throughout Scripture. We serve a God who has never made two snowflakes alike or run out of plans for breathtaking natural landscapes and exotic sunsets. Jesus was so creative and out-of-the-box that He never performed a single miracle the same way twice. He was often challenging religious traditions that limited the greater truths of His Kingdom. It is time for followers of Christ to be known for what we are "for."

All Children Are Born with Passion and Vision

Have you ever seen a bored or listless toddler? Or met a child without dreams? Children are born with an overflowing zeal and passion for life. They possess an abundance of imagination and creativity.

There isn't a five year old who wouldn't consider himself an artist, no three year old who believes he cannot run faster, jump higher, or reach further. Emotionally healthy children overflow with inquisitiveness and enthusiasm. Most children believe they can do anything until an "unbelieving believer" tells them otherwise or until their lives are so filled with meaningless substitutes that passion for the authentic fades.

The challenge to parents is not how to instill passion and creativity in their children but rather how to keep it from dying away! My husband and I love overhearing our kids sharing their dreams. A few years ago on the way to the lake, our youngest son, Joshua, enthusiastically exclaimed, "One day Anna will be a famous singer!" The second to youngest, Christian responded, "Oh, yes, definitely!" Then Wesley added, "And Joshua will probably be the next Josh Groban!" Christian, who can't sing well said, "I'm going to play drums and guitar for famous bands. Wesley dreams and works toward being a professional athlete who brings God glory through sports.

It's never too early to encourage your children to think big and dream the impossible!

As we sat watching the news the other day, Wesley asked, "Mom, what's the most influential thing I could become in life?" Now that's thinking BIG!

Apathy: The Enemy of Passion

One aide said of Winston Churchill, *"Churchill's supreme talent was in goading people into giving up their cherished reasons for not doing anything at all."*

Albert Einstein warned, *"The world is a dangerous place to live, not because of the people who are evil but because of the people who don't do anything about it."*

God is raising up a remnant who overflow with the passion and creativity of Heaven. Because passion is so vital to transformation and bringing God's Kingdom to earth, it remains under constant assault. The message heralded via media, clothing, and music promotes the attitudes of apathy and detachment as attractive and cool. Amongst our youth, who some have even referred to as "generation whatever," it has literally become cool not to care. I asked a parenting teacher what he felt the biggest obstacle facing youth today is and he said "detachment and apathy." This growing trend of indifference is a dream killer for our kids. Why? Because you can't dream if you don't care!

It is disheartening to see so many youth under-challenged and out of touch with their own passions and gifting. The dull, lifeless face of youth is a travesty and should be an oxymoron. Middle-aged adults who have lost their passion and vision are bad enough; children and young teens with no passion is tragic. Why is loss of passion such a tragedy? Because, "The purpose of life is to live a life of purpose."[2]

In her inspirational book, *One Million Arrows*, Julie Ferwerda says, "The enemy wishes nothing more than to coax our kids, if not into rebellion, into pursuing passionless, insignificant, and potentially empty lives. As long as he can hamstring them with apathy, he need not worry about them doing damage to his Kingdom."[3] As parents, we need to be as concerned about apathy as we are about rebellion for either one could ultimately steal the destiny of our children.

Apathy sets in when we have no vision and no purpose. The word "apathy" actually means *without feeling or suffering*. It is the antithesis of passion and vision. If you don't care, you are unwilling to sacrifice or endure discomfort to attain what you desire. In contrast, the word passion comes from a Latin root and means "sacred suffering." When you find your passion, you find what you are willing to suffer for. In essence passion is being willing to suffer for what you love.[4]

Mark Batterson reminds us: *"I'm not convinced that your date of death is the date carved on your tombstone. Most people die long before that. We start dying when we have nothing worth living for."* [5]

In response to the growing epidemic of low self-esteem in mainstream society, countless articles and books are being written in an effort to bolster self-esteem and self-worth in today's youth. What is causing this rising apathy among our young people? I believe that several of the contributors to this growing dissatisfaction are an overabundance of almost everything, the lack of meaningful challenge, and under-cultivated personal talents.

Video games have replaced real play. TV shows and online outlets like Facebook, Twitter, and Instagram have replaced real relationship (Social media can be positive when stewarded wisely.) When children have no vision beyond the next show or electronic gadget and no outlet for significant contribution in their family and community, apathy begins to take root. Apathy sets in when real dreams and aspirations disappear.

Another factor contributing to apathy in some children stems from parents or educators endeavoring to mold them in ways that are distinctly counter to their natural bent. All children can tolerate a certain amount of this; however, when the majority of their time is spent on tasks and activities that are completely foreign to their natural passions and aptitudes, a disillusionment and detachment often begins to grow. This is why the Scriptures exhort parents to "train up a child in the way *he* should go." Consider this— developmental psychologists now estimate that 98% of babies are born with immense creative ability. These same psychologists estimate that less than 5% remain creatively active by the age of eighteen.

So how do we help our children gain strength to resist the cultural tide of apathy and live a life of purpose? For starters, we can help them find and cultivate their unique gifts along with meaningful avenues for contribution. Stephen Covey says this about self-esteem, "I have found that sometimes if people can develop a skill or competency that is in alignment with a fundamental gift or talent that they have, their attitude toward themselves, toward others and toward life significantly improves." [6] Simply put, people feel better about themselves and life when they are naturally good at something.

Deep inside each of us is a God-inspired longing to live a life that makes a difference. The seeds of greatness are planted in every person at birth. Every child has talents, capacities, and intelligences that could potentially remain undiscovered and uncultivated if we don't look for them, experiment with them, and utilize them. When children find their unique design, they are positioned to become an island of excellence in a sea of mediocrity, but not before.

The Good News Is...

Whatever the enemy is up to in our culture—God is up to more! What God is doing in His people and the Kingdom is much grander and more magnificent than any of the schemes of the enemy.

For years, one of the Scriptures that moved me the most was Zephaniah 1:12 which says, "At that time I will search Jerusalem with lamps and punish those who are complacent, who are like wine left on its dregs, who think the Lord will do nothing, either good or bad.'"

This verse is not about punishment, it is about the Lord declaring war on apathy. Apathy believes "God will not do good and He will not do bad." God is in the process of waking up his church, waking up his people as never before! He will manifest himself in contrast to the spirit of the day to awaken His bride—to awaken those who have unconsciously adopted the role of uninvolved bystanders, unable and uninterested in making a difference.

Experiencing God Leads to Passion

Too many believers have no aspirations and no passion. This is ultimately rooted in a disconnection from God and a religious mindset that gives Christians no permission to dream. Believers who are "asleep" to spiritual realities of Heaven feel immobilized and un-empowered to join the cause of advancing God's Kingdom. Some may even want to care, but they don't. On the contrary, believers who are hungry for God and experiencing His presence in a consistent way rarely lack passion or purpose.

You can't authentically experience God and remain passionless. People who experience God on a deep level often find themselves coming to life and beginning to dream. Why? Because supernatural experiences are what ultimately lead to personal transformation and a Holy ambition to bring about change. Hunger for *more* leads to experience, which in turn fuels passion and vision.

The man with an authentic experience carries a fire and vision that mental assertion to doctrines can never match. The man with a theology is always at the mercy of the man with an experience. Satisfaction with good theology is actually what keeps believers from seeking an experience.

In the Hebrew model of learning, truth led to experience, which resulted in understanding. What the Hebrews comprehended was you can never truly understand what you have not experienced. Having said this, seeking revelation through experiencing God and His Kingdom is not a substitute for using our intellectual capacities. As Bill Johnson has often said, "The mind makes a great student but a terrible teacher."[7]

God is the ultimate dreamer, but He is looking for those who will dream with Him. Bill Johnson's book, *Dreaming With God,* revolutionized my understanding of what it means to co-labor with God through dreaming with Him. This book helps believers understand that recapturing their personal inheritance and destiny starts with dreaming the dreams that God has put within them. God's *passion* is to unlock the latent talents, dreams, and creativity in each believer. As believers this is significant because we are not called to imitate the world but to overwhelm it with the creativity and originality of Heaven. And we can never accomplish this if we have no passion and no dreams.

God's desire for us to dream doesn't take away from His sovereignty or encourage our selfishness. Bill Johnson explains, "Abandonment and surrender precede dreaming the dreams of God. People who dream in a fleshly carnal way and then expect God to fulfill their desires are missing an important principle. Just as the Cross precedes the Resurrection, so our abandonment to His will precedes God attending to ours."[8] It is impossible to wholeheartedly seek God's Kingdom and still live a carnal, self-serving life.

When passion and vision stem from hunger for God and encounters with the Holy Spirit, they carry a depth that trumps aspirations resulting merely from self-discipline or self-motivation. The more connected we are to our Heavenly Father, the more passionate we become. When we seek God, He begins to draw out the desires of our hearts. We dream, because we were created to dream.

After graduating from Wheaton College, I started reading biographies about missionaries who lived "by faith." These books contained powerful testimonies of faith that changed my life forever. Lessons like—learning to live a surrendered life is foundational to experiencing God's fullness. However, some of these stories elevated men and women who gave it all away to follow God, including ALL personal aspirations. Some of these stories were influenced by a religious mindset that embraces the notion that loving God means getting rid of all of our personal passions. Anything of material value was put aside. All personal dreams and desires were sacrificed on the altar of serving God. Denying your dreams became a way of proving surrender, proving abandonment to God.

I remember the fear I carried in my heart at Wheaton that "surrendering to God" meant being sent to the most difficult and remote mission field, probably somewhere in Africa where I'd live in a dirt hut, eat snails for dinner, and wash my clothes in a nearby stream. My mindset was sadly, "if I don't want to do it, God will probably make me." I had no grid for dreaming *with* God.

While living by faith is the cornerstone of Christianity, living by faith doesn't mean crucifying all the desires of our heart. God made us to love certain things. As we seek God first, His plan is to give us the desires of our hearts not take them away. "Delight yourself also in the Lord, and He shall give you the desires of your heart" (Psalm 37:4). "Anytime we try to cut away at what God placed in us, we are entering a form of spirituality that the Scriptures do not support, and are contributing to a spirit that works against us having a truly effective witness." [9]

While serving as a missionary in Romania, I read an auto-biography about a woman who lived a radical life for God. This woman walked in signs and wonders and shared about God's incredible love throughout the entirety of her life. Toward the end of the book, this woman expounded in length about her beautiful English garden which she tended and enjoyed daily. She offered detailed descriptions of her antique clocks and ornate furniture, commenting that the more she grew in the Lord, the more beautiful these works of art became in her eyes. She didn't worship her antiques, but she valued their beauty and artistic design more, not less, as she connected to her Creator.

"When we live with genuine passion for God, it creates a passion for other things. While it is possible to value other things above God, it is not possible to value God without valuing other things." [10]

Parents Find Your Passion

"Tapping into my natural gifts is the first and most important step toward living a life of abundance and fulfillment."[11]

One of my favorite movies is *Julie and Julia.* What pervades the entire movie is the power of finding one's passion and then living it out. Julia Child was middle-aged and clearly unaccomplished when she began experimenting and seeking her life's passion. The movie comically depicts her trying hat making, bridge playing, and other activities at which she showed little interest or aptitude. Prior to these attempted hobbies, Julia had worked in copy writing and various roles in the U.S. government.

Julia was determined to find her passion and against all odds entered an astute cooking school in France. If any of you understand the mindset of the French, trying new things or taking on new trades later in life is foreign to their way of thinking. Their motto might as well be, "Leave it to the experts!"

Julia immediately fell in love with French cooking. Imbued with this newfound passion, she soon rose to the top of her class. Without children of her own, Julia Child completely gave herself to her love of cooking. When asked to teach cooking and later develop a French cookbook, obstacle after obstacle presented itself. However, because Julia had so utterly and completely found her life's passion, these obstacles were soon overcome as her vision and lots of hard work paved the way for an expansive career in cooking. Julia Child's determination to find her passion has blessed cooks worldwide and inaugurated a love and understanding for French cooking as well as revolutionized American home cooking.

As I have pointed out in almost every chapter, children ultimately imitate what they see in us more than anything we say or teach. Finding your passion and gifting as a parent will be one of the greatest things you can *do* for your children. For some of you, your passion may not be your full-time job or occupation, although I agree with life coaches who claim that one of the biggest mistakes adults make is not earning a living doing what they love. While using your passion to produce your income is ideal, life does not always turn out that way. What children need to see is that their parents *have* passion and are engaged in cultivating their gifts. If you want them to stretch, you need to stretch yourself. Passionate parents produce passionate kids!

Even if you weren't raised with mentors or parents who helped you discover your personal gifting, history has proven over and over that it's never too late to discover your passion. You are never too old to find those activities that fill you with energy, even when you are half-exhausted; those endeavors and activities that make you feel fully alive. When you discover what you feel you would do for free, you know you have found your passion.

Don't let age hold you back. Benjamin Franklin invented the bifocal lens when he was seventy-eight. Agatha Christie wrote *The Mousetrap*, the world's longest running play, when she was sixty-two. Vladimir Horowitz gave his last series of sold-out piano recitals when he was eighty-four. Beethoven composed his greatest piece, the *Ninth Symphony*, while completely deaf. Colonel Sanders started Kentucky Fried Chicken when he was sixty-five. Laura Ingalls Wilder began writing in her forties and commenced writing the *Little House on the Prairie* series at sixty-five. Moses was eighty years old when God commissioned him to deliver the people of God. Need I go on?

There are a few capacities that deteriorate with age, such as athleticism, but others stay strong and can actually renew and increase for many years. The brain itself continues to generate new brain cells and form new neural connections until the day we die. As more brain research is conducted, the overwhelming science reveals that we retain most brain cells throughout our lives, and the brain has more neurons available than we could ever possibly use. Now this is great news for aging parents. Think about it, we can actually get smarter at any age if we deliberately exercise our brain. How's that for encouraging!

Back to our kids... While cultivating your own gifts is essential, it should not take the place of cultivating your kids. Sadly, I've seen parents who are so utterly focused on developing themselves and fulfilling their destiny, that their own children are developed in front of video games, television screens, and babysitters. Develop your gifts, but don't let it take priority over your children.

We should never underestimate the significance of identifying early-on the place where—what our kids love, and what they are good at come together. Experts refer to this powerful place of convergence in various terms like: being in your element, entering your zone, or finding your personal sweet spot.

I would like to suggest that as believers, we have a third point of convergence that should prove a big advantage. Every believing believer has access to the anointing of God. As a believer, our ideal zone includes natural aptitude, personal passion, *and* the anointing of God. This is a God-sized advantage.

*We don't know who we are
until we know what we can do!*

While some children may defy the odds, most will not discover their passion without the help of others. This is paramount because if we don't *recognize* our gifts we can't *use* them. Many gifts don't become apparent unless there are opportunities to *use* them. Both young and old have amazing abilities and talents that *tests* will never reveal, and thus they often remain undiscovered.

"Take Bart for example. When he was a baby in Morton Grove, Illinois, Bart wasn't particularly active. But when he was around six years old, he started to do something very unusual. It turned out he could walk on his hands nearly as well as he could walk on his feet. This wasn't an elegant sight, but it did get him lots of smiles, laughter, and approval from his family. Whenever visitors came to the house, and at family parties, people prompted Bart to perform his signature move. With no further cajoling—after all, he quite enjoyed both his trick and the attention it generated—he dropped to his hands, flipped up, and proudly teetered around upside down. As he got older, he even trained himself to go up and down the stairs on his hands.

None of this was of much practical use, of course. After all, it wasn't as though the ability to walk on his hands was a skill that led to higher test scores or was marketable in any way. However, it did do wonders for his popularity—a person who can climb stairs upside down is fun to be around.

Then one day, when he was ten, with his mother's approval, his grade-school physical education teacher took him to a local gymnastics center. As he walked in, Bart's eyes bulged in amazement. He'd never seen anything so wondrous in his life. There were ropes, parallel bars, trapezes, ladders, trampolines, hurdles—all kinds of things upon which he could climb, cavort, and swing. It was like visiting Santa's workshop and Disneyland at the same time. It was the ideal place for him. His life turned in that moment. Suddenly his innate skills were good for something more than amusing himself and others.

Eight years later, after countless hours of jumping, stretching, vaulting, and lifting, Bart Conner stepped onto the mat in the gymnastics hall of Montreal Olympics to represent the United States of America. He went on to become America's most decorated male gymnast ever and the first American to win medals at every level of national and international competition. He has been a USA champion, an NCAA champion, a Pan-American Games champion, a World champion, a World Cup champion, and an Olympic champion. He was a member of three Olympic teams, in 1976, 1980, and 1984. In a legendary performance in the 1984 Los Angeles Olympics, Bart made a dramatic comeback from a torn biceps injury to win two gold medals. In 1991, he was introduced into the U.S. Olympic Hall of Fame, and in 1996 into the International Gymnastics Hall of Fame.

Conner now facilitates the passion for gymnastics in others. He owns a flourishing gymnastics school with his wife, Olympic champion Nadia Comaneci. They also own *International Gymnast* magazine and a television production company.

Athletes like Bart Conner and Nadia Comaneci have a profound sense of the capacities of their physical bodies, and their achievements show how limited our everyday ideas about human ability really are.[12]

Perhaps your family is athletically-challenged. Well maybe you have a budding entrepreneur living in your midst. Ken Robinson summarizes Richard Branson's life story from a personal interview with him. "Sometimes getting away from school is the best thing that can happen to a great mind,"[13] reflected Branson.

Sir Richard Branson was born in England in 1950. He attended Stowe School, and was very popular there, making friends easily and excelling at sports. He was so good at athletics that he became the captain of the soccer and cricket teams.

He also showed an early flair for business. By the time he was fifteen, he had started two enterprises. Neither business was particularly successful, but Richard had an obvious aptitude for that kind of thing. What he didn't have was an affinity for school. His grades were poor, and he disliked attending classes. He tried to make a go of it, but it just wasn't a comfortable fit.

At the age of sixteen, he decided he'd had enough and left never to return. His teachers recognized his intelligence, capability, and his relational gifting—but he was clearly unwilling to conform to the school's standards. Commenting on Richard's decision to drop out, his head teacher said, "By the time he is twenty-one, Richard will either be in jail or a millionaire, and I have no idea which it will be."

After leaving school Richard needed something to do with his life. So he decided to become an entrepreneur. His first real enterprise was called "Student," followed by other various ventures. Richard Branson eventually reached the billionaire status, and his empire now includes Virgin Atlantic Airways, Virgin Cola, Virgin Trains, Virgin Fuel, and lately Virgin Galactic (the first commercial endeavor to send people into space). His teacher was right—at least on one count.

Most parents would love to see their children discover their unique design and incredible potential. Not much would excite us more than our children spending their lives doing *not* what they are *good* at but what they are *great* at. Now let's take a look at how we can practically help our children.

> *Like a ship without a sail, a lack of understanding about divine gifting can keep us from going where the winds of Heaven desire us to go.*
>
> — Larry Randolph

Tips for Helping Your Kids Discover Their Passions

Discovering the point where what your kids are good at, intersects with what they love.

Pray

This is simple, yet profound. As a parent, ask the Holy Spirit to help you identify the gifts residing in your children. Ask the Lord to show you what your children need in order to fulfill their destiny and purpose. My prayer journal is laced with one-line prayers for my children. I especially love to pray for divine connections—**connections that connect your children to their destiny.**

Even from my limited personal experience I can assure you that God is ready and eager to answer prayers like these. It is His absolute delight to provide open doors, divine connections, clues, and mentors. He already knows your children down to every hair on their head.

He will connect you with that perfect piano instructor, soccer coach, or art teacher. Perhaps a friend or mentor may just happen to mention something they see in your child that you had yet to notice. Your child may show a sudden interest in a new activity or sport. Or God may even give you a dream. A few years ago I dreamed that our youngest son loved playing piano, and lo and behold, the Lord was revealing a musical gift and passion to me.

Ask the Lord to keep you from missing the divine connections He is sending your way. One day I was up skiing at Mount Shasta with my children. A friend "coincidentally" shared that tryouts for the musical "Annie" were the very next day. My ears perked up as I thought, "This must be from the Lord; Anna would love to be in that musical!" Anna was enthusiastic about trying out so the next day we prepared some songs and drove to the auditions. Anna braved the auditions (which those of you familiar with theater, know is more difficult than performing the actual musical), and we went home to wait. The following evening the cast was posted online. Anna and I could hardly wait to check. We pulled up the website and were amazed at what we saw: The role of "Annie"- Anna Shupe. We were yelling and running around the house shouting praises to God. Well, Mom was the only one running and shouting; Anna took it all more in stride.

Experiment

Finding your child's gifting is a process, so don't get frustrated when talents don't just come floating to the surface. Children often don't know what they love until they try it. Experimenting takes time, but it's time well spent. There is nothing more fulfilling in life than finding what you were born to do and doing it. However don't be afraid to change directions when you see that something is not a fit for your child.

Engage your children

Ask your children questions. What would you do if you could do anything in the world? What would you be if you could be anything or anyone? What are you thinking about when you're daydreaming? What has God put in your heart to do? What is the best solution for such and such a problem? What excites you the most? What 'impossibility' is God calling you to? What are you really great at doing that you enjoy? What is your favorite game to play?

Don't impose your passions onto your children

It is important that you are helping your child find his or her gifting and passions, not imposing your own. Rather than expecting them to follow your template, seek to understand who they are, and how they are made. Children are not clones or puppets to be merely "figured out" and manipulated by you the parent.

Your child may have a passion for soccer while the rest of the family only likes camping and hunting. In this case, get a soccer ball and pursue soccer with your child. Or maybe out of all your athletes, you have one musical, artistic child. Wanting to make your children like you is faulty at best and usually stems from a religious or performance mindset. So be careful not to replace THEIR dreams with YOUR goals and desires.

As your children get older, you are there to help cultivate their passions and steer them toward their destiny. During the teen years especially, think of yourself as a coach on the sidelines advising and encouraging them as they begin to play the game of life for themselves.

Help them stay focused

As parents your job is to help your children stay focused and develop the ability to work hard. By far, the majority of great musicians and Olympic athletes will quickly attest that their parents *made* them practice and often would not let them quit, particularly if they discerned an authentic aptitude and passion.

Becoming excellent at something takes LOTS of practice, and kids will not practice consistently without outside accountability. In later years those same adults are thanking their parents for their help and exhortation. I have yet to hear grown children say, "I wish my parents had made me practice less."

Already in his first years of piano my son Josh has spoken of quitting, but I often remind him that the music will get more and more fun as he develops his talent. Better said, the best is yet to come. This is usually enough to send him back to the piano to practice more. For violin and other strings this is even truer.

Watch them when they are young
Since our children were very young, we have inquisitively watched them for clues of their natural inclinations. It is astonishing how clearly children's gifts and passions begin to reveal themselves at early ages. Left to their own devices or during their free time, what are they drawn to? What kind of things do they like to play at? What kind of things do they like to talk about? What kind of questions do they ask? What do they get most excited about or absorbed in (excluding video games)? What fills them with more energy than usual? When they are playing games, what role do they assume?

Since age three, Anna was singing worship songs with a perfect pitch, and lifting her hands to God in worship. She was also dramatic and verbose. Today, she is acting in plays, singing, worshiping, talking, and giggling a lot!

Wesley was always moving, jumping, running, and keeping us all laughing with his incredible wit and candor. Around the age of six, we watched the movie *Chariots of Fire* and he said, "Mom, you know what my favorite line is?" I said, "Which one?" He replied, "When I run I feel God's pleasure!" This was very telling coming from a child of six years old. I knew he had a sports/evangelism call on his life. Wesley absolutely LOVES sports and continues to entertain us with his canny comments and rhetorical prowess. He also has a perceptive gift for seeing global trends in politics and economics.

Christian is our comedian and financier. He has always loved entertaining anyone who will laugh. "Don't get him started," is a recurring thought of ours. For years Christian has been passionate about business and finance. I can't do anything or plan anything without him wanting to know, "How much does it cost, Mom?" "How much will we make?" "Are we *miwyoneres* (millionaries) yet Mom?" We call him Christian Trump and encourage him to change the world as a businessman. And yes, he plans on it.

Joshua Caleb has a spiritual antennae and personality that leaves us all wondering what he will be one day. He has an innate compass for justice. When he was three years old, Josh and his siblings were over at Grandma's watching a movie (Actually he had fallen asleep on the floor.) During the movie a white person threw something in the face of a black man (a scene depicting discrimination). Instantaneously, Josh awoke out of his sleep, shot up into the air, and pointed at the TV yelling, "Freedom! Freedom!"

To Josh, things tend to be black and white. He is tenacious, goal-oriented, and continually seems to be tuned in to the heavenly realm. His strong leadership gifting, coupled with his compassionate heart make for a unique combination. We affectionately call him our benevolent Napoleon.

Look for mentors and coaches

While parents often see potential in their kids, the value of mentors and coaches can't be overstated. Mentors are role models who are excellent in their fields and can often see things in your kids you cannot. Effective mentors will emphasize strengths and abilities, not weaknesses and disabilities. They will take your children from where they are to where their *potential* can take them. The right mentor will be able to communicate your child's potential so clearly that he or she will be able to see it themselves.

Abilities and aptitudes are incredibly diverse and specific, which is why mentors are so important. Your child might be gifted and passionate about violin but not about cello. They may be awesome at golf and terrible at basketball. They may love water painting but not sketching with pencils. Or they may be gifted at writing poetry but not short stories... The more clearly you and your children can pinpoint their specific aptitudes, the easier it will be to excel.

A good mentor will exhort and encourage your child, and cause them to stretch beyond what he or she thinks is possible. Most children experience encouragement from their parents, but when an outside mentor or role model believes in them, it often gives them hope and vision that stays with them for life. Our daughter Anna has a very high soprano voice. She never really grasped the reality and uniqueness of her gift until an outstanding new voice teacher told her that she possessed a voice range that literally reminded her of Kristin Chenowith. Unbeknownst to this voice teacher, Kristin Chenowith is Anna's absolute favorite soprano singer. She is presently regarded as one of the most gifted sopranos in the country. How's that for specific encouragement from a mentor? Anna's love for opera and Broadway soared to a new level after these affirmations.

A good mentor believes in your kids and will make it known. Again and again when famous men and women have been asked, "Who had the most influence in your life?" The answer was always, "Those who believed in me."

Finding that right teacher can be life changing for your child. I always say there are teachers and there are TEACHERS! The life-changing teachers have passion, excellence, *and* a gift for teaching. Search and pray for the right teachers and mentors for your kids; it is another matter that is well worth the effort.

To further inspire your children, you can get them books and videos or visit museums and special events that are connected to their sphere of interest. Reading biographies of those who have similar passions can also be extremely helpful.

Conclusion

As parents, we are the ultimate mentors for our children—our job is to consistently help our children see their potential, worth, and irreplaceable role in the world around them. A good leader is someone who affirms worth and potential in others in a way that they come to see it in themselves. This is our leadership role to our children.

If we are willing to inspire them toward passion for God and passion for the gifts He has put inside of them, it is highly likely that they will become much more than an average member of society. It is probable they will become a beautiful expression of God's Kingdom on earth.

Discussion and Discovery

1. Do you feel you have experienced God in a way that has awakened your passions and dreams?

2. In what ways have you been affected by an attitude of apathy? Do you deal with apathy in any specific areas? What do you sense the Lord is saying to you about this?

3. Why is apathy so detrimental to young people?

4. Do you feel you have discovered your own innate talents and natural gifting? If so, what are they?

5. How have you helped your children in these areas? What tips or ideas are you especially drawn to implementing?

Optional Assignment

Spend a few minutes listening to Jesus about these areas. Ask him for guidance and wisdom regarding yourself and your children. Write down what you sense and feel the Lord is saying.

ENDNOTES

[1] Larry Randolph, *Original Breath* (2009), 155.

[2] Larry Randolph, *Original Breath* (2009), 140.

[3] Julie Ferwerda, *One Million Arrows* (2009, WinePress Publishing), 21.

[4] Kevin Hall, *Aspire* (New York, NY,Bookwise Publishing, 2009), 72.

[5] Julie Ferwerda, *One Million Arrows* (2009, WinePress Publishing), 27.

[6] Stephen Covey, *The 8th Habit* (New York, NY, FREE PRESS, 2004), 184.

[7] Bill Johnson, *When Heaven Invades Earth* (2004, Shippensburg, PA), 47.

[8] Bill Johnson, *Dreaming With God* (2006, Shippensburg, PA), 31

[9] Bill Johnson, *Dreaming With God* (2006, Shippensburg, PA), 37

[10] Bill Johnson, *Dreaming With God* (2006, Shippensburg, PA), 113

[11] Bill Johnson, *Dreaming With God* (2006, Shippensburg, PA).

[12] Ken Robinson, Ph.D., *The Element, How Finding Your Passion Changes Everything* (2009, Penguin Books), 33-35.

[13] Ken Robinson, Ph.D., *The Element, How Finding Your Passion Changes Everything* (2009, Penguin Books), 225.

.

CHAPTER SIX

Developing Perseverance

I Want to Play Drums,
I Just Don't Want to Practice

Perseverance is the hard work you do
after you get tired of doing the hard work you already did

— Newt Gingrich

erseverance means being willing to suffer for what you love. Have you ever wondered what the most important character trait is for personal success and lasting achievement? Not surprisingly, perseverance is near the top of the list. Many of the men and women who have changed history unanimously ranked it as the most important character trait for living out your personal destiny.

Think about it, without dreams and passion nothing of significance would be accomplished in the world, as a life void of passion is not worth repeating. However, passion without perseverance becomes just another *passing dream*. Achieving greatness or accomplishing great feats takes character steeped in perseverance! As Reggie White, a nine-time All-Pro NFL player, said, "The best athletes are always in the stands."

Sadly studies reveal that about 2% of people actually finish the race of life feeling as if they have lived the destiny that God put in their hearts. Many factors contribute to the tragic existence of abandoned dreams and unmet goals. We live in a country that is still free and full of opportunity, which begs the question "Why?" The answer lies in the truth that it is easy to dream, paying the price to achieve your dreams is where hard comes in. Every once in a while a young person may have the will power to defy social, economic, and family constraints, but more often conditioning and environment play a highly significant role in whether a person fulfills his or her potential. In other words, having the genes to be a champion is not enough. Our cultivated character must undergird our dreams and goals! Graham Cooke points out in his book, *Qualities of a Spiritual Warrior*:

> "Important spiritual disciplines such as fortitude, persistence, stamina, and perseverance are not part of the vocabulary of many modern churches. We have mostly an escapist theology that means we back down at the intimidation stage or don't even show up for the real fight. As part of our ongoing training and development, the Lord must, of necessity, allow us to experience life issues that are protracted and not easily solved. That is, He prolongs some situations in order to develop us at a much deeper level.[1] Being in tough circumstances for an extended period, without learning or becoming what is required, means that we have waited out the Lord—not waited on Him." [2]

Our children will not all aspire to the level of Olympic athlete or world-renowned performer, but God has specific areas in every child at which they can excel and become "great." All of us are carefully designed by our Creator with incredible potential that we can cultivate beyond the level of mere mediocrity. While some children struggle with low self-esteem because of critical and demanding parents with unrealistic expectations, I believe many more children have low self-esteem stemming from the lack of challenge and self-development. Personal development is foundational to personal growth, maturity, and emotional fulfillment.

When we identify and help our children cultivate the areas they are passionate about, we will see their self-esteem soar.

The book of Proverbs is full of verses heralding the rewards of tenacity and hard work. Proverbs 12:24 begins, "Diligent hands will rule…" Proverbs 22:29 says, "Do you see a man skilled in his work? He will serve before kings; he will not serve before obscure men." God promises to bring those who develop their skills and talents to serve before kings.

Good Habits or Innate Talent?

If you are like me, you may have questioned whether famous athletes, musicians, or scientists are really that much more gifted than the rest of us. Is greatness reserved for elect individuals born to do extra-ordinary feats and reach the summits of human potential? What role do parents of Olympians, famous musicians, or prominent business leaders play in cultivating their high level of success? Is it mainly genetic or concerted cultivation on the part of the parent that produces such astounding individuals? The answers to these questions are becoming increasingly clear as more and more research is conducted and released. The advocates of lots of practice and hard work are winning by a landslide over the divine-design promoters. Studies of highly successful athletes and musicians now reveal that ultimately it is the hours that go into accomplishing goals and dreams that determine the outcome.

Olympic swimmer, Summer Sanders, believes, "champions are raised not born." The following common threads were uncovered in a survey amongst parents of Olympians. Parents of Olympians stressed that success comes not primarily from inborn talent but lots of effort and practice. These parents emphasized to their children the value of hard work, the importance of follow-through, and the attitude that hard work pays off. Olympic parents were also good examples. They believe that children follow *not* what we say but what we do every day. Thus they modeled diligence and reminded their children regularly about the importance of tenacious work and giving life their all.[3]

The more psychologists study the careers of the gifted, the more they have discovered how *small* the role innate talent plays and how *large* a role preparation and hard work play. For extraordinary success there must be a certain level of aptitude, but the rest is consistent practice and time.

In the early 1990's psychologist K. Anders Ericsson and two of his colleagues conducted experiments to test the role of talent versus hard work in world-class violinists. All the violinists studied started around the age of five but practiced varying amounts. They repeated their experiments comparing amateur and professional pianists. The same patterns emerged in each group. The amateurs practiced about three hours a week over the course of their childhood, and by the age of twenty they had totaled two thousand hours of practice. The professionals, on the other hand, steadily increased their practice time. By the age of twenty, both the violinists and the pianists had reached about ten thousand hours.

The amazing thing about this study was that they could find no "naturals" who floated effortlessly to the top. Nor could they find any hard workers who worked harder than everyone else but simply did not have the talent to make it to the top. Paramount in their findings is this truth: people at the top didn't just work harder or even much harder than everyone else; they worked much, much harder! What the evidence revealed is that there is absolutely no "fast track" for high achievers.[4]

Now let's delve a little further into the function of practice and hard work as it pertains to high performance and great achievement. One of the best compilations of research regarding the link between talent and achievement is the national bestseller, *Talent is Overrated*.[5] This book explores the overwhelming scientific evidence regarding the link between talent and achievement discovered after decades of analysis over a wide range of fields. It reveals that while talent may play a small role in great performance, 99% of great achievement is linked to hard work and the right kind of practice. Even amongst the most prolific high achievers, one can expect to find someone who has worked extremely hard and put in many, many hours of focused and specific practice.

Does all the scientific research and evidence revealing that talent is not the main ingredient for exceptional achievement mean talent and innate ability are non-existent? Personally, I don't think so; however, if a person can attain amazing heights of ability with *average* aptitude, then imagine what is possible when what you are passionate about and have aptitude for is combined with hard work and the right kind of practice. The possibilities are endless.

Talent is Overrated offered chess as an example.[6] Most people assume that world class chess players have incredibly high IQ's. Research revealed that many of the most renowned chess players actually have average IQ's, and some international chess players even possess below-average IQs. What they all *did* have in common was lots of deliberate practice and hard work. The same findings of average aptitude being developed into world-class achievement, was found in almost every field from sports to music and business to science. What can we conclude? Great achievement and performance is up to us more than we may have imagined or have been led to believe. Great performance is not reserved for the few or the elite. It's available to anyone who is willing to—you got it—pay the price. As far as our kids go, when we find what they have a passion for— great performance and maybe even extraordinary performance is possible if certain principles are applied.

Practice or Deliberate Practice

We've all heard from our parents, coaches, and mentors about how important practice is. We often hear people say, "Practice makes perfect!" This simply isn't true. While practice is crucial to quality achievement, practice in and of itself may not produce much if it isn't the right kind. In fact, some practice doesn't make us better at all, and practicing a skill incorrectly could even make us worse. If practice doesn't take us past our present limitations and beyond the comfortable, if it is no more than going through the motions, we may actually never excel or improve. It's not practice but the right kind of practice that makes us better. Practice doesn't make perfect; perfect practice makes perfect.

I recently read the autobiography of William F. Buckley who was one of the most influential conservatives of the last century. In his life story, he shared about his experiences with his childhood piano teacher. Buckley was one of six children. His beloved piano teacher regularly stayed in the Buckley's home on Monday, Tuesday, and Wednesday and gave all six children forty-five minute lessons three days in a row. In turn, the children were to practice forty-five minutes every week-day as well as Saturday, being excused only on birthdays or special holidays. Buckley recounts the great adoration all the children felt for their loving but strenuous teacher. Her love of music so impacted the siblings that several resolved to become concert pianists. Outside of her fervor and encouragement, her methods of teaching and enforcing practice were what made her so effective. Once, in an effort to enforce "due diligence," she emerged out from *under* Buckley's piano as she "caught" him practicing in a lackluster manner. Yes, this accomplished pedagogue was willing to hide under her pupil's piano to enforce and instill the lesson of focused practice. She continually stressed that practicing without focus or pushing beyond the comfortable would result in little to slow progress. While this incident is humorous, the lesson to take away is that there is practice, and there is deliberate practice. Deliberate practice is what leads to progress and high achievement.

According to the findings in *Talent is Overrated,* deliberate practice has several ingredients. The first is the concept *that **deliberate practice develops specific skills.*** It involves working on *specific elements* that need improvement. "The great soprano Joan Sutherland devoted countless hours to practicing her trill—and not just the basic trill, but many different types. Tiger Woods has been seen to drop golf balls into a sand trap and step on them, then practice shots from a nearly impossible lie. The great performers isolate remarkably specific aspects of what they do and focus on just those things until they are improved and then it's on to the next aspect."[7] Great soccer players break down specific skills and work on them repeatedly. Good practice takes a person beyond his or her current capabilities, and builds the skills that are most crucial.

The second element is that *deliberate practice is mentally demanding*. "Nathan Milstein, one of the twentieth century's greatest violinists, was a student of the famous teacher Leopold Auer. As the story goes, Milstein asked Auer if he was practicing enough. Auer responded, 'Practice with your fingers and you need all day. Practice with your mind and you will do as much in one and half hours.'"[8] If a child can focus hard mentally while practicing the piano for twenty minutes, it could be more productive than one hour of "going through the motions."

 The third element is *deliberate practice isn't always fun*. Doing what we're already good at can be enjoyable, but practicing difficult skills that make us better usually hurts. We've already discussed the importance of finding what your children are passionate about. Parents need to keep in mind, in the words of Amy Chua, that *almost nothing is fun until you're good at it*. This is even truer for kids—especially children who are learning musical instruments. Your child may express monumental zeal toward a particular instrument only to suddenly lose interest when lack of ability quickly reveals itself. For very young children, parents should endeavor to keep practice fun and short. Remember that passion in small children usually comes and goes. Most young children don't possess the maturity to practice diligently without guidance and exhortation; thus parents shouldn't be thrown by a child's waxing and waning passion.

One last important element is that *productive practice requires regular feedback and coaching*. Practicing and even practicing hard is limited without quality feedback. Profitable feedback helps a person understand the process. When people can grasp where and why something is going wrong or how they can improve, they will be eager to enhance their skill.

The Role of Great Coaches and Teachers

One of the most vital roles of parents is finding the right coaching or training for their children. If we look behind the curtains of the lives of children who seem to have drive and tenacity, we often find an inspirational parent or coach. Behind Tiger Woods you find Earl Woods—a golf fanatic and a gifted pedagogue. Behind President John Quincy Adams, you find President John Adams who none will dispute was an accomplished and involved teacher going to all lengths to develop his son John. Behind Olympic athletes, research reveals parents who, if not skilled teachers themselves, at the very least found the very best mentors and coaches for their children.

Your child may have an aptitude and passion for music, art, or sports, but most young people do not possess the long-term vision or work ethic to achieve greatness without a role model or a parent's help. Looking for that right instructor is like panning for gold. What research shows is that top-performing adults were raised by parents who spent lots of time and energy finding the right teachers and then driving back and forth to lessons or training. It's often the determining factor to long-term success and motivation for an aspiring young person.

Great trainers will give feedback that keeps your child progressing and encouraged. If children are only offered negative feedback or constructive feedback is missing, they soon lose heart. When children are left to develop themselves, it's no surprise they eventually quit. It is hard enough to stick with things as an adult; children have even less emotional capacity for long-term goals. When good guidance is absent, there is little chance they will persevere.

Setting Goals

The importance of setting goals is not new information for most of us, yet it is often the determining factor in achieving success. Without goals, achievement and follow through will be unrealistic and difficult to attain. Because of this, it is vital that you set realistic and practical goals with your children. When goals are too high and unrealistic, children get discouraged and lose interest. When goals are too low, easy, or unchallenging, children become apathetic and bored. The sweet spot is for children to be continually stretched beyond what is comfortable but not so stretched that it is overwhelming and out of reach. In the same way that not making kids practice can keep them from going anywhere, pushing them too hard can cause them to give up as well.

Another key to goal setting is specificity. The greatest achievers thought through *exactly* how they intended to achieve their goals. Poor performers don't set goals, mediocre performers set vague goals, but great achievers set specific and clear goals. Goals should be process-oriented and include clear and specific skills and strategies. These kinds of goals help children form a distinct mental map of where they want to go. Productive goals will help a child *see* or *envision* the rewards at the end of hard work. The more a person can *visualize* what they are going for, the more willing and motivated they will be to pay the price to get there. Vision is vital; it's what gives children the drive to succeed.

Lastly, write down goals. When goals are written down it actually creates pathways in our brain making it much easier for us to focus and remember. Writing things down literally stimulates cells at the base of the brain that help us remember and pay attention. It brings clarity and sharper focus.

A Word About Starting Young

When children are still young it's important to let them experiment with various sports, activities, and instruments in order to discover where their aptitude and passions reside. However, if children wait until late teen years to settle on a specific skill, they sometimes lose the advantages of early starters especially in specific areas. For instance, "In a few specialized fields, such as baseball pitching and ballet, the body can be adapted in critical ways only at early ages, after which the bones calcify and the changes become impossible; the pitcher will never get his arm back and the dancer will never turn her feet out as fully as possible." "A study of professional pianists found that the more practice they did before age sixteen, the more myelin they had in critical parts of their brains."[9] That being said, keep in mind that other skills are not as impacted by age. My oldest son, Wesley, discovered his absolute love and passion for golf at the age of sixteen, which hasn't hindered his progress in the least.

A supportive but structured home environment
has been shown to be one of the crucial reasons
top-performing adults have reached great heights in achievements.

Closing Thoughts About Practice

Tenacious practice is often underrated in our society. While making life fun certainly has its place (especially under the age of six for academics) so does hard work and tenacity. The satisfaction of accomplishment feels good, but it starts with hard work. To get good, you have to work and practice diligently, and most children will not choose this on their own.

Because of our cultural over-emphasis on self-esteem, comfort, and fun, parents are often afraid to push or hold their children accountable. While other cultures have no problem requiring their children to practice musical instruments two and three hours a day, many Western parents are apologetic and insecure about making their children practice a mere thirty minutes a day.

Parents need to develop an internal confidence that it is okay and even vital to push their children in a healthy way. Perseverance and diligence lead to competence and *competent kids become confident kids*. When children learn to persevere at a skill or overcome a weakness, an internal confidence is formed that allows them to apply that same fortitude over and over again in life's situations. Learning the truth that hard work and consistent effort have huge rewards is invaluable for children.

> *It's not that I'm so smart,*
> *it's just that I stay with problems longer.*

— Albert Einstein

I recently talked with a woman who raised several very accomplished children. Having personally witnessed her son's amazing musical accomplishments, I was eager to discover her philosophy for helping him reach and cultivate his potential and passion for music. What she shared undergirded the principles of deliberate practice as well as the normal childhood patterns of wavering commitment.

It all began at the young age of five when her son begged her to play piano. She agreed to purchase lessons and a piano but told him in return he would play daily until at least eighteen years of age. Further, if he practiced well he only needed to practice twenty-five to thirty minutes a day. Now this may sound like an extreme agreement to make with a five year old, and personally I was kind of surprised; however, time revealed this woman's keen discernment. As we've already discussed, it is vital to let your kids experiment and then settle on what they want to stick with *after* they've had ample opportunity to discover what they love. This wise mom let her children experiment with various sports and activities making their own choices in many areas. But as far as piano, her agreement with him was for the long-term. For all of you who feel a wave of pity for this boy, let's take a look at the worse case scenario. Worse case scenario—this kid decides at eighteen that he never wants to play or see a piano again. What has this young man gained from his long-term agreement? A lot of character. He has spent a total of twenty-five minutes a day being committed to something he didn't always enjoy and sometimes even monumentally dreaded. Welcome to life as a responsible person. It's crucial that kids do things every day that they don't feel like doing because that is real life. Children who never do things they don't "feel" like doing don't usually fair well in the real world.

Back to our story which, by the way, does have a good ending. This prudent mother was ever attentive and would often exhort her son from the kitchen if she heard him practicing half-heartedly. Within a few short years this boy was winning contest after contest composing beautiful musical pieces. By thirteen, if other children saw his name on the competition list, they knew their chances of winning were slim. He also went on to master several other instruments. While practice was occasionally a battle in high school, this young man eventually decided on a full-time career in music and is widely known for his rare achievements. At eighteen years of age as he left for musical college, he wrote his dedicated mom a letter in which he specifically thanked her for implementing her agreement and "always making me practice." It's also interesting that while this young man came from an affluent family, his mother encouraged him that if he was willing to live on lesser means, he should make a living out of what he loved. He presently spends his days doing exactly that—teaching students singing, composing, and playing instruments as he passes on his passion for music and musical instruments.

Is Drive Internal or Is It Developed?

One of the biggest questions surrounding passion and drive is where do people get it? Like talent, I think most of us assume that you are either born with drive or not. We assume you are either born to make life happen, or you are born to sit by while others make life happen. Here again, the majority of us will have to adjust our long-held beliefs to embrace what research has revealed. While all children are born with innate passions and proclivities, and there are those rare cases of children who can hardly be restrained from practicing, for most children drive and passion increase over time or appear in later years. In short, drive and initiative are mainly cultivated and learned.

Why is it so important to exhort your children to take initiative and try new things? Because future high achievers seldom start out as high achievers. Parents of Olympic athletes universally reported that they have found it vital to instill *drive* in their children.[10] This drive is what motivated the aspiring young Olympians toward victory. These parents understood that passion isn't fully formed at birth, nor does it suddenly burst forth out of nowhere. Consider this statement about initiative by a famous leader, "I can lead a thousand men but I can't drag two."

Cultivating initiative and drive are invaluable if a person is to discover and live out his or her life's purpose. Sometimes parents need to get creative and brainstorm with their children to help jump-start the process of developing a passion and skill. Maybe your children want to drum for a famous band or play guitar for a local youth group. Perhaps they dream of being a professional athlete, famous news reporter, cutting edge film producer, or like our son Christian envision themselves becoming the next Donald Trump-minus the hair. Maybe your children dream of being an elementary school teacher, local fireman, police officer, or government official. Passion and drive develop over time as children are encouraged and spurred on by parents and mentors. But get ready—once your children develop a *can do* spirit there is no limit to what they may accomplish.

Children will often play an instrument or practice a sport for years motivated by parents only to find their drive becoming more and more *intrinsic*. Reminding children of the rewards of diligence, practice, or the process it takes "to get there" keeps them focused and encouraged. Keep in mind that while an adult can labor without reward, satisfaction, or encouragement for days and even years, for a small child, an hour can seem like an eternity! The smaller the child the more frequent they will need praise and encouragement, and the less time they can "practice" without breaks. It takes discernment to perceive what *age-appropriate perseverance* looks like for your child, but it's essential if you don't want your child to burn out.

Our seventeen-year-old daughter can play piano without constant input; however, my eight-year-old son who has just begun piano needs moment-by-moment encouragement. I stay close by while he is practicing so I can admire the beautiful notes. He thinks he is already composing on the level of Beethoven and Mozart—I wish that I had earplugs! What matters most though is that—it is "music to his ears!" Applaud their efforts today, and tomorrow's excellence and accomplishment will take care of itself.

Don't Let Them Quit Too Soon, They'll Thank You Later

"There are a lot of starters in the world. Who doesn't love to start new and exciting things? Starting is the easy part. The hard part is finishing. It is finishing that separates those with passion from those without it."[11]

While it is healthy and beneficial for children to experiment with various sports, musical instruments, and activities—as I've said already—at a certain age a child needs to stick with some of them. The average kid in today's culture quits the minute he or she doesn't "feel" like continuing or when things get too hard or too boring. In our instant gratification "give it to me now" culture many children have not learned what it means to persevere, and because of this they miss out on the internal joy of cultivating their gifts or mastering new skills.

Barna studies revealed that parents of "spiritual champions" encouraged their children to go deep and not wide, encouraging them to excel in one or two areas rather than skimming the surface with dozens. Pursuing excellence in what they did was possible because their parents protected them from burnout resulting from over stimulus or too much pressure from too many activities. These parents took a different path from the typical parent who allows their children to try out everything and anything, quitting before they develop any level of competence.[12]

Condoleezza's Story

Condoleezza Rice began playing piano at the tender age of three and was fluently playing Bach and Beethoven before her feet could reach the pedals. Both her mother and grandmother encouraged her love of music and trained her in piano. At the age of ten, after successfully and joyfully playing for years, Condoleezza decided she wanted to quit playing piano altogether. Her mother's wise response was, "You are not old enough or good enough to make that decision." And then she added, "When you are, you can quit." Condoleezza continued playing several hours a day for years to come. For the most part she genuinely enjoyed the physical and mental challenge of learning piano. Meanwhile her parents went to all lengths to support her piano playing even taking out a $13,000 loan to buy a grand piano on which she could practice. After her sophomore year of college, Condoleezza applied and was accepted to study piano with great pedagogues such as Edith Oppens in a summer music program. During the piano program, in spite of working extremely hard, she realized that although she loved piano, she did not love it enough to rise to the top of this profession or make it her life's full-time focus.

Confident in her change of heart, she sat her parents down to deliver her decision. Knowing her mother was mainly responsible for her love of music and initial pursuit of this career, she wasn't sure what to expect as a response. However her mother just smiled and said, "Do you remember when I told you that you weren't old enough or good enough to quit? Now you are old enough and good enough. For the rest of your life your piano will always be there for you." Many years later as National Security Advisor, Condoleezza had the chance to play with Yo-Yo Ma and as Secretary of State she played for the Queen of England. During her years as provost at Stanford, Condoleezza decided to take even more lessons to enhance her mastery of piano further proving that her love of music would be something that she would always cherish![13]

It's interesting to note that in addition to the hours Condoleezza Rice practiced piano daily, for many years she also practiced figure skating two to three hours each morning. When did she sleep you may be wondering? Apparently not much as she rose around four or five AM to get started with her day which included skating, followed by attending a rigorous private Catholic school and later doing homework and practicing piano. On top of this, she graduated high school at the age of fifteen.

Back to skating—although she became a highly skilled skater her aptitude for ice-skating was not nearly as natural as her music potential, mostly due to her body type which hindered her leverage for jumping. Still, until around the age of sixteen, her father took her to the rink before dawn for many years. What did she get out of ice-skating for hours each day? Condoleezza recalls that she loved the challenge of skating, claiming that it was this particular sport that trained her in both discipline and perseverance. She felt it taught her more about character than even the piano because it was challenging to work really hard, fail at the moment of truth, and have to get back up and do it all again the next day. And perseverance is precisely what it embedded in her character. The lesson to be taken from her life is that even though she did not engage in a full-time career in figure skating or piano, developing both of these skills taught her character traits that she would later transfer to what became her biggest love—foreign relations with an emphasis on Russia. When Condoleezza discovered her love of Russia and foreign policy, she pursued these with a tenacity and perseverance seen in few. In later years, President Bush claimed that it was Condoleezza Rice's extreme knowledge and abilities that literally changed the course of history as it pertained to Russia and the Cold War.[14]

Every good parent faces the challenge of when to back down and when to push their children forward into scary or uncharted waters. Initially when it came to the sport of wrestling, all of our sons encountered a certain degree of fear. I've learned that overcoming both fear and pain is par for the course in the sport of wrestling. On several occasions after arriving at tournaments during their first year, we found ourselves having to push our kids—letting them know they *had* to wrestle. Again this may seem harsh, but when your child loves something or is in the process of trying something new, but they are also afraid, you can make all the difference in the lifelong habits your child develops. Will your child develop the habit of quitting or breaking through? Will your children learn to do things even if they are afraid? Will they learn to push past their comfort zones or take the easy and comfortable route? Equally important, don't be afraid to change streams when you can see something is not a fit for your child. Figuring this out often takes time. Experimenting and trying new things is part of the price and the process. So be flexible, but don't let them quit too soon. Help them persevere, but make sure they are persevering at the right things. If the enemy can't get you to give up, his second strategy would be to get you to persist, but at the wrong things.

Douglas MacArthur said, "Age, wrinkles the body. Quitting, wrinkles the soul."

Discussion and Discovery

1. After reading about perseverance why do you feel this character trait is so important to cultivate in your children?

2. How has culture shaped your confidence in *pushing* or *not pushing* your children in a healthy way?

3. What stuck out to you about practice or deliberate practice?

4. What changes do you feel you could make in your own life regarding perseverance and practice?

5. How were you parented in this area?

6. What are some habits you feel you need to implement after reading this chapter?

ENDNOTES

[1] Graham Cooke, *Qualities of a Spiritual Warrior* (Brilliant Book House,2008), 76.

[2] Graham Cooke, *Qualities of a Spiritual Warrior* (Brilliant Book House,2008), 80.

[3] *Lessons We Learned from the Moms Behind the Olympic Athletes*, News Blaze, August 27, 2008.

[4] Malcolm Gladwell, Outliers (2008, Park Avenue, NY), 39.

[5] Colvin Geoff, *Talent is Overrated* (2008, London, Penguin Books).

[6] Colvin Geoff, *Talent is Overrated* (2008, London, Penguin Books), 46.

[7] Colvin Geoff, *Talent is Overrated* (2008, London, Penguin Books), 68.

[8] Colvin Geoff, *Talent is Overrated* (2008, London, Penguin Books), 71.

[9] Colvin Geoff, *Talent is Overrated* (2008, London, Penguin Books), 171.

[10] Jamie Woolf, *What Can We Learn From the Moms-in Chief behind Olympic Athletes?*
Blog Post August 17, 2008.

[11] Kevin Hall, *Aspire, Discovering Your Purpose Through the Power of Words*, (2009, Bookwise Publishing), 84.

[12] George Barna, *Revolutionary Parenting* (2007, Carol Stream), 121.

[13] Condoleezza Rice, *Extraordinary, Ordinary People* (2010, New York, Three Rivers Press), 162.

[14] Condoleezza Rice, *Extraordinary, Ordinary People* (2010, New York, Three Rivers Press).

CHAPTER SEVEN

Raising Risk-Takers and Successful Failures

Teaching Your Kids How to Risk and Fail

Success is the ability to go from one failure to another with no loss of enthusiasm.

— Winston Churchill

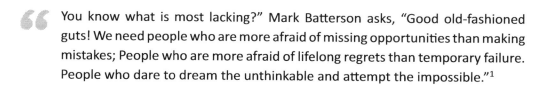

You know what is most lacking?" Mark Batterson asks, "Good old-fashioned guts! We need people who are more afraid of missing opportunities than making mistakes; People who are more afraid of lifelong regrets than temporary failure. People who dare to dream the unthinkable and attempt the impossible."[1]

Risking comes natural to an emotionally stable child. Normal children start out filled with a desire to try new things, discover the world, and take risks. When children are young, they don't worry about being wrong or attempting something brand new, and yet somehow they pick up from adults and our Western education system that mistakes are bad. Getting it right is what counts. Public schools, in general, are fostering kids who are afraid to try and afraid to fail. Our education system is stifled by a performance mentality that applauds success and has little room for mistakes and failure.

Dr. Ben Carson, a famous neurosurgeon, has written a wonderful book about risk taking called *Take the Risk*. In his book he discusses the choices and thought processes behind some of his personal risks. He points out, "In our culture, security has become an obsession. It dictates everything from public policy to Madison Avenue's commercial appeals, from medical care to education and personal family life. We buy every kind of insurance—from life insurance to replacement policies for our cell phones to provide us with the security we think we need. What we're buying and what everyone is selling us is the promise of 'security'. And yet the only thing we can be sure of is that someday every one of us will die."[2]

Most would easily agree that people today are more sensitized to risk than ever before in history. The truth is without real risk history would never have been changed for the better. All of the most important developments in science, medicine, history, technology, music, art, and sports occurred because someone was willing to take a risk; someone was willing to step into the realm of the uncomfortable and attempt the impossible. Sadly, we celebrate risk through our reality TV shows and blockbuster films and yet are often unwilling to take any ourselves. If we refuse to step out of our comfort zones, try new things, or dare to think unconventionally, we are most likely trading a life of freedom and possibility for a life of security.

> *Far better is it to dare mighty things than to rank with those poor spirits who neither enjoy much nor suffer much.*

> — Teddy Roosevelt

Unfortunately, at the other extreme, there are people who seem to take all the wrong risks. Being foolish by taking inappropriate risks ends up hurting you and those around you. People with a lottery mentality often take foolish risks due to an unwillingness to work hard and to take the real risks that would cost more than a few dollars for a prize ticket. People who make decisions without the input of others or never weigh their decisions at all are not a picture of good risk taking.

Ben Carson's Academic Risks

After successfully completing an undergraduate career at Yale with honors, Ben Carson entered his first year of medical school at the University of Michigan. He was confidently unintimidated by all the rumors of the rigors of medical school until he found himself in six to eight hours of lecture a day, exposed to enormous amounts of information.

Ben recalls that to describe the amount of information they were required to learn as "overwhelming" would be a grave understatement. He performed poorly on the first set of comprehensive exams. Shortly afterwards, an advisor informed him that, although he was intelligent, he did not have what it took to succeed at medical school. This was devastating news for someone who had planned on being a doctor since he was eight years old! His dreams crumbling around him, Ben Carson headed home that evening. He decided to do what had become a lifelong habit, he prayed and asked God for wisdom. After fervently praying, he began to assess his situation in terms of risk. He asked the question, "How can I turn this situation around?"

Instead of heeding the foreboding prediction of his advisor, Ben decided to take a risk and completely change the way he was studying for his classes and exams. Ben realized that he was not an auditory learner, so the long lectures were difficult for him to retain. If he wanted to succeed, he needed to capitalize on his best learning methods. He knew that he learned best through reading and repetition so this is what he resolved to do. He took an even bigger risk when he decided since he wasn't learning through listening to lectures, he would quit going to class altogether. Instead he began reading the medical material extensively and creating flash cards for himself. He did not completely ignore classes, as he was able to obtain written notes from "scribes" (medical students who earned extra money by typing detailed notes of lectures and selling them). He obtained these in-depth notes and then studied them thoroughly.

What Ben discovered was that he absorbed much more information at a much faster speed than when he attended class. To ensure optimal understanding he made extensive use of old exams reading them from several years back and analyzing the most important questions. For Ben Carson, skipping lectures in no way meant taking the easy way out as on most days Ben read from six in the morning until eleven at night. He read on every medical subject as widely and extensively as possible. After discovering these new methods, there was little risk of him receiving bad marks on exams. More importantly, this risk allowed him to pass medical school with flying colors going on to become a world-renowned brain surgeon. His extensive reading and in-depth study proved beneficial throughout his long medical career. He would often recall materials he'd studied years earlier and come up with solutions or insights other physicians missed or did not understand.[3] His story serves to illustrate that risk often encompasses more than attempting a daring feat. Risk involves thinking in new ways, weighing alternatives, being uncomfortable, or stepping into unknown spheres. There are physical risks, occupational risks, relational risks, financial risks, emotional risks, being silent is a risk, doing nothing is a risk; the list goes on and on.

Today Dr. Carson is most famous for having performed very risky innovative surgeries in which lives often hung in the balance. During the course of his life, he developed a very simple strategy for weighing risks.

Whenever he was faced with challenging situations, he evaluated them using the following four questions:

- What is the best thing that can happen if I do this?
- What is the worst thing that can happen if I do this?
- What is the best thing that can happen if I don't do this?
- What is the worst thing that can happen if I don't do this?

He used this simple formula when contemplating the risk of his first attempt at a hemispherectomy (the removal of one entire half of the brain), a ground-breaking surgery that made headlines around the world. Maranda was a beautiful, brown-haired four-year-old girl. She had suffered her first grand-mal seizure at eighteen months. Her second came two weeks later, and by her fourth birthday she was experiencing as many as one hundred seizures a day, some only three minutes apart. The seizures were coming so quickly that the danger of choking was too great to allow her to eat. She took in nourishment through a naso-gastric tube.

In this condition and with no quality of life left, Maranda would soon die. Doctors and clinics around the country could find no solution for her strange condition. Experts told Maranda's parents there was nothing they could do. However, Maranda's parents refused to give up, and their case divinely came before Dr. Carson.

At this point in Maranda's life, the only hope of curing the seizures involved a hemispherectomy. Dr. Carson explained to the parents that this dangerous surgery could cause severe brain damage or other limitations, and possibly Maranda would even die in the operating room. The alternative to this risky surgery was that Maranda would get worse and die on her own. The parents decided to take the risk.

The night before the operation Dr. Carson told Maranda's parents what he told all patients—to pray and that he would do the same. The following day, after a long and complicated surgery (ten not the planned five or six hours) the entire left half of Maranda's brain was successfully removed. Dr. Carson and his medical team sewed her skull back in place and sutured her scalp.

Now, the wait. As they wheeled her out of the operating room, Maranda's mom leaned down to kiss her when Maranda's eyes flickered, and she said, "I love you, Mommy and Daddy." All were amazed. They had just removed half of this little girl's brain, the dominant half that controlled speech, and she had talked! She could hear, think, and respond! A miracle had occurred all because parents and a surgeon were willing to take a very big risk![4]

Modeling the Right Attitude

Children develop their attitude toward failure and risk from their parents and the mentors in their lives. If parents themselves are overly careful or afraid of failure, children will pick up this same mindset. Have you ever made comments that might hinder your children's risk-taking abilities? Or asked questions focused on results and not effort? "What if it doesn't work?" "Be careful of getting hurt." "What will so and so think?" "Don't mess up." Or maybe you have overtly processed the areas in which you risked, negatively focusing on your failures instead of framing them as stretching and growing opportunities. The main point here is that if you want your children to have a healthy view of failure, you must exemplify one yourself.

Before a person can become great at something, they will first do it poorly. The Bible says, "The righteous man falls seven times and gets back up again" (Proverbs 24:16). It's important to create a family culture where it is okay to fail—a culture that embraces and encourages RISK. One of the greatest ways to implement the principle of encouraging risk is making sure to delight in your children's feats when they are small. When your child falls off her bike and you praise her effort encouraging her to get back on and keep trying, you are cultivating an overcomer and a risk-taker. Repeating this kind of scenario over and over in a child's life is what creates good lifelong patterns.

It's our job as parents to help our children enjoy the process of discovery and exploration. When they fail, you can encourage them with stories of how you have failed or with stories of how others have failed and gone on to accomplish great things. Then you can assure them that all things are possible for those who keep working and trying. Help them *enjoy the process and embrace the challenge* of learning and risking.

Teach your children to view failure and risk as stepping stones to success. Teach them that most failure is a good thing because the more you fail, the more you grow. The more you try, the more you are going to fail, but the more you fail, the more experience you will get. Larry Randolph says it best, "Failing is the natural consequence of trying. Failing doesn't make you a failure; never trying makes you a failure." Tell your kids about the baseball legend Babe Ruth. "In the year that he broke the record for the most homeruns, he also broke the record for the most strikeouts. Time and again he was willing to risk failure for a chance at success. He never looked for the perfect pitch—he just swung the bat! The result was an incredible .690 lifetime slugging average that has yet to be topped."[5]

Abraham Lincoln's story may be one of the best illustrations of a life where failure became the pathway to success, and persistence was the tipping point to a fulfilled destiny. Born into poverty, Lincoln was faced with defeat throughout his life. He lost eight elections, failed twice in business, and suffered a nervous breakdown. He could have quit many times, but he didn't, and because he didn't quit, he became one of the greatest presidents in the history of our country.

A Sketch of Lincoln's Road to the White House

1818: His mother died.

1831: Failed in business.

1832: Defeated for legislature.

1832: Also lost his job – wanted to go to law school but couldn't get in.

1833: Borrowed some money from a friend to begin a business and by the end of the year he was bankrupt. He spent the next seventeen years of his life paying off his debt.

1834: Ran for state legislature again – won.

1835: Sweetheart died and his heart was broken.

1836: Had a total nervous breakdown and was in bed for six months.

1838: Sought to become speaker of the state legislature – defeated.

1840: Sought to become elector – defeated.

1843: Ran for Congress – lost.

1846: Ran for Congress again – this time he won – went to Washington and did a good job.

1848: Ran for re-election to Congress – lost.

1854: Ran for Senate of the United States – lost.

1856: Sought the Vice-President nomination at his party's national convention – got less than 100 votes.

1858: Ran for U.S. Senate again – again he lost.

1860: Elected president of the United States.

Lincoln was defeated more times than he won, but his life was certainly no failure. Abraham Lincoln's life epitomizes the truth that the road to success is often paved in failure and hardship.

Another Wrestling Story

One weekend, after just learning a new style of wrestling, our oldest son Wesley informed us he was not going to the tournament the next day. He made several excuses to stay home. We realized that Wesley, who has a little of a perfectionist bent, was afraid to lose at the new style of wrestling. At 11 PM that evening he was pacing the house, battling whether to let the fear of new challenges and the fear of failure "tell him what to do."

We told him he could choose to stay home from the tournament, but if he stayed home there would be plenty of yard work to do. We wanted Wesley to make his own choice while providing a little extra incentive NOT to stay home. In real life quitting almost always is accompanied by negative consequences.

Wesley woke up early the next morning and asked his dad, "Do I really have to go Dad?" Jeff responded, "No, it is your choice if you want to quit, but I want to remind you about all the yard work." Wesley answered, "Okay, no problem, I am NOT going," and pulled the pillow back over his head.

Disappointed in Wesley's decision, Jeff went and sat in the living room. As a dad he knew how important it was that Wesley learn to push through his fear—for Wesley's passion to succeed to outweigh his fear of failure. With this in mind, Jeff decided to pray and wait. Ten minutes later, Wesley emerged from his room and announced, "I am going!" This should serve as a reminder to never underestimate the power of prayer in your children's lives!

The wrestling match was several hours from home, and circumstances did not allow Jeff and me to attend. Wesley called us in the afternoon ecstatic even though he had lost his first match. He was so proud of himself for wrestling and facing his fears. By simply participating in the tournament, the fear had lost its emotional grip on Wesley.

Everything I've ever done that's valuable is something I was afraid to try.

— Amy Chua

Warning to Parents

For children to develop a healthy understanding of failure, they need to be able to experiment without fear of criticism. If you are a critical parent, your children will struggle with risk taking. If you are quick to show disapproval at a child's mistakes or are easily disappointed when your child doesn't meet your expectations, your child will likely either lose the heart to try or become obsessed with getting things perfect. Unhealthy performance patterns often result from demanding parents. When a child is not afraid of failure, he can use his best energy to improve his performance rather than sinking into self-defeat because of overly critical or demanding parents. As far as excuse-making goes, kids will often make excuses when the consequences don't allow a way out, or the fear of failure is too great. Too much parental pressure on a young mind can result in confusion, fear, and excuse-making patterns.

However, if you are the kind of parent who brags on your kids (not false praise) and then is willing to do whatever it takes to help them succeed, your children will have plenty of confidence to try new things and embrace challenges. It is said that behind every great man is a great woman, but I would also propose that behind all great kids are parents who believe in them. Children feel it when parents have "big belief" in their abilities, and it gives them self-assurance and joy to endure the process.

As parents we need to understand our children's unique design and propensities and parent accordingly. If you have a child who is prone toward laziness or taking the easy route, you will want to push that child forward in a healthy way. If you have a child who is too hard on themselves, you will want to encourage that child to enjoy the process and lighten up. The better we understand and deal with our own personal weaknesses, the less chance we have of passing them on. Encourage risk and effort, not perfection and performance!

William Wilberforce Changes the Landscape of History

William Wilberforce characterized a life of taking risks, pushing past failure, and persevering like few others. Several summers ago I read a biography about him with my two oldest children, and then we watched the film, *Amazing Grace*, which excellently depicted Wilberforce's tenacious and forceful life.

Young William's formative years were challenging and painful as he entered the world sickly and almost blind. At the tender age of nine his father died, and his mother unable to care for him, consigned him to the care of other family members.

Under the nurture of relatives, Wilberforce first heard stories from the famous preacher and hymn writer Reverend John Newton. However, Wilberforce's early Christian influences waned during his college years at Cambridge University where he was known to do little else but play cards, drink heavily, gamble, and practice his incredible gift of wit, entertaining all who would listen.

Later, while on holiday in the south of France, a devotional book by an English clergyman found its way into his hands and ultimately his heart. Wilberforce was convicted of his sin and embraced the unspeakable mercies of His God and Savior. Assured of salvation and in love with His newfound Savior, Wilberforce possessed a fresh fire and burning desire to labor for those in need of justice.

He entered politics winning a seat in the British parliament in 1780. Slavery at that time in history was considered "essential" to the economy of England. "Slaves were picked up in West Africa and brought in chains to England in ships without sanitation facilities. Once ashore they were fattened to disguise the ravages of months of poor nutrition and seasickness. Then they were oiled and paraded naked before buyers so that their physique could be assessed and market value assigned. In the ten years following 1783 one British seaport alone shipped 303,737 slaves to the New World. In no time Britain, the world's leader in the trade, had supplied three million to French, Spanish, and British colonies."[6]

Wilberforce began his campaign to abolish the slave trade in 1787. This endeavor would consume most of his time and energy until his death. As the forerunner in parliament on the abolition of slavery, he used his seat to present bill after bill contesting British slave trade. He was defeated over and over sometimes by a mere two votes.

Rumors and slander circulated throughout the public sector as Wilberforce championed his cause while facing numerous failed assassinations and lack of support from fellow members of Parliament. Bouts of sickness and failing health strained his emotional fortitude, but Wilberforce never gave up. His tenacity and perseverance finally culminated in a victory of social justice that would change the lives of countless slaves forever. In the year 1807 Britain permanently outlawed the slave trade.

Following this victory Wilberforce then began to work toward not only the abolition of slave trade but also slavery itself. He wanted all slaves freed! Decades later, and three days before he died in 1833, he heard that the House of Commons had passed the law that emancipated all the slaves in the British Colonies.

Having lived to see his lifelong dream realized, his health suddenly worsened, and he died during the night of July 29, 1833. His crusade against slavery was so far-reaching and impactful that it later paved the way for America to also free her slaves.

It is interesting to note that on the 24th of February 1793, decades before Wilberforce would live to see his final victory, a tired eighty-eight year old man penned these words to Wilberforce, "Unless God has raised you up... I see not how you can go through with your glorious enterprise in opposing that execrable villainy.... You will be worn out by the opposition of men and devils; but if God is with you, WHO can be against you? Oh, be not weary in well doing. Go on, in the name of God and the power of his might, till even American slavery, the vilest that ever saw the sun, shall banish away before it."[7] One week later John Wesley (father of the Methodist movement) was dead. The letter he wrote to William Wilberforce would be the last letter he would ever write.

Discussion and Discovery

1. Why is learning to take risks so important?

2. Do you struggle to take risks in your own life? If so how has this shaped the way you parent?

3. What can you do to encourage your child or children in this area?

4. How have you viewed failure in your own life?

5. What can you implement in your parenting to help your children develop a healthy perspective toward failure and risk?

ENDNOTES

[1] Mark Batterson, *Wild Goose Chase,* (2008, Multnomah Books), 145.

[2] Ben Carson, *Take the Risk* (2008, Zondervan), 7.

[3] Ben Carson, *Take the Risk* (2008, Zondervan), 94-96.

[4] Ben Carson, *Take the Risk* (2008, Zondervan), 44-45.

[5] Larry Randolph, *Original Breath* (2009), 109.

[6] http://www.victorshepherd.on.ca/Heritage/wilberforce.htm.

[7] John Holzmann, *William Wilberforce God's Politician* (1996, Littleton CO), 60.

CHAPTER EIGHT

Balancing Protection and Freedom

*Insights and Tips
for Navigating Media and Technology*

*One of the worst ways a parent can damage a child
is be too permissive.*

— Dr. John Curlin

This may sound extreme at first, but if you take a look at what is happening in the lives of many young people today, it doesn't take much to recognize the truth in this statement. Dr. Curlin and his wife, Leeba, have successfully raised seven Godly children who are now raising their own families. After decades of working with parents why does he make this point? Because children without appropriate boundaries experience fear and insecurity far too early. Those without enough guidance and parental authority are often emotionally lost. While not having enough freedom can produce robotic or rebellious children, excess freedom too early has the potential to backfire like a cannon facing the wrong direction. It's easy to observe that some of the "freest" kids are often the most insecure; in contrast when children feel protected, they feel loved!

This doesn't negate the obvious principle that all children need increasing freedom and responsibility as they mature. The point is that too much freedom too early creates insecurity and confusion in the same way that too little freedom quenches uniqueness, initiative, and can result in insecurity. I would like to propose that, as a culture, we have generally over-emphasized freedom and under-emphasized responsibility. While incrementally increasing freedom is important, increased responsibility has much more to do with maturity than freedom.

Personality and makeup vary from child to child, as does the age when they are ready for life's challenges and temptations. However, parents today often mistake healthy protection for unhealthy control, and thus forfeit chances to present age-appropriate choices to their children. Yet fear-mongering media has parents terrified to let their kids play in the front yard or ride around the block for fear a kidnapper will snatch them away. It takes some real thought to separate cultural fears and mindsets from true wisdom and common sense in these areas. All of us have been taken in, at one time or another, by fear-based media that would have us believing some of the most elementary things in life are "just too dangerous for our children." By the way, if you'd like to check crime statistics, it's safer for our children to play outside or ride their bike to a friend's house today than it was in the 80s.

It is encouraging to see all the new parenting books emphasizing relationship with, and connection to, your children—as opposed to adherence to rules and regulations as the bottom line and end goal of parenting philosophy. Yes to the relational emphasis! Healthy parenting is more than keeping our children safe by merely regulating their outward behavior or protecting them from any and all potential negative influences.

The tension for parents is protecting and guiding children, while simultaneously granting increasing freedom, choices, and responsibility. The adage that parents should be working themselves out of a job couldn't be truer. Our long-term parenting goal should be to raise mature, self-reliant lovers of God, which fundamentally involves putting more decisions into the hands of our children over time. In some areas they need more protection and guidance than society seems to believe, while in other areas they are capable of much more than we could ever imagine.

The two ditches for parents, according to Paul David Tripp in his book on teens, *Age of Opportunity*, are isolation and assimilation. The isolation ditch involves parenting your children in such a way that they are isolated from all cultural trends and worldly temptations. These children tend to look and feel completely out of touch with society around them.

This isolation mentality endeavors to avoid anything and everything that is potentially worldly. Isolationism begins with the false premise that if you keep your children from "knowing evil and experiencing the world," they will choose good. Or to put it another way, if you protect your children from the world, then by a process of osmosis they'll choose what's right. While avoiding certain things is vital to protecting children from damaging situations, avoidance patterns that emanate from a "sin is out there" paradigm mistakenly focus on outward behavior when sin is inherently an issue of the heart.

The opposite ditch of isolation (a family that is too legalistic and too religious) is exemplified by the Christian family that has assimilated so much of the world and secular mentalities that it's hard to tell any difference between them and the world they seek to influence. This kind of family is much more prevalent than the former. These families, in an effort not to isolate their children, set no boundaries between what is culturally accepted and what is Biblically mandated. These kinds of parents often want to be "popular" with their kids and the members of society they socialize with. Their desire to be culturally acceptable deafens them to a God-conscious Christian life.

This mindset overemphasizes cultural relevance, thus neutering any ability to model Jesus and live as the salt and light to the watching world. Rather than isolation or assimilation, David Tripp encourages parents to live in what he coins "redemptive interaction."

Redemptive interaction entails teaching our children, and especially our teens, to understand and interact redemptively with culture without slipping into compromise. Our end game is to raise teenagers who are eventually fully able to interact with the culture around them without becoming enslaved to its idols.[1] Redemptive interaction means living amongst our culture while exemplifying Christ-like character and modeling Kingdom principles.

How do we live a life of redemptive interaction?
We must teach and disciple our children in Christ-like character!
The best way is not "spiritual boot-camp" or a list of do's and don'ts
but instead by leading and modeling them toward a dynamic
and life-changing relationship with Jesus.

— Wendy Tang

Entertainment & TV
Too Much Freedom Can Lead to Serious Bondage

While there is no perfect formula for balancing freedom and boundaries, a few decades ago our grandparents would have been horrified by what we consider freedom when it comes to entertainment. The kind of sexual and violent material that most elementary and preteen children watch on a daily basis would not have been considered moral for even adults to watch. We live in challenging times and need to think through what "FREEDOM" really is and what is simply assimilating the culture around us.

- The average child spends more than fifty-three hours a week with media [2]
- Seven in ten children have a TV in their bedroom (71%)
- A third of all children six years old and younger have a TV in their bedroom (36%) [3]

Barna Group surveys substantiate that overly self-regulated children do far worse as adults than children with more hands-on parents. Surveys disclosed that parents who raised spiritual champions were most protective of their children in the area of *media*. Media was a *big issue* for the parents who raised healthy, thriving kids. Further, surveys with young adults confirm that most of them believe parents are usually too lenient with their children where media is concerned. "When I was growing up, I never would have said this," said one young spiritual champion, "But now as I look at the lives of my childhood friends, the ones I envied because they had so much freedom when we were growing up, their lives are a mess." [4]

Another adult spiritual champion shared, "I look at my classmates today and realize how twisted their thinking is, not because they're bad people, but just because they've been exposed to so much garbage without any kind of filter or analysis. Self-regulation failed with my friends; parental regulation worked wonders for me." [5]

"In fact, the unwillingness of parents to closely monitor and limit media was listed by spiritual champions as a glaring fault of many parents. Giving children the freedom to determine their own media diet was ranked as one of the most insidious weaknesses of today's parents, producing outcomes that will haunt their children—and our society—for years to come." [6]

So why is watching inappropriate things so harmful in the long run anyway? Science reveals that humans possess around fourteen billion brain cells. Thankfully we are not in danger of running out of intellectual capacity. The bad news or good news depending on what we watch—our brains retain *everything* we take in. The brain absorbs every single thing we encounter and stores it away either in our conscious or subconscious. Input of information is easy; it's getting bad stuff out that's almost impossible. Once something enters your mind, without a miraculous intervention, (which our God certainly can do) it's there forever. Children's brains have high levels of plasticity, meaning they absorb new information like sponges. "As kids move into the teenage years, especially when they are between eleven and fifteen, their brains are at such a critical stage of development that the patterns they form will be a foundation for the rest of their lives. A 2008 study proved that what kids watch in TV and movies impacts their future actions." [7]

Through her years of research, Dr. Lorraine Day found that: "Children watch an average of forty-three hours of TV per week (now closer to fifty-three); while watching they rapidly become almost hypnotized. It has been shown scientifically that within minutes of beginning to watch TV, the brain changes from the alert brain waves (beta waves) to the hypnotic waves (alpha waves) where the judgment center of the brain is bypassed. So the violence and decadence that the child sees, bypasses the judgment center in the brain and is implanted in the child's brain without any ability on the child's part to decide whether what they see is right or wrong. The brain accepts the violence and decadence without any moral judgment being applied to it. It then becomes part of the child's permanent subconscious." [8]

Good Parenting
Involves Protecting the Innocence of Your Children

Why am I focusing so much on media? Because, media including video gaming, can literally drive the culture in your home. On an even more serious note, it can steal the innocence of your child. It's no secret that this generation faces exponentially more temptation than most of us encountered in our childhood. "In 1950 the average child saw little to no television and what they saw on television was stable, two-parent families who generally interacted with respect. Today, the average child watches around seven hours of television per day." [9] Before 1971, TV producers were not even allowed to say "toilet" on a show because it was considered inappropriate.

Should we really believe that there is no correlation between violence and immorality in our nation and graphic media imagery, when the same media directors promise to affect buying behavior by a thirty-second commercial? We monitor media to keep from putting our children in moral situations in which they will likely fail. Children ultimately mature through testing, responsibility, and choices, but when we allow too much temptation it actually sets our children up for failure. You can put an honest, wholesome, and God-fearing child in a situation that is too much for them and it will cause them to stumble.

The biggest risk to parenting today is all the other parents who aren't.

—Dr. Ben Carson

If you send a young child to a party where you question whether parents are going to allow indecent movies, to assume that your child will have the courage to make the right choice is unrealistic. Yet, a mature, older teen is often capable of wise decisions. Close friends of ours shared that their teen son literally ran home (four miles away) when he found his school friends were watching dirty movies.

We personally don't allow our younger boys to spend the night where parents have installed cable into their children's bedrooms, and children are allowed to select their own media diet. Installing unlimited cable into a young boy's room in the name of freedom is an example of setting children up for failure. What if that child can't say no to sexual content at the age of ten—he or she may develop a stronghold and secret addiction that would take years to heal. There is a lot of soft porn on cable, and most people get hooked on "hard porn" *after* they've become desensitized to "soft porn."

Saying "no" to most of Hollywood is not isolating your children—it is freeing them to develop creatively and wholesomely. As a result of ingested media, children and teens make choices concerning their sexuality and other areas that will affect their lives for years. Parental guidance in media consumption sets children up for success.

More About the Porn Facing Our Young People

The Bible tells us that, "A prudent man sees danger and takes refuge, but the simple keep going and suffer for it" (Proverbs 22:3).

While we should not succumb to fear, I believe we must be fully aware of what our children face when it comes to this issue. The last thing I want is for this information to cause anyone to be overly afraid. However, it's been proven that until people are fully aware of how harmful and serious something is and their conscious is fully awakened, they will not take action to deal with the issue at hand.

The following are a few statistics that parents should be aware of. They are already somewhat dated, so the ages at which children begin viewing porn is probably younger and more widespread due to smart phones and the 24/7 access to the Internet for many children.

- Before the age of 18, the average child will witness over 200,000 acts of violence on television, including 16,000 murders.
- Boys exposed to violent sex on television, including rape, are less likely to be sympathetic to female victims of sexual violence.
- The video game *Grand Theft Auto: Vice City,* rated M, was the best-selling video game among teens and preteens. In it, players can simulate having sex with a prostitute and then kill her.
- More than half of teens report getting most of their information about sex from television.
- Number of pornographic websites: 4.2 billion.
- Daily pornographic e-mails: 2.5 billion (8% of total e-mails).
- Websites offering illegal child pornography: 100,000.
- Sexual solicitations of youth made in chat rooms: 89%.
- Worldwide visitors to pornographic websites: 72 million annually.
- Average age of first Internet exposure to pornography: 11.
- The single largest consumers of Internet pornography: children ages 12-17.
- 15 to 17-year-olds having multiple hard-core exposures: 80%.
- 8 to 16-year-olds having viewed porn online: 29%. [10]
- Divorce cases involving one party with an obsessive interest in porn: 56%. [11]
- Roughly two-thirds (67%) of young men and one-half (49%) of young women agree that viewing pornography is acceptable. [12]
- More than half of sexually experienced guys would rather give up sex for a month than give up going online for a month. [13]

Craig Gross started a website, www.XXXChurch.com, as a resource for Christians struggling with pornography. "In a nonscientific poll he conducted, 70% of Christian men admitted to struggling with porn in their daily lives. A whopping 76% of pastors surveyed admitted to struggling with porn at some level."[14]

Internet porn is a serious issue facing children and young people today. Dani Johnson reveals, "Based on the professional opinions of therapists I've interviewed, pornography is currently the number one addiction in the United States of America. Professionals with PhD degrees who have been counseling for more than 30 or 40 years say that pornography is the greatest epidemic that has ever hit this nation."

Dr. Lavonne Atnip, explains that pornography is far worse than any other addiction, "This is the strongest of all addictions in the last 35 years and has a greater effect than any of the drugs of the 1960s, 70s or 80s. It's more powerful than crack with same effect on the brain as crystal methamphetamine."[16]

No average parent would let their child walk into a strip club or enter a porn video shop, and yet some of the most horrific porn is only one click away. Not to mention many of the porn sites that are often accidentally stumbled upon are actually designed to trap users, making it difficult to leave the site without watching more porn.

Parents should understand that it's not merely "bad or rebellious" kids who get hooked on porn, as almost no child would intentionally look for porn unless they have been exposed first. *Keeping Children Safe Online*, writes, "90% of children aged between eight and sixteen have viewed pornography on the Internet, in most cases unintentionally while attempting to do homework."[17] Tragically, many of the children now addicted to porn were on the computer doing a normal search and ended up in a full-blown pornography site. The natural curiosity of "normal" children makes it hard for them to keep from investigating further. Parents also need to be aware that girls are getting hooked on porn as well. While it remains a larger issue for boys, there are many girls who have stumbled across porn and found themselves secretly accessing it on a regular basis. One in three visitors to pornographic websites are women.[18]

The following scenario may be the most telling regarding the seriousness of pornography and our youth that I have heard to date. "As a guest speaker at a parent-teen conference called *ReConnect*, hosted by the ministry, *Generations of Virtue*, Fred Stoeker shared a shocking story. He had been invited to speak at a popular Bible college, and a week before his arrival the school had sent an anonymous poll to the students regarding their pornography usage. His question wasn't, 'When is the last time you viewed pornography?' It was, 'How often do you view pornography?' The poll results were unsettling to say the least; 100% of men and 87% of women said they view pornography at least once a week."[19]

While porn is definitely the most harmful and destructive online behavior, parents must also come to grips with the deluge of media impacting our children in a wide range of venues. The best book I've come across to help parents navigate the online waters is *Guardians of Purity—A Parent's Guide to Winning the War Against Media, Peer Pressure, and Eroding Sexual Values* by Julie Hiramine. This book is full of practical help and great insights to equip parents in guiding their children toward purity in a world that is doing the opposite. Julie points out, "When we were kids, we had to go to the mall or out to a restaurant to see our friends; now our own children just hop on their computer or mini-computers (i.e., cell phones) to do the same thing. Sure, there were ways for us to get into mischief, but usually that did not happen under the same roof, let alone the same room that our parents were sitting in! Now kids don't even have to walk out the door to get themselves in trouble. We as parents have to realize that being online is like being in a house with no parents home."[20]

Each year the amount of time the average child spends online or on an electronic device is increasing exponentially. Real relationships are being replaced by virtual relationships with kids spending excessive time playing video games, texting, and using social networks. Facebook, Instagram, Twitter, and Tumbler (and other forthcoming social networks that will evolve before this book even hits the market) present a growing challenge to the emotional welfare and purity of our kids.

We must engage this challenge because if our child falls prey in areas like pornography, other parenting principles will be of little help or significance until these strongholds are dealt with. Yet we need to keep in mind that God Himself is more powerful than any schemes of the enemy. While we shouldn't be unaware of the devil's plans to steal territory in our children's lives, we can find great hope that if we engage the battle and follow the Lord's leading our children can remain pure and healthy! Our children can avoid the pitfalls that keep many adults from living victoriously and become part of the world's solution rather than a casualty of the current culture-war. Take courage; God will honor your efforts.

Tips for Stewarding Technology and Protecting Your Kids from Porn

Purpose to engage the battle. Don't be apathetic or inactive about the online behavior of your child. Decide to become involved and aware. It may be painful, uncomfortable, or overwhelming at times, but God is on your side. He wants your family to walk in freedom, and He will provide you with wisdom, support, and tools.

Develop a plan with your children. In our home we have prepared our children for not "if" but "when" the porn temptation comes their way. Help your children understand that if they look at pornography, it will put thoughts in their minds that will torment them for years. Don't teach from an attitude of fear, but prepare them for scenarios where other children may attempt to show them porn via cell phones, in locker rooms, or at their home computers. Being informed and proactive could save a lifetime of strongholds and hidden addictions.

Don't just give rules; give your kids a vision for the awesome blessings in store for those who walk in purity and righteousness. Remember, your sons will some day be someone else's husband. Raise them like you want your daughter's future parents to be raising their son. One of the biggest motivators for young people is a vision for the future. By the teen years all normal teens are beginning to dream of a lifelong soul mate. Let them know that God is preparing special spouses for them and that He has an amazing love story planned for their lives. Teach them that what God has planned is better than the modern-day romances portrayed by Hollywood.

Encourage your children to develop face-to-face relationships. Help them see that if you *only* know someone online, real depth and meaningful connection can't take place. In real life relationships develop by spending quality time with people. Virtual relationships are often shallow and sometimes even deceptive. I've seen some pretty disturbed people attempt to present themselves as normal and healthy online. This can become a serious danger for a child who hasn't fully matured. Think about it—even adults are being deceived.

Venues like Facebook or Pinterest can be fun places to voice ideas, communicate with friends, or express creativity when they are used with good judgment and accountability—just be careful to help your child engage these with discretion.

Monitor younger children. Our older teens go on Facebook without us (although my oldest son has no interest in social networks—he'd rather play golf—thank you Jesus). However my extroverted, tween, loves connecting—the more connections the better. Because he is still somewhat young, he has to have me or his older sister around when he goes on Facebook.

Put some kind of monitoring software on all computers that kids have access to. Sadly, parent after parent has shared with me how their child stumbled on porn accidentally and then became addicted. It's happening increasingly through cell phones—most of the time in the middle of the night while parents and siblings are sleeping. This is why filters and accountability are so vital. A great website is www.CovenantEyes.com. Covenant Eyes offers teaching tools as well as accountability and filtering protection. Once you get a filtering system in place, make sure to monitor it. Having a filtering system that you don't know how to use or don't check won't do you much good.

Limit the overall use of media. Setting boundaries on the amount of time a child can spend on any type of screen helps keep technology from taking over the culture of your home. I confess I have occasionally day dreamed of gathering all the screens in my home, bundling them up in a canvas bag and throwing them off a local bridge. All you moms out there who are constantly getting your kids off of one screen or another know how I feel. I love and appreciate the ability to access information and chat with long-distance friends, yet helping my children steward their time and relationships via technology can be frustrating at times. Picturing yourself on that bridge with all the electronics might be just the humorous picture you need to carry on!

Put all smart phones in a basket at night. You may want to make a place in your house to gather all iPads, cell-phones, iPod Touches, etc. so you can have a media-free time each day and more importantly—at night. Remember, if children have a smart phone in their room at bedtime, it's like leaving your kids at home without adult supervision. Even for older teens putting phones in the basket at night is helpful, trying to go to sleep with texts buzzing can seriously hinder sleep. Who knows what fellow teens may say or send in the middle of the night. As far as sleep, teens already struggle to fall asleep without all the buzzing and beeping. Many teens are texting each other all through the night and parents still wonder why their grades suffer or their kids look so tired all the time. Don't fall for the "it's my alarm" excuse; just go buy a cheap alarm clock that buzzes and beeps *in the morning*! Your children can do without their phone for eight hours.

Keep computers in public, high traffic areas. Have your children and teens use laptops in areas where they can be seen by other eyes. We've encouraged our children to hold each other accountable. This way it's not just Dad and Mom's eyes that are watching;

siblings are helping each other!

Set a good example. As a parent you can't insist that your children watch wholesome media and then watch indecent movies and shows yourself. If you are sneaking off to watch *Desperate Housewives* with other desperate women, you can't expect more from your kids. Your children won't develop moral standards if you don't model them. We can fool our friends, church mates, and co-workers, but we will never fool our children. We really must be and live out all that we want them to become. Believe me, I sometimes wish this weren't so, but children have the equivalent of a PhD in psychology when it comes to spotting hypocrisy.

Cultivate media discernment. Exposing your children to good quality films makes it easier for them to identify quality media overall. This generation has some wonderful producers who are sending timely and powerful messages via the film industry. I remember in the 80's when *Karate Kid* was one the best movies out for teaching values. Today there are many along the same lines and frankly much better in both quality and values. While it may have taken a little searching, our family has discovered lots of wonderful movies with warriors, adventure, sports heroes, and life-changing lessons.

But keep the following insight by Stephen Covey in mind, "It is true that there is much good on TV—good information and enjoyable, uplifting entertainment. But for most of us and for our families, the reality is more like digging for a lovely tossed salad out of the garbage dump." [21] Cable is probably not the best place to find quality movies and shows. As you seek wisdom in making choices about media, make sure you help your children learn to discern for themselves. Asking questions and engaging in family dialogues are great ways to help your children cultivate their own discernment and core values. Engaging their minds and discussing values is as important as rationing and screening media selection. Ultimately you are grooming your children to make wise choices *without* your intervention. So don't just watch movies—discuss them! Don't just make rules—teach values!

Say NO to movies with high levels of sexual content. Study after study reveals that children who watch sexual content will pursue sexual activities and outlets. It's that simple!

Keep strong relational connections going in your family. When children experience the goodness of God and the fulfillment of healthy relationships, resisting temptation and deceptive habits will be much easier. Children with thriving emotional connections to family are much less likely to fall into porn or other destructive patterns. Because when kids are socially, emotionally, and spiritually fulfilled, they will not look for love "in all the wrong places." Children need wholesome friends and strong community, but what they need most is for their favorite people on the planet to be living under their own roof.

Lead them toward a dynamic, thriving relationship with Jesus. Children don't have a junior-sized Holy Spirit. Encourage and teach them how to hear the voice of God and follow the leading of the Holy Spirit. Children falling in love with Jesus and learning to obey His voice are some of the best protection against the traps of the enemy.

Don't fear what other parents think. When you are tempted to cave in to the peer pressure of looking like the overly strict parent, ask yourself what you would choose if you weren't afraid of what other parents thought. Being overly conscious of what others think is a form of "fear of man." People are valuable and important, but don't let their opinion keep you from doing what you know is right. I have often had to remind myself as it's never fun to go against the flow, that it is my job to train and raise my children. My husband and I are the ones who will be ultimately accountable for our choices concerning our kids. Many parents know intuitively what the right thing is to do, but because of peer pressure they waver and lose confidence in their "gut feelings." Ask God for wisdom, decide what you feel is right, and then stick to it. When you are not afraid to "be different" from what is culturally acceptable (maybe even at your church), your children will learn the same. Courageous parents create courageous kids.

Model your convictions. While we've discussed the importance of age-appropriate protection, the fact remains that children develop most of what they believe by watching their parents.

When we were missionaries in Romania, I used to take our children to the local grocery stores to buy food. Porn is quite rampant in Europe and more unabashedly displayed publicly than in the States. As I was checking out of the store one day, the checkout clerk was bagging my groceries in plastic bags with full-scale naked women on the outside. I stood in the line and informed the clerk that I refused to take groceries bagged in pictures of naked ladies. The cashier looked shocked.

Romania, being a former communist country, was not used to people speaking their opinions and convictions so freely. After digging around the back of the store, the lady finally emerged with suitable plastic bags. Meanwhile, the people in line were getting a friendly little lesson in morals, and so were my children.

On a funny note, my parents once shared with me a story about my great grandmother who was a Belgian Catholic raised in an aristocratic family. She was once vacationing in the French Riviera in the late 1900s where lo and behold—the French pioneered the practice of nude beaches—even back then! My grandmother was meandering along the sandy shores when she happened upon a completely nude man. She immediately approached the man and exclaimed assertively, "You sure would look a lot better with your clothes on!" So maybe my forthrightness is more genetic than I realized. Thank the Lord for the example of our grandparents!

For more tips on Internet protection, go to www.ProtectKids.com. Furthermore, please remember that while pornography addictions may be hard to overcome in the natural, we have a supernatural God who can deliver and free us if we are serious about pursuing purity. While we should take heed in this area, we don't want to lose sight of how powerful our God is to deliver and heal His children! There is nothing too big for Him! More and more ministries are springing up to help people get free of these addictions.

A Word About Overnights

Our family doesn't have a hard and fast RULE about overnights. However, after interviewing numerous counselors, seasoned parents, and reading stats regarding this issue, it seems worth addressing.

In his book, *Have a New Kid by Friday,* Dr. Kevin Leman says; "Overnights should be rare, especially when your children are young. Children need to be home, and today's kids are home less and less." He then asks, "How well do you really know the family that your child would be staying with? There's a difference in letting your three year old stay at Grandma and Grandpa's for the night and letting your seven year old stay at his little league friend's house overnight. Do you know for sure that there is no pedophile in that home?" [22]

In over 20 years of ministry to children and families, my husband and I have been surprised again and again with what we have discovered in this area. Some of the most seemingly wholesome leaders we have personally known, turned out to be pedophiles or regular pornography users. We've counseled too many young people who were exposed to porn first at a slumber party or abused by a friend's brother or dad while spending the night at another home.

As our kids have gotten older, there are families that we trust with our children overnight—but not many. Ask the Lord to give you discernment about when to say "yes" and when to say "no." Don't doubt your own discernment, but keep in mind that in this particular area it's better to err on the side of being too cautious than on the side of being too careless.

It is fun for teens and preteens to occasionally spend the night at each other's homes. As parents, we should care about what our kids care about but not at the expense of losing their moral innocence! Don't play Russian roulette with your children. The stakes are too high!

Teach Your Children to Value the Wisdom of Authorities

It is interesting to note that science now substantiates that the brain doesn't fully mature until around the age of 25 ("That explains a lot," I hear many of you parents thinking.) Training young people to embrace the wisdom of their parents and mentors could save them from a boatload of trouble and lifelong wounds. Though there is certainly a delicate balance between teaching your budding teens independence and emphasizing the importance of retaining respect for the wisdom of authorities and mentors.

A powerful example of the benefits of trusting the wisdom of your parents comes from the life of one of the Curlins' daughters, a contemporary of mine at Wheaton. During college she was dating a young man with whom she felt she was deeply in love. Their commitment was nearing engagement but as the relationship progressed, the parents rightly observed that this relationship was not affecting their daughter in a healthy way.

She became increasingly introspective and insecure in her relationship with God, manifesting a lack of peace in her life. While the parents did not dislike this young man, they began to discern that he was not the kind of guy that would bring out the best in their daughter. Their personalities were decidedly incompatible.

Finally, her father intervened and helped his daughter bring an end to the relationship, something she most likely would never have done on her own. Their daughter was around 20, but because she knew and trusted her father's wisdom and love for her, she made the painful choice to follow his advice. She was willing to embrace discomfort and trust that sometimes others can see things you cannot—especially your parents! She was willing to trust someone more than she trusted herself.

Initially, breaking the relationship off proved grievous and distressing. Doing the right thing does not always feel right or comfortable at the time. When it comes to relationships, everyone needs wise counsel outside of themselves. Next to our relationship with Jesus, choosing our future mate will be the most important and impactful decision we will ever make!

For this young woman, not too much time passed after that event when she met someone else at Wheaton College. Wow, this guy was truly a match made in Heaven for her! His encouraging, confident personality complemented her artistic, introspective, and sometimes melancholy, make-up.

The Curlins' daughter presently lives in Panama where her husband is a successful business missionary who was instrumental in taking a Panamanian airline public. She has used her artistic, creative abilities to decorate homes for those living on a limited budget, and inhabitants of the poorest areas of Panama. Today she is more grateful than ever that she took the advice of her parents and so is her husband! Embracing Godly advice and waiting for God's best is always worth it in the end.

Living From the Inside Out

Ultimately, children will *behave from the heart*. It's mandatory that we help our children internalize Biblical principles and that we exemplify a life flowing from relationship with God. Children do best when they cultivate a personal desire to submit to God through experiencing the father heart of God. Christianity can only be truly lived from the inside out. *"You cannot build enough fences without. You must build them within."* [23]

We were never created to be controlled from the outside in. As we equip and prepare our children to withstand temptation, we must not lose sight of the fact that the best protection entails casting vision, building values in our children, and making sure their emotional needs are met.

When children are young, we are their protection; but as they grow older, they must increasingly be governed internally. *"If a child is believing things that are not true and desiring what is wrong, there is no way that he will do what is right. So the goal of parenting is not to focus on getting right behavior, but to shepherd the hearts of our children. Heart response and heart change are our focus because we know that what controls the heart will control the life."* [24]

Two Trees in the Garden

Consider the Garden of Eden. It contained two trees, the "tree of life" and the "tree of the knowledge of good and evil." Only one tree was forbidden. Why was the tree of the knowledge of good and evil right in the middle of the garden? Because when there is no choice, there is no true freedom. God ultimately wants relationship not control.

All relationships involve both responsibility and choice. Children learn the strength of handling freedom by making choices. The end game is not protection, it's equipping children to be confident and strong in the midst of life's temptations and challenges. Training involves freedom to choose. The older children get, the more responsibility they have for their own moral choices. As children mature, their choices will be motivated more and more by relationship — their relationship to God and those around them.

Gregg and Sono Harris, parents of Brett and Alex Harris, who wrote *Do Hard Things*, and Joshua Harris who wrote, *I Kissed Dating Goodbye*, have helped families to raise leaders for over 25 years. They describe parenting by using the example of a greenhouse.

"When you want to have a strong crop in the future, you often have to start plants in a greenhouse, allowing them to get a good root system established. Ultimately, your goal is to transplant them to the field where they'll bear their fruit. But as they grow, that transition is a process. As they mature, you move them to a cold frame where they can harden up and learn to handle the changing temperatures. They're no longer getting all the nurturing they were in the greenhouse, but neither are they exposed to the full force of the harsh winds and the elements." [25]

Next to giving too much freedom too soon, the worst thing a parent can do is raise overly-protected children who have no grid for real life. *"Children will not be content to be protected and guarded. If you squeeze too hard, they will slip out of your grasp as sure as a wet bar of soap. You can't just drive kids, you need to let them steer."* [26] Giving enough freedom often means facing and dealing with our own issues of fear and control which can stem from our personal inability to trust God with our children.

It's sad to see, but when parents endeavor to hold on to children too long, or use excess isolation, children will often break loose, and parents then miss the opportunity to offer age-appropriate choices. If we let go of our children a little at a time, we can incrementally give them more freedom, saving the shipwreck that often happens when kids are overwhelmed by too much freedom too fast. Use good judgment in protecting the innocence of your children, but keep the end goal in mind: raising self-reliant leaders, initiative takers, and lovers of God.

Lastly, as a parent it is easy to let fear overtake you when you spend too much time considering the temptations facing your children in our rapidly changing world. I was recently watching the latest version of the movie, *Emma*, and heard the father say to his daughter, "You have not known FEAR until you have children." How true that tends to be! Please remind yourself as many times as you need that the Lord is on your side and that He loves you and your children more than you could possibly imagine.

Discussion and Discovery

1. Between the two pitfalls of assimilation and isolation, where do you feel you need to make adjustments? In what ways do you need to live more counter-culturally?

2. Are there areas you feel you give your children too much freedom or not enough? Pray and ask the Lord how you can make healthy adjustments.

3. Are there areas in which you've over-emphasized freedom and under-emphasized responsibility? Pray and ask the Lord how you can make changes in these areas as well.

4. Were you raised with too much freedom or not enough? Were you over-controlled or under-guided?

5. What does your own heart tell you about the effects of television on your children? What changes could you implement in this area?

6. Which tips about media and protecting your children from porn do you plan to implement in your home?

Optional Assignment

Spend some time listening to Jesus and let Him show you what you are doing right and then ask for wisdom in areas you need to adjust. Write down what you hear and feel. Write down some goals as the Holy Spirit leads you.

ENDNOTES

1 Paul David Tripp, *Age of Opportunity* (1997, New Jersey), 158.

2 Mark Prensky, *On the Horizon* (October 2001, MCB University Press), Vol. 9 No, 5.

3 Victoria J. Rideout, Ulla G. Foehr, Donald F. Roberts, *Generation M2: Media in the lives of 8-18-Year-Olds*, Kaiser Family Foundation, January 2010, http://www.kff.org/entmedia/upload/8010pdf.

4 George Barna, *Revolutionary Parenting* (2007, Carol Stream), 87.

5 George Barna, *Revolutionary Parenting* (2007, Carol Stream), 73.

6 George Barna, *Revolutionary Parenting* (2007, Carol Stream), 73.

7 Julie Hiramine, *Guardians of Purity* (2012, Lake Mary, FL), 45.

8 Dimitri A. Christakis, et al., *Early Television Exposure and Subsequent Attentional Problems in Children,* Pediatrics 113 (2004): 708-13

9 Stephen Covey, *The 7 Habits of Highly Effective Families* (1997, Golden Books), 121.

10 A. C. Huston and J. C. Wright, *Television and Socialization of Young Children,* in T. MacBeth, ed., *Tuning in to Young Viewers* (Thousand Oaks, Calif.: Sage), 37-60.

11 Covenant Eyes Website: http://www.covenanteyes.com/

12 Enough is Enough, "Pornography Stastistics," http://www.internetsafety101.org/Pornographystatistics.htm

13 The National Campaign to Prevent Teen and Unplanned Pregnancy, *That's What He Said: What Guys Think About Sex, Love, Contraception and Relationships.*

14 Jason Rovou, 'Porn & Pancakes' fights X-rated Addictions, CNN.com, April 6, 2007, www.cnn.com/2007/US/04/porn.addiction/index. html (June 2008).

15 Dani Johnson, Grooming the Next Generation for Success (2009, Destiny Image), 60.

16 Dani Johnson, Grooming the Next Generation for Success (2009, Destiny Image), 61.

17 www.safefamilies.org/sfStats.php.

18 Ropelato, "Internet Pornography Statistics."

19 Julie Hiramine, Guardians of Purity (2012, Lake Mary, FL), 29.

20 Julie Hiramine, Guardians of Purity (2012, Lake Mary, FL), 12-13.

21 Stephen Covey, The 7 Habits of Highly Effective Families (1997, Golden Books), 125.

22 Dr. Kevin Leman, Have a New Kid by Friday (2008, Grand Rapids, MI), 158-159.

23 Michael Pearl, Avoiding Vacuums (NGJ Calendar 2011), 2.

24 Paul David Tripp, Age of Opportunity (1997, New Jersey), 49.

25 Julie Ferwerda, One Million Arrows (2009, Enumclaw, WA), 60.

26 M. Pearl, Jumping Ship (2007, Pleasantville, TN), 41.

CHAPTER NINE

Education & Intelligence

Discovering How Your Child Learns Best

Don't let schooling interfere with your education.

— Mark Twain

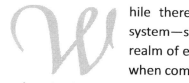hile there are certainly good elements about our education system—some foundational features ought to be challenged. The realm of education is presently one of the more antiquated fields when compared with the innovation taking place in other spheres such as business, media, medicine, and the arts. Recently, a well-known educator was lamenting the fact that public education has remained virtually unchanged for the past one hundred years. All in spite of mounting evidence revealing that the current style of educating the next generation is only optimally effective for a small fraction of students in today's schools.

What is really the goal of education anyway? William Yeat's understanding of the heart of education stands the test of time. He is famous for his notion that, "Education is not filling a bucket but lighting a fire." I would also add that true education should involve the discovering of *your* fire.

It is becoming ever apparent that a *majority,* not a *minority* of students do not fit the current one-size-fits-all system of educating children. Sir Ken Robinson, a world-renowned creativity expert and author of the best-selling book, *The Element*, believes that the existing system of education is actually dislocating many people from their natural talents and is in need of a radical shift from standardized learning to personalized learning. In his talk titled, "Schools Kill Creativity," he promotes the idea that human resources are often like natural resources and are buried deep within a person, thus you have to *look* for them. You must generate the circumstances and environment for them to reveal themselves. Since human talent is incredibly diverse, education needs to move away from cloning, pigeonholing, and conformity toward customization and personalization.

Consider what Walter Isaacson said of Einstein. "As a young student, he never did well with rote learning. And later, as a theorist, his success came not from the brute strength of his mental processing power but from his imagination and creativity." Einstein would often play his violin in his kitchen late at night, while pondering complicated problems. Then suddenly he would announce, "I've got it!"[1] Einstein never functioned well in the traditional education model, and yet he is a celebrated and legendary genius.

The biggest problem today is that education has failed to adjust to radically changing times, in which the skills and aptitudes required for optimal success are fundamentally shifting in response to emerging global trends. Ken Robinson believes that in the future creativity will be as important in education as literacy. His work with organizations and businesses involves helping them understand that creativity and intelligence are blood relatives. A person can't be creative without acting intelligently. "Similarly, the highest form of intelligence is thinking creatively."[2] Creativity, intuition, emotional intelligence, and independent thinking are already in high demand in most companies. To learn more about these cultural shifts read the fascinating book, *A Whole New Mind, Why Right Brainers Will Rule the Future* by Daniel Pink. This book explores emerging wealth-creation trends, accentuating the tidal wave of emerging creative, right-brained careers and entrepreneurs. It can serve as an invaluable tool for parents to better understand and prepare their children for a swiftly changing world with very different future job opportunities.

Successful careers will progressively involve right-brained job skills in which art, design, and creative thinking will play a vital role. In greater numbers, the purely left-brained careers will be outsourced overseas and produce less income. The premise that outsourcing has been over-hyped for the near future, but under-hyped for the long run, will most likely prove true. Those who will have the greatest future job advantage will be skilled at utilizing both hemispheres of their brains. If you haven't noticed the swell in artistic design in almost every product on the market, just observe the artistic creativity displayed in anything from the latest car models to the various artistic toilet bowl cleaning brushes sold at Target. Art and creativity are becoming an integral part of every industry that touches our daily lives.

Businesses across the globe are looking for employees who are creative, intuitive, and can think independently. Companies will also seek out employees who can quickly adapt to change, as the rate of change will exponentially increase. Thus flexibility will be a valuable and sought-after skill.

> *The principle goal of education is to create men who are capable of doing new things,*
> *not simply of repeating what other generations have done*
> *~men who are creative, inventive and discoverers.*

— Jean Piaget

Missed Opportunity

While many children in our country *are* being educated, the unfortunate component of education for many students is one of *missed opportunity*. Ideally the education system should *help* children discover and develop their natural abilities, but often schools unintentionally hinder individual talents and capacities. Intelligent, gifted, and creative children think they are not because the present system often stigmatizes, or remains ignorant of children's unique gifts and talents. Sadly, as Ken Robinson emphasizes, children whose minds work differently (and this is most likely a majority) often feel alienated and even stupid. Too many graduate from school unsure of their personal capacities and innate talents, mainly because schools in general have a very limiting and small-minded view of human intelligence. Even more tragic is when adults have finished high school or college and have lost their love of learning entirely. Some even lose it as early as elementary school.

Think about it: considering a child spends seven to eight hours a day in school for thirteen years (approximately 17,000 hours before the age of 18), the effectiveness of the school experience should be evaluated. What kind of results would we see if after basics were taught, at least three hours a day was utilized toward developing students' natural gifts and passions? Imagine if musical children spent a good portion of their day learning music, scientifically-inclined children focused on their particular field of interest, and children who love business were taught leadership and marketing skills.

Homeschooling was certainly partly birthed out of a desire for faith-based education, but I believe the bigger motivation for many homeschool parents is the aspiration to give their children a tailor-made education. These parents desire their children to work hard and learn extensively, but only in an environment that uncovers and stimulates their natural gifts and aptitudes. While many challenges are involved in the quest to create an environment for optimal education, positive breakthroughs are taking place in Western education. Certain sectors of public schools are implementing greater means of reaching children who learn and think differently. Charter schools are springing up across the country that offer more opportunities to develop arts and creativity, or cultivate specific skill sets. Many of these Charter schools offer two or three-day weeks to accommodate parents who want to take part in their child's education but may not feel equipped to manage it all. I was a part of this kind of Charter school in California and loved it.

I believe that in the future, effective education models will adopt a primary mission of developing children through unique styles of learning. The *cutting-edge* schools will move away from standardization and toward customization. In these environments teachers will be *students of their students,* mining for the *sweet spot* where students' innate gifting and aptitude meets their personal passion. These will be environments where kids want to learn and can discover more about their unique design.

Marva Collins, founder of Westside Preparatory School in inner-city Chicago, is considered one of the world's greatest teachers. Her astounding impact on education lead to invitations by both George H. W. Bush and Bill Clinton to become Secretary of Education, but she turned them down in favor of teaching one student at a time. She believed that there is a brilliant child locked inside every student. She forsook busy work and rote memorization, replacing it with active participation and a demand that the students practice self-discipline. She believed the teacher should make learning contagious and create an environment in which one idea sparks another."

Marva was able to take children who had been told they were illiterate and help them become fluent in language. They were able to read from the greatest writers—Plato, Socrates, Homer. 'Throwaway' students began quoting Shakespeare. Eventually, and with a lot of hard work, graduates of Westside Prep were accepted at Harvard, Princeton, Columbia, Oxford, Yale, and Stanford. She said this about teaching, "I have discovered few learning disabled students in my three decades of teaching, but I have discovered many, many victims of teaching inabilities." She focused on identifying and magnifying each student's unique gifts.[3]

Escalating studies exploring multiple intelligences and diverse learning styles have served to prompt the urgency to reform current educational processes. One recent expert in brain and genius capacity found that every single individual has genius capacity. The key is finding out *where* your personal genius resides. It's interesting to note that the word "genius" literally comes from the Roman word "genuinus," which means *what you were naturally born with*.[4] Yes, genius manifests when we discover what we were naturally born with and utilize it.

Multiple Intelligence Discoveries

Controversy will continue to surround the question of human intelligence with its intricate and multifaceted nature. Most of us would have to erase our mental slate regarding what we know and think about intelligence in order to embrace what is being discovered.

Intelligence is extraordinarily diverse and as unique as an individual's fingerprint. One of the most profound insights by Sir Ken Robinson was the assertion that we are asking the wrong question. People often want to know "How intelligent they are?" but the right question is instead, "How *are* they intelligent?"

Psychologist Howard Gardner, a professor at Harvard whose work regarding multiple intelligences has profoundly impacted mindsets toward education (particularly in the United States), developed one of the most accepted theories. In addition, Dr. Caroline Leaf, a current brain scientist and coach who has spent twenty-five years studying the brain, has compelling insights regarding intelligences as well. Her book, "The Gift in You" explores the science of the brain and the unique blend of gifts and learning capacities within each individual. She expounds on intelligences in detail and offers tests to discover your own gifting as well as your children's.

Howard Gardner's study uncovered seven predominant intelligences at work in people. His work showed that individuals have primary intelligences, but each person also possesses all the intelligences in a unique blend and in varying degrees. These assorted intelligences work together and are interconnected. All seven intelligences are needed to live well—thus the more individuals understand their unique blend, the more powerfully they can capitalize on their innate design. Discovering which intelligences are strongest is key to developing personal gifting and capacity. The following list by Howard Gardner is a general overview of the distinct intelligences as they pertain to children, along with some insights by Dr. Caroline Leaf. (For an in-depth study on multiple intelligences please see Dr. Caroline Leaf's books and DVDs.)

Intrapersonal Intelligence These children are very aware of their own feelings and possess an innate capacity to understand themselves. They are often introspective, and can easily shift between thoughts, deal with decision-making, as well as focus and analyze easily. Intrapersonal thinking allows a person to stand outside of himself and analyze his own thinking. Strengths of this intelligence are self-knowledge and the ability to self-regulate using their will to direct their behavior. Some professions suited to a high intrapersonal intelligence include: judge, counselor, philosopher, elder, and attorney.

Interpersonal Intelligence These children are leaders among their peers; they can understand and work well with people. They are good at communicating and can easily "read" other people's emotions and feelings. "Social interaction, listening, sharing, building relationships, giving and receiving love."[5] Interpersonal gifting allows one to motivate, lead, manage, and mediate between others. This relational IQ often carries an ability to discern about others, perceive motives, or distinguish if a person can be trusted. Those with a high interpersonal intelligence flourish by connecting with people and are energized by relationships. Some professions suited for this intelligence include: politicians, religious leaders, salespeople, and public relations.

Linguistic Intelligence These children enjoy writing, reading, telling stories, and are sensitive to the meanings of words and sounds. Children with this gifting can often speak or write effectively. Speaking is something these children do a lot of. Children with this kind of gifting often use language as a primary means of communication. They like to argue, persuade, entertain, and teach. Professions for those with high linguistic intelligence include: authors, poets, lawyers, speakers, and speech-writers.

Logical Intelligence These children usually have high logical intelligence and are interested in patterns and categories (typically very mathematical). They like mathematical procedures and have a high capacity to analyze problems logically, detect patterns, and reason deductively. These children are often drawn to strategy games and problem solving. Some professions that coincide with this gifting include: scientists, physicians, CPAs, engineers, computer programmers, and analysts.

Spatial Intelligence These children are visual/spatial learners. They think in images and pictures and can perceive color, light, shapes, and depth. Visual/spatial learners see and imagine things in their mind's eye. As their teachers teach, they imagine and visualize. They may like puzzling, drawing, painting, or making crafts, and they often day dream. The back part of the brain is the part that is utilized when we imagine and form mental pictures and images. Some professions suited for high visual/spatial intelligence include: artists, architects, sculptors, CEOs, photographers, and pilots.

Musical Intelligence These children can often sing well, compose music, play musical instruments, make rhythms, and attune to sounds. They also have an innate ability to "read between the lines." Musical children often have keen intuition and can easily feel when things are right or wrong. These children tend to make decisions based on feelings. High musical intelligence professions include: composer, conductor, singer, performer, or dancer.

Kinesthetic Intelligence These children process knowledge through bodily movement and sensations. They are often gifted athletes, or good at crafts and woodworking. They have good coordination and approach problems physically. "By definition, this is a tactile, energetic, multisensory type of thinking that involves control of body movements, the ability to co-ordinate yourself and the capacity to handle objects and things around you skillfully. These kinds of thinkers need to touch, feel, and move things around. To understand and retain information, they have to maneuver or experience what they learn." Or better said, they have to *move to think*.[6] Kinesthetic learners are often labeled "busy bodies," "hyperactive," or "ill-behaved." They process information through movement thus the traditional classroom is less than ideal for this kind of learner as they need to move to think and learn. Professions for high kinesthetic intelligences include: actor, athlete, dancer, surgeon, builder, or physical therapist.

More About Intelligences

If your dominant intelligence is interpersonal, you would learn best by gathering information while interacting with people around you. You would better process information by asking questions because it would jump start your brain's sequence of processing information.[7] This happens to be my dominant pillar of learning so I can relate to this process. I often stop Jeff when he is explaining something and ask a question if I am mentally stuck. This seems to help my brain to process the information he is giving me. I often "ask questions" by researching on the Internet or reading books while internally asking questions the entire time. Asking questions for an interpersonal learner jump-starts brain sequencing and allows better understanding.

On the other hand, an intrapersonal learner is distracted by questions and often wants to ponder things deeply. For them asking questions inhibits learning. The intrapersonal learner will often *not* tell you what they are thinking until a later time. This can be frustrating for the one who processes through questions and lots of verbal feedback.

Each person's unique combination of intelligences has a powerful impact on how he or she functions, learns, and experiences the world. Understanding the natural strengths and unique wiring of each member in your family can greatly enhance your ability to form close relationships built on trust and understanding.

Anna

Our oldest daughter is a classic example of a visual/spatial learner. She thinks in pictures and images. While not as clear with all of our children, Anna's dominant method of learning was noticeably evident at an early age. Even when she was very young, she would become frustrated when trying to explain something and say, "Mommy, just let me draw it for you!" We are extremely different in our learning and thinking patterns. I was so bad at drawing that when I attended school in Europe I constantly received Fs on my attempts at any sort of art. Visual/spatial learning is probably my lowest intelligence, while Anna on the other hand is very gifted at drawing, painting, and using her imagination.

Dr. Leaf explains the doorway into Anna's mind as a visual/spatial learner consists of picturing what people are saying in her mind's eye. Anna sometimes looks off when I am talking to her which is common for the visual/spatial learner as making eye contact can actually distract them when they receive information because it inhibits their ability to picture what you are saying in their mind. Anna's brain processes information by seeing a mental map in her mind as a person speaks to her. These kinds of children are processing information at the deepest level when they don't make eye contact and looking away actually helps them build memory.[8] Some of the children who look away or out the window in a classroom setting are not day dreaming but actually processing and picturing what their teacher is saying. Understanding these patterns is of paramount importance if you consider that possibly 30-40% of children are dominantly visual/spatial learners. Many students might actually love a particular subject if it were taught visually instead of presented in a non-visual way.

> *Ninety percent of what we learn is not what we're taught;*
> *it's how we're taught.*

Anna's second most dominant learning intelligence is musical. She can play songs by ear and often feels things before she understands them intellectually. She exhibits a high level of intuition, allowing her to instinctively feel what is going on around her. When Anna was very young, we were often surprised because at the beginning of a movie (before the rest of the family) she could intuitively pick out the bad guy or predict where the plot was going.

Musical children are also extremely sensitive to tone and sound. They listen to tone more than words. For them whenever correction or instruction is needed, the idea of "soft tones and soft words" is extremely significant. Also with musical children, classical music has been shown to augment their learning experience. Anna loves background music while she is working; for me it is a concentration blocker. Note to parents—there is no evidence that loud rock music benefits anyone's learning experience.

Wesley

Our son Wesley is a kinesthetic and interpersonal learner. His love and aptitude for sports and movement reveals his kinesthetic intelligence. He learns best while moving around. During his elementary years, he was known to begin walking around the classroom sharpening pencils and circling, while unaware he had even left his seat. Teachers often commented on his need to move. Sitting perfectly still and learning is sometimes agony for Wesley, but he loves people so much he still prefers to learn "at school." I asked him what his favorite "subject" was and of course he said, "P.E.". Kinesthetic kids love touch and physical activity of any kind. All three of our boys have a high degree of kinesthetic intelligence, which is often evidenced as they wrestle all over the house and even want to try their moves out on me.

Interestingly, kinesthetic CEOs are now using large balls to sit on instead of chairs so they can rock back and forth while working at their desks. This has proven to significantly improve their productivity and peace at work.

Joshua

Kinesthetic is Joshua's dominant learning style as well. However, Joshua is extremely kinesthetic without Wesley's verbal capacity, thus he tends to express himself physically before verbally. If siblings bother Josh too much, watch out or be ready to duck. We've had to work with Joshua and Wes on keeping their hands to themselves. Joshua is constantly moving during prayer and worship times, as he loves to interact with God through movement. During family worship, Joshua loves to wave flags and leap around the living room expressing himself to the Lord through action. Again, "be prepared to duck" comes to mind when he has his worship flags going. Sports of all kinds are great outlets for boys who have a high level of kinesthetic wiring.

Joshua is also very musical so his intuition and love for sound and rhythm is easy to observe. Like Anna, he has loved worship since he was a toddler. When he was three years old, he so enjoyed the worship time at church that when a friend offered to take him to "Petco" toward the end of worship, he yelled on the way to the car, "Take me back to church; take me back to church!"

Christian

Christian has remarkable relational skills that are a result of his interpersonal intelligence. If emotional intelligence (EQ) and ability to relate with people results in the highest success in the business realm, Christian will be a success indeed! I gave Christian Dr. Leaf's interpersonal intelligence quiz, and he answered a resounding yes on almost every one of the questions. Questions such as: I need people around me a lot, I form friendships easily, I find it easy to tune into the needs of others, I like to influence others, I prefer to lead rather than follow, I thrive on attention, and I can easily work with people from different backgrounds. "Yes! Yes! Yes!" answered Christian quickly and decisively. Christian's love for people of all ages has made him many friends and opened many doors. He also has a gift of humor that adds much to his emotional intelligence.

Within two months of beginning 6th grade at a new school, Christian had made the yearbook four times and become acquainted with many older juniors and seniors who often visited him at lunch just to say hello. Today, Christian knows few strangers while walking the school halls. The downside to his personality might include—being his teacher. I recently attended a back-to-school night where I asked the teacher how Christian was doing. A moment of silence followed by, "Mrs. Shupe, maybe you should go ahead and set up a parent/teacher conference." The teacher proceeded to clarify that while Christian is a fun student, she has literally found no student to sit him beside in which he doesn't visit. Apparently he knows everyone! Ugh, the lectures on being quiet in class will continue.

Having a clear understanding of your predominant intelligence can literally keep you on your path of destiny. Do you remember the story I told about how Ben Carson took the risk to study in a completely unconventional way in order to succeed at medical school?

Well, that is also a perfect example of how his understanding for *how* he was intelligent and *how* he learned best became the difference between failure and success, when it came to his education and attaining his lifelong dreams.

The Power of Reading

Dr. Carson is known for many accomplishments. He became a world-famous neurologist after being the first to successfully separate Siamese twins joined at the head. In addition, he was the youngest Director of Neurosurgery at John Hopkins Hospital, has received sixty-one honorary doctorate degrees, and written three best-selling books. Further he is a professor of neurosurgery, plastic surgery, oncology, and pediatrics at John Hopkins Medical Institution. Why am I sharing all these accolades? Because *The Ben Carson Story* is a story that could have turned out quite differently.

A Little Background

Ben Carson grew up as an at-risk child on the road to a life of academic failure, when his single, illiterate mom approached the Lord in prayer for a solution. After a few days of praying, his mother received a God-inspired plan. She informed Ben (who was in the fifth grade) and his brother, Curtis, that they'd no longer be allowed to watch television every day after school but instead would be going to the local library. The plan went like this—the boys were each required to read two books a week from the local library, accompanied by a written report about each one. If this was completed satisfactorily along with all schoolwork, they could choose two shows a week to watch. The boys assured their mom that she was ruining their lives, and neighbors scolded her for her parenting style, but she stuck to her convictions. Before long, this habit of reading two books a week and writing a report on each one opened up the world of learning and knowledge for these young boys in ways that changed their lives forever. Ben Carson advanced from illiterate to the top of his class within a year and later graduated with honors from high school. He went on to successfully attend Yale University and soon thereafter entered University of Michigan Medical School.

While reflecting on Ben Carson's mom, I was particularly impressed with her keen insights and hunger for advancing her lot in life by carefully observing those around her. Ms. Carson worked long hours cleaning and baby-sitting for affluent families, sometimes three or four families at a time. Ben shared that his mother observed how these successful and wealthy people became successful and what they did once they were. She wanted to know what separated the wealthy for whom she worked from the poor amongst whom she lived. This might be a good place to add that a common trait amongst successful people is that they are usually keen observers of people and the environment around them. Successful people frequently possess an insatiable curiosity.

One invaluable insight Ms. Carson obtained was regarding the general attitude most wealthy families held toward television (which in today's world would include video games). Although they owned multiple television sets—sometimes as many as five or six—they hardly watched them. Instead they spent a large amount of time reading and analyzing materials.[9]

This brings me to the subject of reading. While changes are needed in our current style of education, I remain a firm believer in cultivating our intellectual abilities to the full. The rate at which material comes at us will only increase, and if one can read well, he or she possesses a clear advantage. Historically and today, reading opens up worlds of opportunity.

Studies conducted on top business executives and performers continue to reveal that those who earn exponentially more than the rest are avid and devoted learners. In the business world, the adage that *Earners are Learners* couldn't be truer. Successful businessmen and women as well as entrepreneurs confess to constantly studying and reading books connected to their sphere of business. Studies reveal that the average amount of books top earners read is approximately twenty-four books a year in addition to computer data and articles. Further, the attitude of successful executives is always marked by a hunger for more knowledge and refraining from taking the attitude of an "expert."

Whether you are a visual or audio learner, kinesthetically inclined, or a relational wizard, reading is a skill at which almost anyone can become great. The more you read, the better you will get at it and the more you will enjoy it. Reading opens up the world of information and possibility that has no equal in intellectual opportunity. And for those creative, artistic types, reading has proven to enhance creativity. "Reading actually activates the mind in the same way that we activate muscles when we lift weights. The more active our minds are, the more agile they become, which results in higher levels of creativity. As someone wisely pointed out, 'The mind, once stretched by an idea, never returns to its original dimensions.'"[10]

Watching any kind of screen in excess dumbs kids down. When children watch television, the images and sounds are doing the thinking for them. They don't need to use their imagination, deductive reasoning, or creativity to ponder or extrapolate like one does when reading written material. Reading does the following:

1. Reading activates and exercises the mind.

2. Reading forces the mind to discriminate. From the beginning, readers have to recognize letters on the printed page, make them into words, the words into sentences, and the sentences into concepts.

3. Reading pushes us to use our imagination and makes us more creatively inclined.[11] It is undisputed that "students who excel academically, read extensively."[12] Avid reading produces intellectual accomplishments.

As a result of Ben Carson's Mom's courageous decision to go against the flow of those around her and raise the bar for her two sons, many schools have implemented her program. Students joining the Ben Carson Clubs promise three things: Read two books a week, submit a report on each one, and limit television.

Limiting television and video game access is vital to this program. Outside of parental involvement, very few children will cultivate a love for books if the path of least resistance and instant gratification is readily available. Making tough choices with your children will always require courage and often entails going against the cultural flow. However, the long-term dividends are worth the alternative. Think about it. You could be raising the next world-famous neurosurgeon, cutting-edge politician, innovative scientist, top-notch teacher, or even a future Michelangelo.

Develop Strengths, not Weaknesses

Back to the intelligences and how they work. Exceptional leaders figure out what they do best and leverage it to the max. Brain science now validates the advantage of developing strengths. In the past, people were often told to focus on their weaknesses instead of their strengths. However, the latest research reveals that we actually become "smarter" by focusing on our strengths. The emphasis should rest on identifying strengths, not exposing weaknesses. God has created each person with special strengths, and to glorify Him best we must discover and develop our unique strengths, passions, and talents.

As we cultivate our primary intelligences, our non-dominant thinking patterns actually grow stronger as seen in the following excerpt from Dr. Caroline Leaf's book, "We have had math students who have been failing math. I am thinking of one of my students in South Africa who had dominant musical and kinesthetic thinking and was failing math.

He was desperate to play a musical instrument, but his parents wouldn't allow it until he improved his math grade. I profiled him and showed his parents that the way to get his gift going and pull all his grades up was through his musical learning pillar, since it was the highest. So we got him going on the keyboard, we got him playing the drums, we got him singing, and we got him playing in a little band. What happened? This child's grades in all subjects skyrocketed. He started getting 70s and 80s. His linguistic intelligence wasn't very high, but by developing his dominant pillar, he used his gift to pull all the other lagging pillars up. When he was able to fully learn and express himself through his dominant pillar of thinking, all the other areas of thinking just naturally lifted."[13] Developing your child's strengths is an integral part of elevating their weaknesses. Now that is some seriously encouraging brain science!

Another great story of developing strengths instead of weaknesses is found in the life of Gillian Lynn. "Gillian was only eight years old, but her future was already at great risk. Her schoolwork was a disaster as far as her teachers were concerned. She turned in assignments late, her handwriting was terrible, and she tested poorly. Not only that, she was a disruption to the entire class, one minute fidgeting noisily, the next staring out the window, forcing the teacher to stop the class to pull Gillian's attention back, and the next doing something to disturb the other children around her."[14]

The school thought Gillian had a learning disorder of some sort and that it might be more appropriate for her to be in a school for children with special needs."[15]

After receiving a letter from the school, her parents took her to a psychologist for assessment. After a plethora of questions directed more toward Gillian's mother, the psychologist told Gillian she had been very patient and that he would be going outside the room to speak with her mother for a few moments. Gillian nodded apprehensively, as the two adults left her sitting there on her own. But as he was leaving the room, the psychologist leaned across his desk and turned on the radio.

As soon as they were in the corridor outside the room, the doctor said to Gillian's mother, "Just stand here for a moment, and watch what she does." There was a window into the room, and they stood to one side of it, where Gillian couldn't see them. Nearly immediately, Gillian was on her feet, moving around the room to the music. The two adults stood watching quietly for a few minutes, transfixed by the girl's grace. Gillian's face was pure pleasure. At last, the psychologist turned to Gillian's mother and said, "You know, Mrs. Lynn, Gillian isn't sick. She's a dancer. Take her to dance school."[16]

Gillian attended a dance school, filled with people just like her who had to move to think. She attended this dance school each day and later auditioned for the Royal Ballet School in London and was accepted. She went on to join the Royal Ballet Company and became a soloist performing all over the world. Later in her career, she formed her own dance company producing many successful shows that ran in London and New York. Eventually, she connected to Andrew Lloyd Webber and created the famous productions, *Cats* and *The Phantom of the Opera* with him. Thankfully, this young lady's gifting was discovered at a young age as millions worldwide have experienced the joy of seeing 'Little Gillian's' musicals.

Part of the reason our present education system is so constrained is because it caters to one or two of the intelligences—namely the logical/mathematical and the linguistic pattern of thinking. In fact, most schools teach students as if they all process information the same way, which couldn't be further from the truth. Students are often made to learn in ways that are completely unnatural and counter to their personal learning bent. Not to mention the entire school system is better suited to females who tend to have less need to move constantly. Most boys, on the other hand, love hands-on learning when they are young and have a learning capacity that declines sharply after fifteen-minute intervals. Boys who like to move are labeled ADD, hyper, or misbehaved and often put on medications. Like one educational speaker recently quipped, "Nowadays if you are a real man, they put you on drugs."

Concluding Thoughts

While the latest information is pretty exciting, please keep in mind that there is no quick fix for educators to immediately implement all the growing knowledge regarding intelligences and learning styles. Yet identifying and understanding *how* your child learns and thinks can result in great benefits for your child (and the peace in your home). Also, I don't believe it's realistic or balanced to expect every academic venue to be suited exactly to your child's personal make-up. We all have to spend a certain amount of time doing things at which we aren't very good or that don't come naturally to us, some of us more than others. So while you endeavor to keep "schooling from interfering with your child's education," try to be realistic about your aspirations for your child. Sometimes a right-brained, artistic, musical child struggling and striving to climb the steep grade of Algebra II is just what his or her character might need at that moment.

Discussion and Discovery

1. Reflect on how you were educated. What were some of the positives and negatives of your personal experience with education?

2. What do you feel is your personal strongest intelligence? How does this affect the way you learn?

3. What are some of your children's main intelligences? What are some ideas you can implement to capitalize on how they learn best?

4. What are your thoughts on reading? Is video gaming or media hindering your children from a more stimulating way of learning?

5. After reading this chapter what are some things you can implement in your family's habits to foster your children's growth?

6. Do you feel you have spent more time developing your strengths or your weaknesses? Where do you think changes can be made?

ENDNOTES

[1] Ken Robinson, Ph.D., *The Element, How Finding Your Passion Changes Everything,* (2009, Penguin Books), 50.

[2] Ken Robinson, Ph.D.,*The Element, How Finding Your Passion Changes Everything,*, (2009, Penguin Books), 56.

[3] Kevin Hall, *Aspire, Discovering Your Purpose Through the Power of Words* (2009, Bookwise Publishing), 172-173.

[4] Kevin Hall, *Aspire, Discovering Your Purpose Through the Power of Words* (2009, Bookwise Publishing), 47.

[5] Dr. Caroline Leaf, *The Gift in You* (2009, United States of America), 53.

[6] Dr. Caroline Leaf, *The Gift in You* (2009, United States of America), 57.

[7] Dr. Caroline Leaf, *The Gift in You* (2009, United States of America), 71.

[8] Dr. Caroline Leaf, *The Gift in You* (2009, United States of America), 75.

[9] Ben Carson, *Think Big* (1992, Zondervan), 177.

[10] Ben Carson, *Think Big* (1992, Zondervan), 224.

[11] Ben Carson, *Think Big* (1992, Zondervan), 223.

[12] Ben Carson, *Think Big* (1992, Zondervan), 226.

[13] Dr. Caroline Leaf, *The Gift in You* (2009, United States of America), 82.

[14] Ken Robinson, Ph.D., *The Element, How Finding Your Passion Changes Everything*, (2009, Penguin Books), 1.

[15] Ken Robinson, Ph.D., *The Element, How Finding Your Passion Changes Everything*, (2009, Penguin Books), 1.

[16] Ken Robinson, Ph.D., *The Element, How Finding Your Passion Changes Everything*, (2009, Penguin Books), 2.

CHAPTER TEN

Inwardly Grateful While Outwardly Focused

Cultivating an Attitude of Gratitude and Kids Who Can Serve

Whatever you are intentionally thankful for increases.

—Bill Johnson

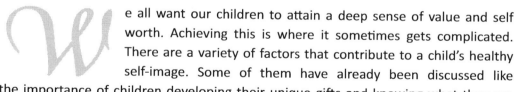 e all want our children to attain a deep sense of value and self worth. Achieving this is where it sometimes gets complicated. There are a variety of factors that contribute to a child's healthy self-image. Some of them have already been discussed like the importance of children developing their unique gifts and knowing what they are naturally good at doing. Then there is the reality that children need to feel the affection and attunement of parents to their needs. Every kid needs to feel—*somebody adores me*, somebody is crazy about me. It's also vital for kids to see that their parents feel good about themselves. Children *feel* secure when they perceive that their parents *feel* secure.

In addition to some of these factors, I'd like to touch on a few other areas that hinder or help the development of character and a good self-image. Roy F. Baumeister, professor of social psychology at Florida State University, was a proponent of self-esteem in the early seventies but has since changed his views. Thirty years later Baumeister now recommends, "Forget about self-esteem and concentrate more on self control and self-discipline."[1] The modern day obsession with self-esteem is not achieving the desired results because as it suggests in the word itself–it's all about *self*.

The reality is no one feels worse than the person who has no control over his desires and views himself as the center of the universe. Have you ever noticed that the most self-centered people tend to be the most unhappy, while other-centered people seem to experience the greatest joy and satisfaction?

The Power of Serving

Children who learn to serve and think of others at a young age have a considerable advantage over the average self-focused child in today's society. We've talked quite a bit about the importance of "developing your kids" and helping them "discover their unique abilities and passions," but if a life of contribution and serving doesn't remain the focal point, "cultivating your kids" runs the risk of slipping quickly into cultivating self-centered ambition.

In their eagerness to raise a "princess" or a "prince," it's easy for parents to neglect the core value of serving. Some parents are so busy making sure their girls and boys have comforts and fun, they unintentionally abandon some of the very training that would foster real security and joy. As with any other character trait, children learn the most about serving by watching their parents serve. If parents joyfully serve and look for ways to bless others, kids will eventually do the same. If parents complain, grumble, and seldom serve outside of their four walls, then kids will adopt these attitudes as well.

It is interesting to examine how the Bible depicts a Godly woman. Many Biblical passages display Godly women as those who had hearts to serve—women who were *industrious,* as well as, *other-centered*. You can find such an example in Genesis 24. In this passage Abraham has sent his servant to find a wife for his son Isaac. Isaac's servant prayed to God and asked in Genesis 24:14, "May it be that when I say to a girl, 'Please let down your jar that I may have a drink' and she says, 'Drink, and I'll water your camels too,' let her be the one you have chosen for your servant Isaac."

Later in the story Rebekah came out with a jar on her shoulder. Isaac's servant, Eliezer, followed his plan and requested a drink. After Rebekah gave him a drink she said, "'I'll draw water for your camels too, until they have finished drinking.' So she quickly emptied her jar into the trough, ran back to the well to draw more water, and drew enough for all his camels" (Genesis 24:19-20).

Watering camels was a difficult and laborious task. Each camel's water capacity ranges from eight to fifteen gallons, so this was by any means no small job. If you do the math, Rebekah was prepared to draw up to one hundred gallons of water for Eliezer's ten thirsty camels. Now that's a true example of an industrious woman with a servant's heart. A woman willing to water one camel was probably hard to find, but this woman was willing to water them all.

In this passage, we also see that Eliezer didn't merely take Rebekah at her word. Rather, he *watched* to see if she would follow through with her offer. What was Eliezer doing? Eliezer was testing this young woman's character. When Rebekah fulfilled her promise, he knew that not only was she beautiful, but also she was also a woman of character.

The same principle of serving applies to boys. As I was listening to the radio the other day, a news reporter was sharing how the latest studies reveal that boys in their teen years need to be working and serving because it is literally how they are mentally wired. Further, the studies revealed that if boys aren't working and serving during the teen years, they often become depressed and dissatisfied. Boys aren't made to sit at home or spend their free time pursuing non-stop pleasure and leisure. The studies also showed that it doesn't even matter if these boys *get paid* for their work and service; what's important is that they contribute toward something or someone beyond themselves. In light of the complaints coming from your teen about hard work, some parents may find this study a little hard to believe, but let me assure you —it is real. In our society we have so cultivated comfort and leisure as a way of life, it literally can take an adjustment period for teens to get in touch with their innate needs and design.

When children serve or contribute, they feel good; in fact, teaching your kids to serve is training them to lead. Great leaders are always great servants. I Kings 12:7 *"If today you will be a servant to these people and serve them, and give them a favorable answer, they will always be your servants."*

Acts of kindness and service affect our brain in a positive way. In his bestselling book, *The Power of Intention*, Wayne Dyer writes about the effect of kindness on the human body. Scientists who studied the brain activity of individuals as they performed an act of kindness for another found increased levels of serotonin, the chemical the brain produces to make you feel good and the common ingredient in antidepressant medication. That wasn't all they found. In those receiving the acts of kindness, researchers recorded the same amount of serotonin as that found in those giving the service. It was further determined that even those observing the acts of kindness produced the same amount of serotonin.[2] So now it's confirmed—serving has a wonderful effect all the way around!

Meet the Little Women

We love having all kinds of families over to eat and fellowship at our home. One particular family with six girls visited us not long ago. My husband and I were so impressed with this family that after they left that evening, we chided each other saying we wished we lived in the times of arranged marriages. I know, I know those days are long gone!

Their six girls are full of personality and engaged with ease in conversation with each of us. The adults didn't get ignored as is often the case nowadays nor were we expected to serve the kids the entire time. Within moments, several of their girls were in my kitchen offering to help and talking to me about all sorts of things. The older girls were checking on the younger ones allowing their parents to visit. They were so entertaining and refreshing to have around that my boys quickly begged us to have them over again.

This family carries the joy and aroma of heaven wherever they go. Another day, I happened upon one of their girls (Rebecca, age 12) at the local farmers market. She had gotten up at 6:30 that morning to help sell bread for their local bakery. As I was leaving their booth, Rebekah noticed that I had more than I could successfully carry back to the car. She immediately offered to leave the booth with her aunt and carry some of my load. On the way to the car, she chatted cheerfully as she asked about our family. I felt great when I left that morning... Wow, kids like that can really make your day!

These parents have successfully cultivated in their daughters a respect and enjoyment for the adults in their world. Honoring and serving others is an important core value to this family. And because values determine behavior, their girls naturally behave in ways that manifest their values. When young people honor adults they FEEL good about themselves. The Bible teaches children to honor their parents and authorities. However, from the way many parents are raising their kids, you would think the Bible read, "Parents honor your children, and it will go well with you..." I'm all for blessing and serving my kids, but we need to teach them that honoring and serving other people is more important than being served.

It is unfortunate that this simple example of joyful and respectful children is rare. Parents who respect their children and children who respect their parents should be the norm, not the exception. As conveyed in the book, *Raising Respectful Children in a Disrespectful World*, "We've substituted self-esteem for self-respect, and in the process we lost our manners. Character development has been de-emphasized and psychological development has become the focus. We began to view them not as fairly durable little people who needed to be taught respect, responsibility, good manners, and the like, but as fragile little containers of something called self-esteem, which could be irreparably damaged with a harsh word."[3]

After emphasizing the importance of cultivating respectful children, it is important to remember that respect is a two-way street. Respect starts with the parent. Parents can't just demand respect—they have to model it. They have to show it to their children on a consistent basis. Another interesting survey I recently heard also appears to agree with the Bible on the issue of respect. This extensive survey uncovers that *what* the most happy and fulfilled people have in common is this—they are living lives with an attitude of respect toward others. Yes, when adults and children live from a posture of genuine respect, they are going to feel happier and more fulfilled.

A Word About Manners

Why talk about manners anyway? Manners, while they vary depending on where you live in the world, are significant because they are a practical way for children to live out the core value of honor. When honor has no way of being practically implemented, it means little to children. Manners are an outworking of the core value of honor.

The Chinese proverbial principle to never treat others in a way that makes them feel small is why serving and manners are so important. The opposite of treating others small is treating them BIG. When we serve others or show respect through heartfelt manners, we are saying to others, **you** *are large,* **you** *are valuable,* **you** *are highly esteemed.* When we treat others rudely or without acknowledgement, they feel insignificant, they feel small.

Using manners causes us to focus on what others feel and on what others need. Sadly, in our modern day quest for freedom of expression and self-esteem, manners like serving, have also become a rare commodity. In much of our culture, children are not expected to humble themselves or extend respect to friends or authorities. Training our children to use manners is more challenging today because in the past as we've already discussed the culture under-girded what parents taught and modeled at home. Today many of the most important core values have become counter-cultural.

Today's parents need to be intentional and focused to foster these kinds of good habits. Part of the challenge is that parents often have to endure opposition as they are stereotyped as uptight, outdated, and unrealistic by other parents who have yielded to prevalent cultural values. In addition, many parents themselves aren't really sure what constitutes good behavior. Some families think because their children are not rude, it means they are polite. But this is no truer than the idea that because your child is not mean, then they must be kind. When a child smiles and with kindness and real gratitude thanks you for having them over, you feel good. They feel good. Manners are all about simple gestures, but simple gestures can have big impact. When it comes to relationships, the little things *are* the big things.

Why are manners important anyway? Syndicated columnist Judith Martin offers this insight: "The attitude that wishes of others do not matter is exactly what manners are intended to counter." Respect lies at the heart of both manners and morals. Yes, manners actually affect morality. Manners that are instilled in the early years become the foundation for moral behavior in the later years.

Teaching children to let older people go through doors first or to keep eye contact when speaking or being spoken to are those little things that cultivate honoring hearts. Teaching the basics: "please, thank you, excuse me, how may I help you, you go first," are basic but powerful. These are the little phrases that when genuine can actually create a culture of honor and courtesy.

In your desire to cultivate good habits, make sure you don't just *drill* manners. Help your children understand all the wonderful benefits of using good manners. I like to remind my kids that "manners will take them far in life," and in today's generation manners are so uncommon that polite kids have a decided advantage. Polite kids literally stand out. My middle son has picked up on this. In addition to how good he feels when adults are honored by his kind words, he has definitely noticed the wonderful advantages that have come his way. He is never at a loss for invitations to people's homes and even has moms making his favorite meals just because he is coming over!

Don't be discouraged if your kids don't use their manners all the time—No kid does. Believe me, I've worked on certain habits for years and seen some good results in one area, while seeing that others still need lots of cultivation and reminders. There are also times when I think we've almost finished training in an area when lo and behold, it feels like we are starting all over again, or even more discouraging, maybe going backwards! To keep our sanity and joy as parents, we have to remind ourselves that parenting is all about the long-term, and training often takes a long time. Be encouraged because in the same way that training is long-term so are the wonderful results. You have a long time to train your kids; consequently, you also get to reap the benefits for a long time.

While outward manners are important, remember that manners are ultimately a matter of the heart. Performance and mere outward compliance is not the end-goal; inward motives for manners are also important when it comes to training. You can train a child's outside behavior perfectly and still not condition the heart. Some of the most well-mannered children can be the most selfish and ungrateful. I'd rather see a backward unmannered child who has a genuine heart for the needs and feelings of others any day over a polished, outwardly polite child who is self absorbed and ungrateful. Plenty of kids say thank you for things they are hardly grateful for (which leads to the next subject of gratefulness).

Be sure to teach manners but focus on the inside first. You are polite to people because you want them to feel, well as the Chinese proverb teaches—Large!

The Power of a Grateful Heart

Being thankful and grateful are essential spiritual keys to obtaining "increase" in our lives. By increase, I am not talking about more stuff. By increase, I mean more of His presence, more peace, more joy, more perspective, more energy, better sleep, better mental health, and last but not least happier kids. If you want to change the atmosphere in your home, focus on cultivating, as the cliché goes, an *attitude of gratitude.*

Gratefulness and thankfulness are a reflection of the condition of the heart. Thankfulness is an act of the will, a choice that goes beyond circumstances, beyond our natural bent. Thankfulness, especially when circumstances aren't favorable, is our sacrifice to God. God gave us this sage advice because He knew the implications were numerous. As everything else He decrees, thankfulness is a mandate given with our best interest in mind. It is so vital to a life of character and blessing that the Bible exhorts believers over and over to give thanks. Ephesians 5:20 teaches us to, "Give thanks always for all things." Psalm 100:4 says, "Enter his gates with thanksgiving and his courts with praise."

If you are dissatisfied with your life, if you are ungrateful and unaware of God at work in your midst, if you are unhappy, or if you find yourself complaining on a regular basis— you may have entered the land of the unthankful—expect to wander in circles. It was because of a lack of thankfulness which manifested in complaining that the Israelites were not allowed to enter the Promised Land. The opposite of gratitude and thankfulness is complaining and grumbling. The Israelites literally spent forty years wandering in circles in the desert all because they were ungrateful. Why weren't they thankful? I propose it was because they focused on what they didn't have instead of what they had. They were dissatisfied with God's provision and complaining took root. They became the prototype of the saying, "It's where people place their focus that causes them to either be grateful or ungrateful."

Gratefulness is powerful because it changes the way we look at things. This principle is wonderfully expressed by Wayne Dyer, "When we change the way we look at things, the things we look at change." If the Israelites had focused on God's miraculous provision of manna and the fact that they had food, they would have felt gratitude and been able to express it. Who knows what kind of blessings (and food) the Lord might have released had they chosen thankfulness.

When it comes to thankfulness and gratitude, children pick up most of their attitudes from watching us. Gratitude like other attitudes is more caught than taught. Children hear whether Mom is grateful or ungrateful. When someone gives you a gift or does something for you, do you express heartfelt gratitude or indifference because it wasn't enough or not quite right? Do you find time to express thanks even when things are not how you expect them to be?

Expressing your gratitude aloud helps your kids learn thankfulness. Saying things like, "That was so nice of so and so to bring you home, that was out of their way," or "Wasn't it kind of that teacher to take extra time to explain that to you," or "That was generous of Matt to let you borrow his favorite book." Cultivating thankfulness starts with the little things, but it has big ramifications.

Spend time at night expressing to God and each other what you are grateful for. Doing this seems to have a supernatural effect by causing our hearts to fill with an awareness of God's blessings in our lives. It would be impossible to exaggerate the rewards of practicing thankfulness. And remember thankfulness is worth cultivating because "whatever you are thankful for increases!"

Entitlement and Overindulgence

While gratefulness can be cultivated in any child, two hindrances seem worth mentioning. First, it is very hard for a child to be grateful if they are continually overindulged. Some kids have so much material stuff and endless entertainment that what would bring the average child great joy means nothing to the child living in excess. Parents often shower their kids with more than they can handle and then complain that they are unthankful.

As parents we have to fight the tendency to give our kids too much, too soon. There is a big difference between love and indulgence. God's love for us knows no limits, yet He does not indulge us. He gives us what is best for us, which is not whatever we want, whenever we want it. Going the extra mile to bless our kids is natural and even praiseworthy; however, as parents it's best to exercise our own self-restraint and give to our children in a way that is most beneficial for them. In the long haul, children aren't very grateful for things they don't work or wait for. By giving them too much too soon we are actually taking away from their joy, not adding to it. Our culture is permeated by an instant gratification "give it to me now" attitude. We rush through everyday life in an effort to get everything we want. Yet, the Bible is filled with scriptures that teach us the power and the blessing of waiting. Hebrews 6:12, "Through faith and patience we inherit the promises."

Waiting is important because learning to wait leads to contentment. Having a contented spirit is a result of being at peace with waiting. If children get what they want, as soon as they want it, they miss out on waiting. They miss the anticipation, joy, and excitement of receiving a desired longing. When children have to wait for something or work to save up for that special treasure, something of little value can mean the world to them. Even the smallest toys or most simple form of leisure can become a wonderful treasure or exhilarating adventure to children who are not dulled by too much of everything. Do you remember saving up for what seemed like an eternity for a particular toy or item and then finally heading to purchase it? Mowing yards, holding lemonade stands, and babysitting to save for something special can bring a child or teen tremendous joy and dignity. Another great way to help your kids attain their desires, especially bigger priced items, is through matching funds. If they earn $100 toward a go-kart, you can match the funds with $100.

It is great to bless your kids, just be careful not to give them more than they can emotionally handle while keeping a grateful heart. On the other hand, sometimes it's important to get your children something without making them work or wait. The Lord LOVES blessing His children. God loves blessing us so much that He also has to use restraint to hold back certain blessings until we can handle the full weight of them. He doesn't make us work and wait for everything we get. He loves gifts and surprises! So every once in a while, for no reason except the sheer extravagance of your heart, just get your kids something they desire. When you do this, they are learning a little about God's heart through your actions as a parent!

Entitlement

I asked a wise man not long ago, "What is the greatest weakness you see in the church today?" He quickly responded, "An entitlement attitude." After pondering this, I believe there is much truth to his observation.

The entitlement attitude is being cultivated from the top down in our country and has infiltrated almost every sphere and system, even the church. The entitlement attitude ranges from very subtle to blaringly obvious. Believers manifest it when they come to church for what they can get instead of what they can give. The wealthy manifest this attitude when they assume because of their wealth or position they should get special favors and privileges. The poor manifest entitlement by dodging responsibility and work while still expecting provision and amenities.

Even as adults, we've come to expect as a right some of the very things that in generations past were considered a privilege. For example, education for centuries was the responsibility of the parent, not the obligation of the state; health care was the responsibility of individual citizens, not the duty of the government. What was a privilege in the past is often expected and demanded by our generation.

Entitlement hinders gratitude because it assumes an attitude of expecting and demanding. One way we foster entitlement in kids is by trying to make life fair all the time. It sounds really good when parents make an effort to always "keep things even," but the problem is that life is seldom like that. If every time one child gets a present or a special opportunity, you feel you have to create it for your other children, then they come to expect life to always be fair. They assume the attitude of claiming their rights or looking for their fair share.

To counter the entitlement attitude teach your kids to work hard and bless others *without* looking for what they will get in return. Teach them to rejoice when a sibling receives an unexpected gift or gets to attend a special event. When children learn to rejoice in the blessings of others, they are positioning themselves to receive and handle their own blessings. But more than anything, the best way to safeguard against an entitlement attitude is to make sure you don't have one yourself.

Discussion and Discovery

1. Why is serving so important for cultivating self-esteem in children and teens?

2. What are some ways you can cultivate serving in your children's lives? What are some ways you can serve as family?

3. How do manners affect self-esteem? Discuss how you feel when others treat you with courtesy and respect?

4. What are some habits you would like to teach your children in this area?

5. Is thankfulness a genuine part of the atmosphere in your home? Do you feel like you model thankfulness to your children?

6. What kind of adjustments can you make to keep from allowing entitlement or overindulgence to affect your children in a negative way?

7. Are there ways you model an entitlement attitude? If so how can you change this?

Optional Assignment

Take some time to repent of wrong attitudes you may be modeling at home. Ask the Lord to give you the grace and ability to train your children in ways that will cultivate character and joy. Spend time writing down ideas the Lord gives you. The Lord promises in the book of James that whenever we ask Him for wisdom He will *always* give it to us. He is eager to fill us with vision and strategy for raising our kids so tap into the greatest source of wisdom on parenting available—ask God in prayer!

ENDNOTES

[1] Interview with Roy F. Baumeister, Florida State University, http://www.fsu.edu/profiles/baumeister/ (accessed April 12, 2006).

[2] Kevin Hall, *Aspire, Discovering Your Purpose Through the Power of Words,* (2009, Bookwise Publishing), 135.

[3] John Rosemond, *From Spock to Rosemond,* Syndicated column, July 25, 2000. Found online at http//www.rose. mond.com/EditorialEExprint.LASSO?-token.editorialcall=91501.112113.n and Schuster, UK).

CHAPTER ELEVEN

Achievement Obsession or Character Cultivation

Making Sure Achievement Doesn't Trump Character Development

It's easy to add anointing to character
–it's difficult to add character to anointing.

—Graham Cooke

hat factors really lead to true maturity and Godly character in young people? In the foreword to the book, *Do Hard Things*, Chuck Norris laments, "Today we live in a culture that promotes comfort, not challenges. Everything is about finding ways to escape hardship, avoid pain, and dodge duty. In the past, young people were expected to make significant contributions to society. Today, our culture expects very little contribution from teens. A sad consequence of such low expectations is that life-changing lessons go unlearned."[1] It's true that much of our culture has come to expect very little from young people when it comes to contribution or the development of their personal gifts and talents. These young people tend to have little work ethic and are often emotionally lost due to the lack of challenge from those around them. Additionally, there is another growing phenomenon in our society that is obsessed with achievement, particularly academic accolades and extraordinary achievements in "extracurricular activities."

In some circles, character development and physical labor or work is waning only to be replaced by long hours of academic study and sports. Character emphasis, the focus of previous generations, has been traded for *achievement* emphasis. Many schools across the country are much harder than in decades past. Middle schools are more rigorous, and many of the top high schools leave even the most intellectually gifted teens studying three or more hours a night. A growing number of parents expect their children to study non-stop while they play the role of chauffeur, tutor, food preparer, room cleaner, and even Gestapo when it comes to checking grades. College-worthy transcripts, college-admissions frenzy, and SAT prep courses have become more important to parents than raising a child with character.

The fixation with academic accolades is partly tied to the growing obsession with getting into college, especially top universities and colleges. Parents feel guilty about the intense academic pressure and over scheduling of their children so they end up with an opt-out alternative when it comes to chores or serving opportunities. When free time is available, parents often reward academic work with leisure times dominated by video games and various other forms of media entertainment. While academics have unquestionable inherent value, the academic frenzy and extracurricular craze is leaving behind many of the lifelong lessons that children learn from physical labor or a character molded by contribution.

Many of us have witnessed young people who are driven to make straight As, play on sports teams, and participate in student government, but who are almost completely unaware of anyone else's needs around them. These kids are so focused on achievement that *they* have become the end game. Parents have bought into the deception that this kind of lifestyle is what it will take for their children to make it in our fast-paced world—so they are not only going along, but they are also pushing and promulgating it themselves. Instead of emphasizing character or other-centeredness, life becomes all about transcripts, sports, and extracurricular activities. Even the mentorship programs like big-brother big-sister are often joined with transcripts in mind rather than a true heart to serve and mentor younger students.

What is the overly academic emphasis producing in our society? While it is producing an educated elite, it is also cultivating some intellectual ignorance. While this is said with partial humor, there are far too many brilliant and well-educated young men in today's world who couldn't build a simple doghouse or start a fire if they were left stranded on an island. Washington D.C. is filled with Ivy league intellectuals who have little understanding of the physical costs, sweat, and toil our forefathers endured to ensure freedom for the generations that followed. The overly academic emphasis has produced an intellectual paradigm, which has in many ways replaced "life in the trenches."

I believe over-emphasis on achievement, if it replaces character development, is unhealthy for young people, but I am in no way downplaying the value of academic achievement and excellence. I genuinely value education as well as the need for kids to work hard at school. Further, I am not promoting a Pollyannaish view of the agrarian days when some children had to work an excessive amount. While we cannot go back to the times when many valuable lessons were learned from "life on the farm" and hard physical labor, we can endeavor to recapture and create avenues for similar lessons to be learned by our children. We can examine the prevailing cultural mindsets and make adjustments where it is humanly possible. Accomplishing this for modern-day parents will take wisdom beyond "conventional thinking." Yet, it is still wonderfully possible for our children to grow in both achievement and character without compromising one for the other.

Contribution Builds Confidence

The segment of culture that is obsessed with kids who are "exceptional at everything" has created a group of teens striving for perfection, not teens with high self-esteem. A teen counselor recently said the most common fear she hears coming from the striving teens today is the fear of disappointing their parents. It's not realistic for every child to be social, athletic, artistic, and an academic champion; in fact, this kind of pressure has left many young people with high levels of anxiety and fragile self-esteem. While kids *developing themselves* is good, out of balance, it simply isn't healthy. Success is more than grades and athleticism. Success and vitality have to do with how our children treat others, contribute at home, or live for something beyond themselves.

Hard working, contributing children are confident because they are not overly focused on *their* needs, weaknesses, and hurts; they are *free* to focus on others. In the same way that the lazy, self-centered child is unhappy when he doesn't get his way, the performance child (who performs only for themselves or their parents) is also unhappy and insecure.

Holy Homework or "Home" Work

A good way to keep academic achievement from getting out of balance is by making sure our kids do their share of *home* work. While I am a firm believer in the "keep them busy" philosophy for the teen years, if "keep them busy" means they have no responsibility and everything is centered around their activities, then we really do our kids a disservice. Why? Because our kids will one day be fathers, mothers, and spouses with families and real-life jobs of their own. When parents have their kids in so many activities that there is no time left to help out at home, they are most likely too busy.

Instead of letting homework become holy and exalted, make sure that the *home* work is also a regular part of your child's life. As my dad has keenly observed, "The problem with life is that it's just so daily." It's important that children live in a real world of daily chores and being part of the family team. Doing laundry, cleaning dishes, mowing the yard, helping cook, vacuuming, and learning to fix broken things around the house are all daily chores at which everyone needs to take part. Teach your kids to work hard in school, but don't let homework become so holy that it trumps *home* work.

Premature Adolescence or Prolonged Adolescence

Which is worse making kids grow up too early or never letting them grow up at all? I don't know, but I guess I'd rather see a ten year old ridiculously trying to act fifteen as opposed to a fifty-year-old man who is still making excuses for his life. Unfortunately, we see both of these growing trends in our society. There are girls in fourth grade who feel pressure to wear make-up, dress like full-grown women who talk and walk like Brittany Spears, and boys who are ashamed to play with guns or play-mobile for fear a fellow preteen might spot them and make fun of their affinity for hands-on-play or make-believe games.

Equally counterproductive to premature adolescence is the latest trend of "prolonged adolescence." Prolonged adolescence is in essence *putting off* the responsibilities and challenges that cause young people to mature. This lack of productivity and responsibility easily becomes a breeding ground for boredom and insecurity. No wonder the peak age for depression is eighteen. While young people obsessed with achievement is unhealthy, young people with no goals or ambitions is just as tragic. Dr. Alex Chediak says, "Generation Y has a propensity to demand more recognition for less effort and to associate self-esteem with mere *being* rather than for *actual accomplishment*." Image and individuality have replaced character and contribution. This line of thought has led to a growing number of depressed young people who, after having endeavored to live a life of *being* void of *doing,* are finding the emptiness of an identity null of character. Some of them perceive there is something very wrong, but in their youth they don't know what it is.

While our teens are physically and genetically ready to take on the world, we are still protecting them *from* the world. "A survey by polling expert Tom Smith at the University of Chicago asked fourteen hundred people that very question: At what age do you think adulthood begins in the United States? The answer: twenty-six."[2] Yes, can you believe it? Twenty-six. For all you parents out there planning your first trip away together on a relaxing Alaskan Cruise to celebrate the new season of empty-nest syndrome, you need to hang tight because according to recent polls you only have eight extra years until little Johnny is ready to leave home.

Not long ago, *adolescence thinking* was completely foreign (even more foreign than children in their twenties living under your roof), but it has become a culturally accepted mindset and contributed to the now entrenched "myth of adolescence." By "myth" I am not denying that they get really strange when they go through puberty throwing many parents into a complete tailspin, but "myth" meaning that prolonged childishness and irresponsibility is now considered normal and even healthy. Being held back from the privilege of what they "could do" and further what they are created by God to do is handicapping and hindering the natural independence stage of life for many teens, and unfortunately, even young adults.

Two Ditches: Over-Protecting and Under-Guiding

Rooted in the latest cultural trends, many well-meaning parents embrace faulty ideas in an effort to help children mature. In our desire to help them grow up, coupled with our fear of being labeled the worst label of the decade, "a helicopter parent," we give our kids freedom but often in the wrong areas. While giving too much freedom in certain areas, we simultaneously hold them back in the very areas they need freedom and increasing responsibility to grow. For example, as we've already discussed some parents install a TV with fully-loaded cable into the room of a ten year old and then say okay, "exercise your freedom"—Oh yes, this will really help them mature. Then there are parents who watch their kids develop an underachieving, apathetic attitude and to keep from becoming the "overly involved parent," they stand by as their children flounder through adolescence all-the-while proudly sticking to their "hands-off" approach to parenting.

The "under-guiding parent trend," according to extensive Barna surveys was *not* the method of choice for parents who raised children that matured into spiritual champions. Instead, these parents chose the role of "involved coach" while at the same time being careful not to smother their children too much. The right amount of freedom and responsibility was something these parents put much prayer and thought into. Parents who raised mature and motivated children did not ascribe to the trendy hands-off parenting styles.

Making adjustments is the constant role of any dedicated parent. As Ben Carson explains, "Parenting seems to demand of us two seemingly conflicting assignments: protecting and pushing. Adolescence, that troublesome transition when our two primary missions overlap, may be the riskiest time for parents and children. If parents relinquish their protection too early, there is enormous risk because kids won't have the judgment necessary to avoid the great dangers of life. But, parents who wait too long or never shift into push mode may hinder the chance for their children to become independent, responsible, mature, and emotionally healthy adults."[3] Wisdom and discernment are needed to maneuver through this season of life.

The scope of these challenges begs the question—what really helps children mature? While many factors contribute to the maturation process, I would like to assert that while freedom is important, it is actually not the main ingredient for maturation. Responsibility and challenge coupled with hands-on coaching and mentoring have a much greater impact on the maturation process.

Real maturity occurs when responsibility,

choices, and guidance are in proper balance.

Until recently, kids were needed for a family's basic survival. We all know from personal experience how important it is to feel needed in life. Throughout most of history, children literally contributed to a family's survival and heritage. Children helped raise siblings, took care of animals, helped run the household, and were often integrally involved in the family business. Competence and responsibility were taught to children as soon as possible. Kids were not only adored, they were needed and valued. "Until the Industrial Revolution came along and turned children into cheap labor, children were the opposite: valuable labor."[4]

Further, the gulf between adults, teens, and children did not exist as all ages worked side by side and lived relationally interconnected. The sitcom worldview that equates adults as "antiquated and out of touch" was unheard of in previous generations. Living daily among children and adults of all ages was one of the main components in the maturation process of children. It's always humorous to hear people ask how "homeschooled" children will acquire their needed social skills. One day, an unassuming mom commented to me (during one of the years that I homeschooled several of mine), "Your kids seem really normal." "Thanks!" I said as I could hardly keep the grin off my face. Has this mom frequented a local junior high lately? Does *normal* occur by being *in school* where no one in the building outside of the teachers is more than two years younger or older than anyone else? I've seen first hand the wonderful social skills that the average junior high student exhibits, and I wasn't that impressed. What has impressed me is seeing kids who talk freely and confidently to a person of any age, which often comes from being around people of many ages. Just to be clear, I have nothing against conventional schools or jovial junior high students—I'm merely making the point that children mature by being around "maturity."

For most of history, with the exception of the industrial revolution, Western children were not exploited; however, they were expected to integrate into society through pulling their load, not parents pulling (driving) them around all the time. "While childhood might have its tender moments, the goal of a child was to grow up as promptly as possible in order to enjoy the opportunities and shoulder the responsibilities of an adult."[5] Parents knew the sooner their children learned to be responsible, the sooner they would mature. Teen years were not expected to be a recess from responsibility where parents expected nothing short of trouble and heartache. Instead, the teen years were harvest time, a time when parents began reaping what they had sown during primary years (and yes, even planning that Alaskan Cruise). The teen years were something parents looked forward to, not something they dreaded or feared. Perhaps we should call this phenomenon of lengthened youth *prolonged parenting* rather than prolonged adolescence since it's the parents who pay the biggest price for this elongated process of growing up.

Parenting Is not About Pampering; It's About Preparing

Historically when children reached the age of thirteen to fourteen they were considered ready for adult work. As Lenore Skenazy says, "Pampering was as far off as Pampers."

The idea of treating children as "cherished cherubs" wasn't out there either. Nothing against adoring our kids, but you get my point. I agree with Lenore who points out what should be common sense. "Children are built to survive." As soon as they can do it on their own we don't need to be doing it for them. The prolonged teen-years syndrome has blinded many of us to the potential and desperate need to stretch and grow amongst our young people. Much of the depression and apathy that today's youth are plagued with is due not to mental illness or abuse, rather it emanates from a lack of being needed—a lack of challenge and responsibility. While some youth are anxious and stressed due to excessive pressure to perform, many others are downcast because of empty comfort and a lack of anyone who really needs their contribution.

Take a look at even the most recent history. Until the last century, teens were fighting battles and running businesses while contributing significantly to their local communities. George Washington was fighting in the army (no need to fight mock video-game battles for little George) and had a job surveying the land of Virginia by his late teens. At the age of fourteen, John Quincy Adams, accompanied by another adult, was sent to Saint Petersburg, Russia, for nearly three years to assist in diplomatic relations. His job—to attain recognition for the new United States. During his teen years, he also published a travel report of Silesia and became fluent in French and Dutch and semi-fluent in several other languages. Mark Twain's father died when he was eleven causing him to go to work. At twelve years old he began working as an apprentice printer in New York. By the age of fifteen, he worked as a printer, occasional writer, and editor of a local newspaper. Another famous apprentice printer was Ben Franklin, who began his career in Boston at the age of twelve. Then there was Clara Barton, a nurse to her father's men by fourteen, and by seventeen years old she was a successful school teacher. Soon thereafter, she cared for thousands of men in the Civil War. Clara is best known as founder of the American Red Cross. The list goes on and on.

Although it's easy to romanticize the days of old or reminisce about the times when children actually thought their parents knew something, I am not advocating we send our kids to the front lines of Iraq or Libya or that we pull them out of school at thirteen and make them tend a farm (that we would have to buy first). I am merely suggesting that we examine our cultural mindsets and make adjustments where possible. Making adjustments, even small ones, can often have significant long-term outcomes. As parents, we can start by giving our kids greater responsibility, while at the same time not being afraid to parent in risky areas where most teens desperately need accountability and guidance.

Our kids can do more than make their beds and complete a little homework. A friend of ours has a son, who attends a rigorous preparatory school. He spent the summer of his sophomore year building their family a guesthouse following the plans his father carefully crafted. This young man completely built a small guesthouse overlooking picturesque mountains by the end of the summer. The guesthouse is now used for adults who want to spend time alone with God, need a retreat, or simply a quiet place to work on writing projects. Another friend of ours had their son, who also attends this same preparatory school, spend his summer working alongside his older cousins to construct an extravagant and intricate deck on the back of their house. These parents noticed that working outside in the hot sun on this building project had their son as happy as they'd ever seen him. You may not have construction projects, but perhaps your boys could mow yards, spend time teaching younger children in sports, or help the elderly with projects around their homes. It is important for teens to engage in challenging, physical tasks.

Our daughter loves cooking, so instead of having her try out a recipe here and there when she has extra time, she makes us whole gourmet meals which take planning, preparation, and hard work. The confidence she has gained from doing the whole meal on her own is fun to watch. In the political arena, there are teens across the country volunteering with political campaigns during summer breaks and on weekends. They organize campaign speech events, hand out flyers, and use their technological aptitude to market and organize via email and online venues.

Proverbs 20:29 says, "The glory of *young* men is their strength." Young men according to Biblical times meant any boy who had gone through puberty. When a young man uses his strength and abilities, he finds significance and identity. This truth is applicable to boys and girls alike.

Serve as a Family

Your family is a powerful team that can accomplish all kinds of amazing feats for God. I am convinced that it is one of the enemy's biggest schemes to get families to live under the same roof while being totally independent and disconnected from each other—the kind of family where "everyone is doing their own thing." Instead, the ideal family culture is one in which the family has some common dreams and goals that are attained by working together.

A study of horses revealed that a single horse could pull an average of 2,500 pounds. The test was repeated with two horses. You'd expect the weight to double to about

5,000 pounds. Not so. Two horses working together pulled 12,500 pounds! God made us to be able to accomplish exponentially more as a team.[6]

Living as a team includes overcoming hardship together. Our family has gone through some financial difficulties over the last few years. My second to youngest son noticed I was fasting for a family in need whom we know. The next day it dawned on me at lunch that he had never eaten breakfast. I asked him if he wanted lunch, and he said, "No thanks!" I then asked why, and his reply was, "I'm fasting for financial breakthrough for our family." His fast didn't last more than a few meals, but I thought this was pretty encouraging coming from a fourth grader. He had noticed his parents pressing in for breakthrough for others, and now he wanted to do the same for us.

"Some of your best time together will be that which is spent in real struggles and challenges to achieve common goals. A child builds self-worth, not by being the center of attention, but by actually conquering a real-world need."[7]

Tips About Work

Cultivating character has a lot to do with work ethic. This is an area we are continually working on with our kids. Below are a few helpful tips I've picked up along the way.

Make work fun This is especially vital when kids are young because they are internally learning to either dread or love work. The secret to teaching children to love work is to start them off with jobs they love. Children should learn to work and play at the same time—but remember work should be *fun* for small kids.

Start them when they are young Children develop their attitude toward work at tender ages because this is when the brain is constructing lifelong patterns of thinking. If Mom does everything for her child until the age of five, a self-centered paradigm has already taken root. Children under the age of two cannot do productive work, but they can be involved. When children are allowed to be involved in adult work like sweeping, cooking, or working in the garage, and it occurs in a joyful atmosphere, work becomes a regular part of their worldview.

Never do for your children what they can do for themselves You hinder initiative in your children when you do for them what they can do for themselves. If a child can get a toy out, a child can put that same toy away. When a child sits and watches his parents pick up the toys, he is learning to be lazy. Yikes! It is so much easier to clean up for them when they are little, but it is not best for them.

Work together as much as possible Don't work for your kids, and don't make them work for you—work together. Children develop a dread of work when work is continually carried out in isolation. We were created for community and relationship. There is great truth in the proverb that many hands make the work light. And I might also add—many hands can also make work fun!

Repaint your own front door, refinish a floor, paint rooms together, plant new flowers, or construct swings, forts, and castles in your yard. Build something onto your house, prepare full meals and take them to new moms, find widows or relatives to help, or set up regular times to help feed the poor. There's no end to the projects you can do together.

Don't hire yard service; let your boys take care of your yard or maybe your girls. Personally I love mowing the yard and can get kind of territorial when it comes to mowing. However, now that our boys are older, my husband is more persistent that our boys undertake this domestic duty, even though I still occasionally sneak out and get behind the mower. Yes, I realize it is rather horrifying to see a mom out mowing the yard while her sons are inside playing the latest version of wii golf.

Leave children with a good feeling about work Do NOT expect perfection. It is crucial that children feel like a success in their early attempts at work. Children do things mediocre at best when they are young. One family who has five children replaced their kitchen counter numerous times due to water damage as their children learned to cook and clean. They didn't focus on the messes that were made but on the progress and skills their kids were learning.

One of the telltale signs of performance parenting is not recognizing what is age appropriate and what is not. The performance dad will snap at the child who doesn't recognize the difference in a flat head screwdriver and a Phillips-Head screwdriver (not that I do either). A mom might berate the child who doesn't see all the dirt on the garage floor or the child who drips water all over the floor while cleaning counters. If children associate cleaning and working with tension and strife, they will learn to dread and avoid work.

However, if children are encouraged and work is fun, they will eventually do things well. If after a job, you feel they need to come back and do things better, join them and make it a time of encouragement. Then stand back and admire what you have accomplished together.

Optimism must run high if you want to cultivate initiative and a love for work—none of us performs well for those who do not believe in us; on the other hand, we will do almost anything to live up to the expectations of those who encourage us and are tolerant of our mistakes and shortcomings.

Admire your child's work regularly and then brag about it to your friends and relatives!

Discourage procrastination You do this by teaching and modeling how great it feels to get unpleasant tasks out of the way. Sometimes my children would come home from school and complete their entire homework pack for the week on the first afternoon. I wanted to take full advantage of this positive behavior so I asked them, "How does it feel to have your entire homework pack all done?" A wave of self-awareness and healthy pride spread across their countenances as they took note of how good it feels to work ahead and be on top of things.

A few years ago, I got up late from an allergy filled night. I found my second and fourth graders, who were both homeschooled at that time, sitting at the dining room table "conquering" their homework (Boys conquer homework you know!) Spotting me, both boys proudly announced they had already done three subjects. Wow, this was the perfect time for a big-time praise. Just for the record, my children don't always choose to work ahead, and some more than others tend to put things off.

Give rewards for hard work When you see your kids going the extra mile or working hard for a prolonged period of time, find ways to reward them. When you have big jobs to accomplish around your home, plan something fun right afterwards. This gives your kids something to look forward to. Life is about work, but life is also about celebration—so make sure you have plenty of celebration planned as well.

Define jobs clearly When weekly jobs are clearly defined there is less potential for misunderstandings especially as children get older. When chores are clearly defined on paper, and your kids are complaining—instead of tension between you and your child—you can let the job chart speak for itself by steering them back to what is defined on paper. Make a system or chart and defer to it. This can alleviate a lot of potential conflict and complaining. When there is no chart or system, everything is always negotiable. Boy, have I learned this one the hard way.

Model a love for work I enjoy cleaning my house and cooking. One day I was pondering why I *like* to clean, and then it dawned on me that during my formative years I had spent many summers in Belgium with my relatives doing these very things. In Belgium, many of the women take great pride in caring for their homes and cooking homemade meals. I internalized these attitudes from my aunts. Even though most of them had full-time housekeepers, they would joyfully work right along side them.

I hope these tips are helpful! May your family come to enjoy the gift of work whether it is at school, at home, or helping your fellow man!

Discussion and Discovery

1. What are the most important components that lead to maturation in young people?

2. Discuss what you think about the growing cultural obsession with achievement and how it affects character cultivation.

3. What are some adjustments you feel you need to make in this area?

4. Why does contribution build confidence?

5. What do you think about premature adolescence and prolonged adolescence?

6. In what ways do you tend to overprotect or underguide your children?

7. What work tips do you want to implement in your home?

ENDNOTES

[1] Alex & Brett Harris, *Do Hard Things* (2008, Colorado Springs, CO), xiii.

[2] Lenore Skenazy, *Free-Range Kids* (2009, San Francisco, CA), 71.

[3] Ben Carson MD, *Take the Risk* (2008, Grand Rapids, MI), 191.

[4] Lenore Skenazy, *Free-Range Kids* (2009, San Francisco, CA), 72.

[5] Alex & Brett Harris, *Do Hard Things* (2008, Colorado Springs, CO), 35.

[6] Alex & Brett Harris, Do Hard Things (2008, Colorado Springs, CO), 111.

[7] Quote by Michael Pearl.

CHAPTER TWELVE

Don't Let the Church Take Your Job

*Insights for Spiritually Equipping
Your Children*

*It's impossible to give away spiritual depth or hunger for God
that we don't possess ourselves.*

I f your child has the best education available, plays two musical instruments, and is constantly in the local newspaper for outstanding athletic achievements, what will it matter in the end if they don't have a thriving relationship with Jesus or a heart for the lost? What if your child accomplishes tremendous feats, but God is not a part of the equation? As parents, we need to think about what takes priority in the lives of our children. Excellence and achievement are important and can bring great glory to God, but they shouldn't be our end game.

Have you ever wondered why so many young people seem to be turning away from God? Current statistics for Christian kids *keeping the faith* aren't very high. Why? Obviously, there are a wide range of factors that play into this dilemma. The weightiest component is probably due to the fact that most parents count on Christian schools and local youth groups to train and equip their children, which has resulted in an epidemic of youth leaving the church. Consider what *Revolutionary Parenting* revealed about this issue, "Churches *alone* do not and cannot have much influence on children. The responsibility for raising spiritual champions, according to the Bible, belongs to the parents. The spiritual nurture of children is supposed to take place in the home. Organizations and people from outside the home might support those efforts, but the responsibility is squarely laid at the feet of the family. This is not a job for specialists. It is a job for parents."[1] Essentially, church starts in the home.

Parents, we have the incredible privilege and assignment of raising up this next generation to love and follow God. Sometimes it is easy to feel like we don't have much influence with our kids, (especially during the teen years), but the truth is we have substantial influence with our children because God created it that way. We are the number one influence in our kids' lives—unless we forfeit that privilege. While youth groups can undergird what's being taught at home, most kids who stay committed and in love with Jesus are those whose parents are investing in them at HOME. Don't give over the awesome privilege of raising tomorrow's leaders to someone else simply because it gets difficult or you come to a place where you don't know where to go. God has entrusted your children to you, and He will equip you with the skills and anointing to accomplish this successfully!

Model a Dynamic Relationship with God

Another pivotal reason children often fail to develop dynamic relationships with Jesus is because they don't see them modeled at home. If you want to see a small revival in the life of your child, you need to have a big one in your own. It's impossible to give away spiritual depth or hunger for God that we don't possess ourselves. This doesn't mean we have to be a perfect parent, but we do need to be *sincere* parents. There's nothing like hypocrisy to turn our children off toward the things of God. Our children need to witness a genuine hunger and love for God, backed by a character that makes "life with God" attractive to them.

Don't Just Read the Bible
Get to Know the Author

Teaching our kids the Word of God is essential. While it's vital to study the Bible to develop sound doctrine and life-giving principles, we need to keep the *primary* purpose for reading the Bible in mind. As Kris Vallotton wisely said, "The goal of reading the Bible is to know the Author. If you know the book but not the Author, you're in deception and the Word of God can actually blind you to the Christ that is standing before you." [2]

"There is a style of Scripture reading that is mainly concerned with finding and applying principles rather than enjoying His presence. This is good but limited."[3] The Bible is full of principles that lead to successful living (which any human being can apply), but as a believer, the ultimate purpose of reading the Bible is *getting to know God*. When we diminish studying the Bible in order to pursue head knowledge, achieve good theology, or find keys for right-living, we enter a form of religion void of power, void of experience. Believers who know the book but not the Author, have in essence "read" God out of their Bibles. As we read Scripture, it is the Holy Spirit who leads us into truth. It takes the Word and the Spirit to arrive at real truth and a deeper understanding of who God is. One without the other leads to deception in one form or another.

When believers value the Bible itself more than the Holy Spirit or relationship with God they enter a subtle form of idolatry. "It's not the Father, Son, and Holy Bible; it's the Holy Spirit. The Bible reveals God, but it is *itself* not God. We are reliant on the Holy Spirit to reveal what is contained on the pages of Scripture... The fear of becoming like some mindless fanatic has kept many Christians from interacting with their greatest treasure in this life—the Holy Spirit."[4] Don't just read the Bible—get to know the God of the Bible. Read your Bible to gain wisdom for Godly living, but more importantly, read it to experience and get to know your Heavenly Father!

Your Kids Need to Experience God

Kids who experience God want to know Him more! God is real, God is powerful, and God is exciting. Your kids need to experience a God who is alive and active; a God who can do great exploits. This generation wants to see signs and wonders—they want to experience God not just know *about* Him. In fact, your children experiencing God is probably the best insurance against a life of pursuing excitement *outside* the walls of the church.

One way for your kids to experience God is by going on mission trips where believers really pray for the sick and see supernatural things happen... Not the kind of mission trip where even if God never showed up, no one would know the difference or the kind of exclusively humanitarian mission trip Christian families take once-in-a-lifetime to appease their guilt for living the "American Dream." I'm talking about mission trips where kids participate in preaching the gospel, healing the sick, and praying for the needs of people.

At the end of their eighth-grade year, two of my older children, Anna and Wesley, got to go on a mission trip to Mexico with students from Bethel Christian School. Both attest that this trip was the most exciting event of their entire junior high experience. In Mexico, the students loved on orphans, did practical works of service, and ministered to the people. They got to pray and prophesy over young people and adults, as well as see people get miraculously healed. Wesley was so moved with compassion for the orphans that he asked the principal if they could bring them all home. Anna loved the trip so much that she plans to go back later to minister in Mexico again—not only that but ministering in Mexico ignited in her a desire to minister in other areas of missions as well.

Getting to experience at a young age what it means to take the gospel to the nations can be life changing for our kids. Our family served as missionaries in Romania for about six years when our children were very small. It was an unforgettable season that instilled a commitment to evangelism and missions that will remain with us forever. We also witnessed first-hand the impact on other families as they joined us via short-term mission trips. Experiencing God through missions infuses in believers the heart of God for the lost like few other experiences.

Taking your children and teens to conferences or camps where they can participate in vibrant worship and hear relevant and anointed messages often creates tipping points for spiritual growth in their lives as well. Wonderful youth conferences are occurring all over the States that are specifically designed to equip youth to walk with God in a powerful and relevant way. When young people get to experience God in corporate settings, they realize they aren't alone in their faith. While it's our job as parents to equip our children spiritually, young people also need to experience community and the wider expression of the body of Christ.

The Power of Prayer

Praying *with* your kids is another way for them to see and experience God at work. Praying together as a family, even if you only have a few minutes to gather, can make a huge difference in the long run.

When I was growing up, my family was introduced to the Gospel at the beginning of my high school years. Within a few short months my entire family gave our lives to Christ.

Because of my lack of spiritual background, I knew very little about the Bible or prayer. I was what you'd call—completely *unchurched*. I couldn't understand why "church people" used the word "Lord" and then sometimes "God," and who was "Jesus" in relation to "God"? I thought Psalms was pronounced "Palms" and "Job" was something you got after college not a person in the Old Testament.

Prayer was a spiritual discipline that profoundly shaped my early spiritual life. Spending time each day getting to know God was emphasized by our youth leaders, thus I quickly experienced the benefits of implementing this practice into my life. Additionally, before school each day my mom made sure we prayed *together*. As an autonomous teen praying *together* was not at the top of my list. However, to this day I still remember how powerful and impactful it felt to pray *together* before leaving for school. I learned by experience that praying together has a supernatural way of bonding us to each other (Matthew 18:33). It builds family connection and connection to our Heavenly Father.

It's also great to write down or journal the things your family is praying about so you can keep track of how God answers. Your family can pray for each other, neighbors, friends, teachers, coaches, various countries, and witness what God does as a result. When your children see and experience God answering specific prayers it builds their faith and encourages them to make prayer a lifestyle. Almost everything in the Kingdom happens as a result of some kind of prayer. Countless men and women who have lost their way spiritually and then returned to walk in the fullness of their destiny will attest to discovering that "someone, somewhere was praying *specifically* for them."

Prayer involves talking to God, but it also involves listening. Ultimately, prayer is about friendship with God. It's about relationship with our Heavenly Father. Have you ever noticed that you often hear God when you are in the midst of worshiping Him? This is because when we focus on Him, we hear Him. A fantastic little book our family read together which is filled with demonstrations of the power of listening to God is *God Guides* by Mary Geegh (missionary to India in the early 1900s). This book was compiled by "Pray America" and is teeming with one to two page testimonies of God speaking in response to believers who intentionally listen to His Voice. It depicts how swiftly and powerfully God acts on behalf of His children when they listen and then fully obey His leading.

In addition to corporate family devotions, it is important for your children to build their own well with God. When your children come and ask you about various situations, exhort them to seek God's wisdom and heart as well. Of course you want to help guide and counsel your children, but it's vital that they increasingly learn to hear and obey the voice of the Lord for themselves. You don't want your child to start learning to hear God's voice when it's time to leave home or go to college. The ability to hear God's voice is an essential skill for all believers who genuinely desire to live out their divine destiny and purpose in God.

You can help your children by asking them questions like, "What do you sense the Lord is saying to you?" "What do you feel the Lord wants you to do in this or that situation?" Ask them what God is revealing to them in their personal time with Him. My husband regularly asks our children *whom* they feel the Holy Spirit is prodding them to pray for. Prayer is about sensing and hearing what God is saying. It's when we develop "eyes to see" and "ears to hear" that we can truly partner with God in fulfilling our destiny. In essence prayer helps us posture ourselves to be part of where the winds of Heaven are *already* blowing.

Exhort your kids to spend *alone time* with God each day—the purpose—*friendship* with God. Don't worry about the length of time. Your kids may start out spending five or ten minutes with God, it's cultivating the daily relational habits with God that counts the most. Teach them that God *loves* spending time with them and is always ready to impart wisdom, direction, and encouragement when they ask (James 1:5). Let them know that they can talk to God about the big things *and* the little things. Encourage them to spend time just letting God touch them with his Holy Spirit. It makes God sad when we only come to Him to ask for solutions and personal requests. Prayer is more about relationship than getting things done. It's about us turning our affections toward Him so we can *enjoy* His presence, experience His peace, and know His heart.

Teaching God's Word

The other habit I learned as a new Christian was the importance of studying God's word. Meditating on God's word and memorizing Scripture transformed my thinking and shaped my worldview. I was encouraged by spiritual mentors to learn not only individual verses but also whole portions of Scripture and smaller books in the New Testament. The Holy Spirit used the Word to ground me in truth and teach me about the ways of God, and I'm pretty sure it helped my memory a lot for college!

My husband and I wanted our children to love God's word from a young age. When they were small, we spent time reading Bible stories out loud and listening to the Bible via CDs and tapes. The ministry, *"Your Story Hour,"* has incredible dramatized audio Bible stories that our kids have loved for years. (This ministry has been creating these wonderful products since 1949). Kids should have *fun* while they are learning the Bible. Sometimes, I encouraged our kids to draw what they were hearing as they listened along. Getting to illustrate their own cartoon version of what they heard provided an exciting way for them to engage and experience each story.

By the way, *Your Story Hour* also has inspiring CDs about historical figures like Thomas Edison, George Washington, Joan of Arc, and numerous other heroic figures. Joshua and I recently listened to a wonderful depiction of the life of Alexander Graham Bell on a two-hour car trip to the airport. Hearing Alexander's full-life story gave me a new and deeper respect for the sacrifice and determination that surrounded the invention of the telephone.

Children Don't Get a Junior-Size Holy Spirit

When your children are young is the optimal time for them to begin to hear God's voice and experience the supernatural. They may be younger and smaller, but they have the same size Holy Spirit living inside of them as a full-grown adult. This Biblical truth has wonderful and profound ramifications if you think about the possibilities. Children experiencing God at young ages and developing the habit of walking in His presence can be life changing. It's actually easier for most children to hear and experience God than for many of us adults. "One of the more offensive concepts that Jesus taught and believed is that children are more ready to enter the Kingdom than most grown-ups— Matthew 11:25. We tend to think that weightier concepts are reserved for the mature. In part that is true. But the really mature, from God's perspective, are those with a child's heart."[5]

I remember driving along the highway when Joshua was about three years old. He was strapped in his booster seat and staring at the scenery ahead—I was thinking to myself, "I sure hope Josh always loves and worships God." Immediately Josh as if I'd just spoken aloud said, "Mom, don't worry I will always love and worship God!" Well, I'm glad we got that settled. Wow! I better watch what I *think* around Joshua!

Another time, Josh and I heard an ambulance approaching rapidly, sirens blaring. Josh was about four years old when this occurred. As he looked out the window with beaming eyes, he pointed right above the ambulance and declared, "Oh look Mom, there come the angels, Mom, look! There they come!" We never told him that angels come to accidents. OK, Ok... Mom wasn't seeing any angels, but I'm sure they were definitely on the way. On an interesting note, when I was a child, I always felt tremendous fear when I heard any kind of ambulance as I didn't like the thought of people getting hurt and maybe even dying. What was historically a place of fear for me, became a place of *comfort and confidence in God* for my son Joshua. This illustrates God's desire to see our children experience victory and overcoming in the same areas where we may have faced defeat and weakness. It's God's plan for the posterity and heritage of our family lines to be in a perpetual state of growth.

Most children are remarkably attuned when it comes to spiritual matters. Until high school, I grew up in an agnostic home where "God" was something we never talked about. I had no idea if God even existed. During second grade, my parents sent me to a school called, "The Sunshine School." (They were hippies back then in case any of you are wondering.) The Sunshine School had no books, pencils, or even desks for that matter. I don't remember doing *any* academics at all during that year. Maybe that's why I ended up liking school so much later on. In spite of the lack of educational training, I do remember our agnostic teacher, "Charlotte," having all the students (About 10-12 students were in the entire school, as you can imagine not many parents were eager to pay for school where you didn't do any *school*.) climb up into the loft where she read to us from the acclaimed novel, "*The Lion the Witch and the Wardrobe*," by C. S. Lewis.

I was immediately enthralled in the plot and imagery and couldn't wait for story time each day. I distinctly recall the description of "Aslan" depicted by Lewis. I remember daydreaming about knowing this "Aslan" personally. "I wish *I* could know "Aslan," was the cry of my heart. I pictured his mesmerizing voice, his soft flowing mane, his tender yet penetrating eyes, and his ultimate sacrificial death on the round table. I envisioned the land of Narnia with remarkable talking animals and mysterious talking trees, a land with luscious green grass and cool rushing streams, a place where time knew no earthly bounds and wounds healed in mere seconds. In second grade and with no Christian moorings, the spiritual truth of "Aslan" was calling and awakening my soul to Christ. Years later I would learn about the Jesus to whom "Aslan" so powerfully pointed. It is still fascinating to me that in my adulthood I can so vividly recall this early awakening to the *reality* of God. My personal testimony serves as just one of many examples of the spiritual attunement of young children to their Creator.

I am grateful that my own children experienced encounters with God at early ages. When our kids were small, we would sometimes gather our entire family and ask God to touch us with His Holy Spirit. During prayer, the kids were often touched in different ways. They also experienced God during worship times at church. Sometimes they would describe how God touched them with a sense of incredible peace or love. Other times, one of them would cry and let us know they were experiencing tears of joy. Occasionally, they enjoyed His presence by shouting and running around. Now and then their experiences were more dramatic. Whether they experienced God subtly or dramatically, we were just grateful they were experiencing God in a tangible way. On a comical note, watching our four kids lay hands on our dog, Revival, to see if he too could get touched by the Holy Spirit, could get pretty hysterical. Ever so often Revival would just suddenly fall over, but I'm not sure if this emanated from the Holy Spirit or a dog-inspired idea to get our kids to leave him alone.

At about seven years of age, our daughter Anna was prayed for by a pastor from Southern California. Within moments Anna fell to the ground and lay as still as a statue for over twenty minutes. Anna was generally wiggly and energetic like most young children, which was the first clue that she was having a real God-encounter. Starry eyed, she finally sat up and thoughtfully shared how she was sitting on Jesus' lap the entire time. Anna expounded about her captivation with Jesus' deep, blue eyes. She recalled how Jesus shared with her how much He loved her and how beautiful she was to Him. She went on to describe his white robe and the breastplate over his chest covered with twelve colorful stones. Unbeknownst to her, Anna was describing the twelve stones depicted in the Old Testament which represent the twelve tribes of Israel. Only an authentic experience could reveal this kind of detail to a child who knew nothing of the twelve tribes of Israel. It is God who orchestrates and comprehends the purpose and significance of each Heavenly engagement. One thing we know for sure—a *genuine* encounter with God—is always a good thing! In God-encounters believers often learn by experience what is impossible to know through human comprehension.

Memorizing and Praying Scripture

Take time to memorize Scripture with your children; this habit will bear fruit for years to come. We kept it simple, but we began memorizing specific Bible verses when our kids were young. In reality, sometimes we were more consistent than other times. It's amazing what you can accomplish by working toward realistic goals incrementally over time. If you teach one verse a week or even two verses a month, by the time your children are teens they will know close to five hundred Bible verses. During the teen years when youth often struggle with worldly temptation and mounting pressure concerning identity and sexuality, having Bible verses memorized (meditated-on is even better) could be the difference in good choices and bad choices. During these years, the brain undergoes massive change causing many teens to feel confused and even disoriented. Most of us can remember doing things during the teen years and looking back we now wonder, "What was I thinking?" You weren't thinking very well—that's the problem.

If young people have no verses or Biblical principles stored in the brain, then when the brain scans for truth and answers in high-risk situations, nothing comes up. That's just one reason why memorizing the Bible is so helpful. In addition to memorizing Scripture, as kids get older, it sometimes is beneficial to study the Word of God as it pertains to various topics. You may want to take a few months to study what the Scripture says about topics like: giving, joy, thankfulness, purity, work, or forgiveness. Our family likes to regularly read the Proverbs. My husband has our boys read chapters in Proverbs out loud as he drives them to school in the morning. Proverbs is teeming with wisdom and practical principles on how to live your daily life and make Godly decisions.

A few years ago a humorous interaction occurred between our two sons, Joshua and Christian. The previous evening, our son Joshua had an encounter in his sleep in which he saw angels and heard God telling him to "Joice"—rejoice. The next day, he was leaping around the house and singing for literally hours. After a morning of observing his "constant leaping, jumping, and singing" (it was starting to get a little annoying), I asked him what was going on. Joshua then proceeded to share his dream from the night before in which he had been told to "Joice!" when he saw God! Christian overheard Josh sharing and immediately popped over, his finger pointing in Joshua's face, he proclaimed, "Joshua, the Bible says you can NOT see the face of God and live!" Josh was very upset that Christian didn't believe him and what began as a stirring testimony quickly turned into a heated argument with possible physical ramifications. Thank goodness we have Christian around here to keep our theology straight.

It's also fun to use Scripture to teach your kids more about prayer. I remember once when the kids were small we used the verse Isaiah 68:1, "Let God arise and His enemies be scattered," to pray over nations. Several of the kids were running around beating drums and another had a flag waving while they took turns shouting, "Let God arise and His enemies be scattered over blank"—They shouted out the name of a country. Kids LOVE shouting so why not put it to good use.

During these years, our kids also loved to dance, beat drums, sing, and move a lot. God is fun and adventurous, and we wanted them to experience Him this way! I can still picture all four of them jumping and shouting out, "God release your kingdom in Africa, God release your kingdom in the United States, God release your kingdom in Romania." Or Wesley shouting, "Come to Jesus, and get your NEW mind!"

Every family is different and will have it's own way of spending time with God and experiencing His presence. It's important to teach our kids about the ways of God, but there is plenty of room for expressing our individual creativity as a family. The main thing to keep in mind is that church starts in the home, and it's our job to equip our children to hear God, experience His presence, and follow His Word.

A Word About Teens

Many parents are mystified and dumbfounded as teens travel through adolescence. While teen years can be fruitful and fulfilling, they also present a wide range of new challenges. Part of the "myth of adolescence" for parents is that while teens look like adults on the outside, they are still "under construction" on the inside. Teens themselves waffle between breaking away to establish their own identities and still expecting the comfort and guidance they have become so accustomed to over the years.

So why am I talking about "teen turbulence" in a chapter about spiritually equipping our kids? Well, because after hearing about our children's encounters with God, I didn't want parents to be mislead with the notion that our family *always* experiences an idealistic and euphoric devotional home life. Or that our children are *always* excited about pursuing their relationship with God. Life is real, and it is sometimes confusing and messy. More importantly I wanted to touch on teens, because it's during these years that spiritual equipping may be the most important. Parents more than ever need to "stay the course" of discipleship and devotion to God in spite of the vicissitudes of adolescence. As for parents—the teen years are perhaps the best opportunity you will ever have to develop your leadership qualities and spiritual depth.

Parents need perspective, hope, and perhaps even some of that professional knowledge from the "experts" when it comes to teens. Consider this, "Over the past twenty years, neuroscientists have learned that the teenage brain radically changes its structure in adolescence. The period between the age of ten and puberty is a period of vigorous production of brain cells followed, between the ages of fourteen and seventeen, by a period of pruning back, when gray matter thins dramatically. The brain becomes more streamlined and efficient. But the frontal lobes, the areas of the brain responsible for rationality and modulation of impulses and desires, do not reach full development for girls until twenty-four or twenty-five and for boys until twenty-nine. Judgment and wisdom, (executive function) live in the part of the brain that is last to mature."[6]

Understanding the psychological and neurological altercations of teens can help parents make sense of their teen's shifting behavior and attitudes. Having three teens myself, I empathize with fellow, bewildered teen parents. Navigating the teen years often stirs in me upcoming book titles like "What All Teens Wish Their Parents Understood," or "What Not to Expect from Your Teen." If there's ever a season parents need some help, humor, and clear strategy, it's during these years!

Parenting takes more faith at the end than at the beginning.

—Jeff Shupe

Take devotional time as an example. After watching our young children encounter God with hunger and tenacity, witnessing the fluctuating passion toward God from older teens can be perplexing. Undergoing adolescence affects the way teenagers see themselves, others, and their relationship with God. You may be confused, but remember they are *more* confused. Your teen may no longer eagerly wave flags, raise their hands, and shout praises to God like they did at five. Teens can certainly have HUGE hearts for God, but in my experience to expect the same kind of childlike exuberance is often unrealistic, especially during the years when teens are most conscious about their image. Prepare for some inconsistency might be a good first tip when it comes to teens. Oh and definitely plan on persistence when it comes to gathering busy teens for evening devotions.

I must confess that previously in my own idealistic view of the teen years, I imagined my teens and I would glide through this season conversing over spiritually and globally significant topics all the while observing an ever-increasing maturity and spiritual depth in their lives. Today's reality—on some days, I'm just thrilled when they *think* about the future or beyond their immediate concerns. As far as visions of our teens dancing before the Lord, well those have given way to figuring out creative schemes for evading local school dances where spirituality is the farthest thing on most teens' mind. Don't get me wrong, there has remained spiritual hunger during adolescence, it's just come with greater turbulence than I envisioned.

Part of the tension during teen years is due to a sharp decline in cultural and societal values. Even more tension results from the socialistic anti-God agenda being unabashedly promulgated through our education system, media, and government. Fifty years ago, parents could send their children to secular schools without much concern that family, Biblical, and relational values would be constantly under-mined. Today's parents can no longer expect secular institutions to under-gird family values. Quite the opposite, "all inclusive tolerance is demanded" —with the exception of tolerance for a Christian worldview.

All "humor and brain science about teens" aside, if you want your teen to journey through teen years as victors and overcomers, then you have to respond to the times in a way that is equal to the challenge. You can only build a successful family from the inside out. The Kingdom values and relational connections in your home must be stronger than the culture surrounding your kids. Ultimately, we are preparing our children to be salt and light to a lost world. The challenge for today's young people is "mingle and associate with the lost, but don't take on their values or habits."[7]

Only God can reveal to each family how, when, where, and to what degree to send our children among the worldly systems. After prayerful consideration, my husband and I decided to send two of our children to a local preparatory school for the high school years. Having equipped them as best we could—we prepared for continued intentionality and involvement in the lives of our teens and LOTS of prayer.

What have our kids learned? Over recent years, our teens have learned that being a young person devoted to Christ can be challenging and even painful at times; holding to Kingdom values will test a young person's devotion to God. Staying home while most other teens frequent the latest R-rated movie can feel lonely, and being one of the only students in high school who doesn't attend the "planned parenthood" sex education week where youth are indoctrinated with the latest socialistic amoral agendas about sex, life, or absence of life in the womb, and homosexuality isn't fun when you are a teen. Think about it, teens are going through the greatest neurological and physiological changes since toddlerhood while being challenged to stand strong amidst the worldly mores surrounding them.

On the other hand, our teens have experienced the significance and joy of impacting the lives of other young people. They're learning that the same teens who frequent all the latest movies experience loneliness too, only they are lonely in the crowd. They're learning that living lives of courage and love for God fuels other teens with courage to do the same. They're learning that Jesus is with them in everything and at all times. They're also learning that you get strong by being tested! As for our family, we've gained a genuine love and enjoyment of all kinds of kids and families. Even with all the challenges, it's proven a great blessing and privilege to share God's love in secular environments.

Don't get short-sighted or discouraged during the tougher days. Partner with God in leading your family with confidence. Persevere in building a Kingdom family culture!

When the teen years are said and done, it is highly probable that your teen will evolve into a highly-functioning, God-loving member of society. So press on, stay focused, keep your sense of humor, and enjoy the never-a-dull-moment teen years!

Discussion and Discovery

1. What is a realistic goal you can set for teaching your children the Bible? Come up with a simple plan for memorizing Bible verses.

2. How often do you feel it is possible to meet together as a family to worship, pray, and read the Bible? Set some goals with your husband or with the Lord if you are a single parent.

3. Pray about the possibility of taking a mission trip together as a family. Write down your thoughts about the subject of missions.

4. What are some long-term spiritual goals you want to aim for in the lives of your children? What are some practical things you can do to move toward these goals?

ENDNOTES

[1] George Barna, *Revolutionary Parenting* (2007, Tyndale House Publishers, Inc.,), 38.

[2] Quote by Kris Vallotton.

[3] Bill Johnson, *Dreaming With God* (2006, Shippensburg, PA), 140.

[4] Ibid, 142.

[5] Ibid, 131.

[6] Wendy Mogel, *The Blessing of a B Minus,* (2010, Scribner), 22.

[7] Bill Johnson, *Dreaming With God* (2006, Shippensburg, PA), 103.

Concluding Thoughts

*A*fter working through an entire book on all the different ways you need to train and equip your children and then on top of that how you need model all of these traits—you may be feeling a bit overwhelmed. You might be ready to throw in the towel or send your children off to a boarding school where nuns would raise them instead. You've just read about teaching your kids how to overcome, how to work, how to persevere, how to risk, how to fail, how to learn and how to serve. In addition, you are supposed to be a relational parent enjoying all aspects of this calling so your children will feel enjoyed and loved. For many of you, this seems like an impossible mission.

Well let me bring you back to where this whole book started—remember what Stephen Covey says about families? "Good families—even great families—are off track 90% of the time!" It's not being perfectly on track that produces great families; it's having a sense of destination and aiming for it that matters most. When we put our best energy into the things that matter most in life, our efforts will always bear fruit. When we're trying to live out what we believe, struggling and even striving to move in the right direction, our children will usually accept our values and adopt our principles.

As you evaluate the present and look toward the future, remember that more than anything we teach or endeavor to train into the lives of our children—our children will become very much like us. One of the best things we can do for our child is to become what we want to see them become. Passionate parents create passionate kids, kind parents create kind kids, confident parents create confident kids, insecure parents create insecure kids, selfish parents create selfish kids and on and on we could go.

Certainly kids can overcome any instability and lack of character we pass down to them. In a similar manner, they can rebel and not take on our positive traits. However in general, they will become a lot like us. When we grow and change, they tend to grow and change.

Yet, the tension lies in the fact that no matter how much we endeavor to become what we want to see our children become, we are still works-in-progress. We have to do our best and then trust the Lord. I like what Graham Cooke says about emotional healing, "The Lord heals you 80% and then he gives you friends." Ultimately as parents, our hope and confidence shouldn't depend on our abilities or the lack of them, but in the Lord's desire and ability to strengthen and guide us along the way. While writing this book, I've regularly dealt with my own insecurities and failures as a parent. Like each of you, I have areas of strength and areas of weakness. Some of you come from great homes, which gives you a head start compared with the average parent. Others come from extremely dysfunctional homes, leaving you with a lot to overcome. The rest of you fall somewhere in between.

Regardless of where you find yourself on the parenting spectrum, God knows everything about your situation. He sees the whole picture, past, present, and future. He knows your personal capacity as a parent. He knows your strengths; He knows your weaknesses. He knows your deepest desires, and He knows your greatest fears. He knows what you face, and He knows the solutions for these dilemmas. You serve a God who is eager to imbue you with the anointing and wisdom to succeed in raising a healthy family. In the same way that you want your children to look to you as a parent, God wants you to look to Him as your Father.

As you look to your Heavenly Father for wisdom and strength, I exhort you to work on the areas that He highlights to each of you. Remember, God only asks us to work on specific things during specific seasons. His yoke is easy and his burden is light (Matthew 11:30). Don't get overwhelmed in parenting; instead, make a decision to give it your all, but trust God in the process and leave the results to Him.

The Big Picture

In closing, I would like to invite you to reflect on the Big Picture. If as a society, we focus our attention on the family structure, we can affect crucial change around us, yet if we don't focus on the family, we may continue to fight on a thousand fronts needlessly. Why? Let's take a look at Roman history. Edward Gibbons is considered by many, as the world's most renowned historian and expert on the decline and fall of Rome. In his epic study regarding Rome's demise, the following are the undisputed reasons for the "Fall of Rome" in order of their significance.

1. The breakdown of the family structure
2. The weakening of a sense of individual responsibility
3. Excessive taxes and government control and intervention
4. Seeking pleasures that became increasingly hedonistic, violent, and immoral
5. The decline of religion[1]

Yes, the number one reason attributed to the Fall of Rome was—the breakdown of the family. History could repeat itself, but it doesn't have to. I wanted to share this tidbit of history to help parents see just how valuable it is to raise the kind of family that manifests God's heart and values on Earth. Raising a Godly family affects our future and our posterity. While this book is about the family, family in and of itself is not the end game. The purpose of a great family is to make a difference in the world around us. As a believer, raising a successful family is more than raising healthy and happy children; it's about raising children who will influence their culture as they walk in their God-ordained destinies and become passionate followers of Christ. Ultimately, parenting means touching the globe through our children and our children's children. The positive ramifications of this are endless! So as your consider the Big Picture—May God grant you incredible vision and purpose for your family! May He grant you authentic joy and deep hope along the journey, and may He richly bless your family for many generations to come!

ENDNOTES

[1] Edward Gibbon, *The Decline and Fall of the Roman Empire, in Great Works of the Western World*, vol. 37-38 (Chicago: Encyclopedia Britannica, 1990).

Revolutionary Parenting

A Summary

The book *Revolutionary Parenting* was written by George Barna, a world-renowned researcher who founded *The Barna Group* — one of the most respected statistics groups of the twenty-first century. After conducting a series of in-depth surveys, as well as thousands of interviews with young adults and their parents, *Revolutionary Parenting* presents and explores the common denominators that were implemented by successful parents. According to *The Barna Group*, more than 75,000 parenting books are presently glutting the market representing various theories, philosophies, and assumptions as to what makes a great parent and what produces a great child. But none have actually weighed the tangible outcomes of these parenting theories. Through statistics and comprehensive surveys, *Revolutionary Parenting* measures the results of what *actually* works to produce spiritual champions, in contrast to what current parenting trends claim to work. The following is a summary of some of the main points taken directly from the book with a few of my own thoughts added here and there. Please purchase the book if you would like to hear more about what these surveys revealed.

- Most parents talk a better parenting game than they play, largely because they have vague notions about the process and product. Few adults have clearly and comprehensively thought through their role as parents. Most of the parents interviewed in recent years had a survival-based philosophy rather than a goal-oriented philosophy. However, parents of spiritually transformed children showed that they had a refreshingly unambiguous notion of their role.[1]

- Americans have a tendency to repudiate facts that discredit what they believe to be true. The more sensitive people are to the criticism raised, the more likely their initial reaction will be to reject the facts of the argument. Yet, research reveals that it is possible to perform one's parenting functions well if certain parameters are in place.[2]

- People's lives are shaped primarily when they are young. Research related to child development and spiritual growth showed that the spiritual war occurring in an individual's life is largely won or lost by the age of 13. What parents do with their children before the teen years is of paramount importance.

- Spiritual champions live in ways that are very different from the norm. So do their parents.

- A major condition for success that we discovered is that those who produce spiritual champions embrace parenting as their primary job in life. Parenting is their full-time job; the job they get paid to do is simply an addendum.[3]

- Research showed that churches alone do not and cannot have much influence on children. In fact, the greatest influence the church may have in affecting children is by affecting their parents.

- Revolutionary parents fight cultural enticements and emotional temptations to embrace society's dominant parenting philosophy — not because they are renegades or contrarian but simply because they want to do what is right not according to social norms but upon Biblical principles. It causes little stress to revolutionary parents to parent differently from what is culturally acceptable.[4]

- The depth of love that revolutionary parents had for their children, translated into an intense sense of mission to prepare them for life. These parents knew that to affect their children's lives, their love had to be manifested in authentic relationship. They were striving to fulfill a dual role of real friend and that of authoritative coach. Research showed the average amount of time revolutionary parents spent in dialogue with their children ranged between 90-120, minutes a day while the typical American family registers less than 15 minutes of direct parent-child conversation each day.[5]

- Revolutionary parents had clear, measurable parenting goals and held themselves accountable. One parent quoted, "That unless I sat down, thought through where we were going as parent and child, how I was going to get there, and then developed some steps or milestones along the way that would show me whether or not I was making progress, my efforts quickly deteriorated into satisfaction with getting through the day without doing anyone bodily harm. Having a plan and some benchmarks was really important for me." Parents identified dimensions of life that made a significant difference and focused on those elements.[6]

- Most parents acknowledge their children are unique but tend to parent each one identically. Revolutionary Parents do not buy into that line of reasoning. They operate from the line of reasoning that because each of their youngsters is unique, their parenting responses must be unique as well. Yes, there are golden principles for educating and disciplining. For instance, they may believe that showing compassion to their children is necessary, but what constitutes compassion for one child (such as allowing a normally diligent child to miss school for a minor ailment) might be detrimental to another child (reinforcing a lackadaisical child's manipulative tendency). Revolutionary parents took the time and made the effort to learn the unique nature of each of their children and to build a parenting framework around each child's distinctives.[7] One-size-fits-all approach to parenting is easier but it certainly does not produce better results. These parents were students of their children.

- Revolutionary parents had basic expectations for all their children but gave them freedom to express themselves in personalized ways that were consistent with those values. The right blend of freedom and limitations proved to be a taxing proposition for most of these parents. Like an unending chess game where you want EVERYONE to win.[8] They endeavored to find the balance between protection and age-appropriate freedom.

- Revolutionary parents had a core philosophy of advancing their children at a pace that was natural for the child. They held this position even when teachers, family members, or friends expressed disapproval. "You can't worry too much about how other people judge your decisions… They are not responsible and they are not living with the child. They can do what they want with their children; but I have to live with the consequences of my choices for my children." Focus on the needs of your children NOT the reaction of outsiders.[9]

- One-hundred percent of the revolutionary parents interviewed agreed that the most important focus of their children's training was the development of Godly character. Spiritual champions have the advantage of being raised by parents who are more concerned about the love they show fellow students than whether they outperform them.[10] Character was more important than performance.

- Eight out of ten Revolutionary parents said they were heavily involved in every aspect of their child's life.[11]

- Most parents today try to balance their own needs and the needs of their children, seeking to limit their input in relationships and decisions of their children as much as possible. Their view is that providing general guidelines and allowing children to learn through trial and error is the best course of action. Revolutionary parents, attempt to subjugate their own breadth of needs in order to partner with the child in every dimension of his or her life. The balance is where to draw the line between helpful assistance and overbearing intruder. The parent's job is to be there to help them learn and make right choices. The tension was related to becoming too involved, and smothering the child.[12]

- Revolutionary parents saw themselves as a parent not a best friend.[13] But they were also friends with their children.

- Spiritual champions experienced consistency and dependability in their home environments. They said they could always count on what their parents said being carried out. It was a relief to these kids that there was order in the universe, even if it was only on their property. Lack of consistency can be the undoing of a parent. Adult spiritual champions attributed their character partially to the consistency of their parent's efforts, while young adults who are not living a transformed life today frequently noted that their parents lacked consistency.[14] Most parents know cognitively what to do but are unwilling to make the sacrifices necessary to be consistent.

- Parents who raised spiritual champions saw themselves as the primary spiritual developers of their young children. They didn't just drop their kids off at youth group they wanted to know what was being taught and how kids conducted themselves. In contrast, the typical parent simply wanted to know the time and place to drop their kids off and weren't concerned with content, atmosphere etc.[15]

- Revolutionary parents raised their children with God. They knew they were not alone.[16]

- Revolutionary parents did not fight every battle. While some parents claim that you must win every battle, over 96% of revolutionary parents said you would wear yourself out and lose your relationship with your child if you fought them over every circumstance in which you disagreed.[17]

- Revolutionary parents wanted to know what company their kids were keeping. If their child was outside the home after dark, another child's parent had to be present. They were adamant about knowing the facts. "Where are you? Who are you with? What is the activity? When will you be home? Were things we needed to know," said one parent of one of the most popular kids at school. "If we were lied to or our needs were not met by their choices, while out and about, there would be a price to pay...." "...when kids saw their parents were serious and willing to enforce the penalty, they complied very well... they always test you."[18]

- Three out of four Revolutionary parents admitted to helping their kids choose their friends. Most of these parents did this discreetly without the kids realizing it.[19]

- The average preteen spends more than forty hours ingesting media content. Revolutionary parents explained to their children the problems embedded in the media content. Spiritual champions listed the unwillingness of parents to closely monitor and limit media as a glaring fault of many parents. Giving children the freedom to determine their own media diet was ranked as one of the most insidious weaknesses of today's parents, producing outcomes that will haunt their children, and our society, for years to come. Seventy-three percent of revolutionary parents placed a lot of emphasis upon protecting their children from negative influences.[20]

- Revolutionary parents did not follow a clear-cut pattern regarding discipline. But they were consistent in a discipline approach and stuck to it embracing discipline as fruitful and necessary. They felt discipline was one of the most challenging aspects of raising children. A consistent principle that emerged among Revolutionary Parents was their ability to contain their anger and frustration. They got upset with their children but were able to channel their emotions toward positive and productive solutions.[21]

- Barna nationwide studies among young adults pointed to verbal abuse as one of the most serious mistakes made by parents. A surprisingly large number of baby busters criticized their parents for saying things that were permanently hurtful.[22]

- Parents who raised spiritual champions left no doubt in the minds of their children that they were in charge and their children recognized this. "Children need parents to be strong and in charge—not to the point of crushing their spirit or disallowing participation in decision making, but someone who has the final say and takes responsibility for decisions made. If a parent refuses to be in charge, you get the inmates running the asylum."[23]

- Revolutionary parents tended to provide their children with logic and explanations regarding their rules or standards. When their children asked for explanations or reasoning behind decisions, they gave it to them. They encouraged their children to think and ask questions.

- Modern trends have accepted the idea that quality time with your children can substitute for quantity of time with your children. Studies done over the last 15 years showed that this pattern has hurt both parents and children, leaving a large proportion of young adults feeling as if they were not adequately parented and a shockingly high number feeling they lacked a father figure.

- When The Barna Group asked young adults what they felt were the most significant mistakes that America's parents have made, the second highest ranked mistake was not spending enough time with their children. (The failure to provide appropriate discipline was the top-ranked deficiency.)[24]

Revolutionary parents rejected the cultural spin and remained committed to spending lots of time with their children and also having times of intense focus and memorable experiences. Revolutionary parents did not perceive amount of time to be the main factor but a combination of factors including:

- Highly engaged—Being emotionally and intellectually present as well as physically present.

- Investing time—They understood that unless they invested substantial amounts of time, they would not have deep relationship with their children.

- Willing to listen—The most important skill in spending time was listening to what the child said. Extraordinary parents said that too many moms and dads are so busy completing their agendas they do not hear what's on the minds of their children, and thus miss great opportunities to connect at a deeper level and take advantage of life-changing moments offered by their young ones.

- Balancing soft and hard — Revolutionary parents described seeking to reach a balance of openness and vulnerability along with being the authoritative coach. Being too soft and touchy feely was thought to dampen their potential leadership; being too strong and directive could break the child's spirit or disrupt the relationship. Finding a sweet spot in between the extremes was said to be a difficult journey but one worth the effort.[25]

- One of the nonnegotiable behaviors of great parents was their insistence on faith in God and following Biblical principles as the driving force behind the household culture. Many of the parents did not have a stringent scriptural trail.

They were more likely to deal with Bible content once or twice a week and selected Bible passages that addressed a specific incident or event that made God's word relevant to their kids.

- Revolutionary parents did not come from a theologically liberal or spiritually complacent group. They had vibrant relationships with God, which their children "caught."

- LOVE was the method of revolutionary parents! Spiritual champions confirmed that their parents loved them into the presence of God. Even when spiritual champions confessed to trying their parents as adolescents, they said it was their parent's consistent love that made God's love ultimately real to them.

- Revolutionary parents considered salvation important but opted for a lifelong emphasis on discipleship.

- These parents prayed consistently. If anything, it seemed like they loved their children into the Kingdom of God.[26]

- The parents interviewed recognized the importance of developing the habit of serving others and sought ways to inculcate that in their children's lives. In younger years this included pragmatic acts of service, like cutting a widow's lawn or doing kind things for others. Later service shifted to mission trips, taking care of the elderly or other more overtly spiritual acts of service. These parents also served as an entire family regularly.

- Most American parents make an effort to help their children make good decisions. However, revolutionary parents approached this a little differently. Their aim was to teach their children how to think independently, basing their choices on core principles.[27]

- Revolutionary parents found it important to protect their children from burnout. They prioritized competing opportunities so that their youngsters would not suffer from unnecessary fatigue. One parent voiced, "I wanted my kids to have lots of experiences and to develop the discipline to pursue excellence in what they did, but I did not want to put too much pressure on them to achieve a wide range of activities." They helped choose what their kids got involved in, and simply expected them to do their best and keep striving to do better. The spiritual champions themselves grew up and appreciated the fact that their parents didn't overdo it. They selected a handful of activities and asked them to go deep rather than broad. "I benefited greatly from the idea of excelling in one or two areas rather than skimming the surface in a dozen."[28]

Some of the parents interviewed had well-honed intuition about parenting, but most worked HARD at parenting and studied the Bible to grasp the principles that would lead to success.

The Bible gives surprisingly little specific instruction on parenting. More guidance is provided about spiritual maturity in adults because God knows that parents in effect produce children in their own image. Therefore impacting parents will always impact the children. The Bible is a guidebook for life, but doesn't tell us too specifically how to do most things. There is no simple set of rules or one-size-fits-all pattern that would guide all churches. "God respects our idiosyncrasies—in fact, He created them—and He appreciates the ever-changing, unique circumstances in which we find ourselves. To make life more exciting and challenging, He gives us room to develop creative Biblical solutions to the problems we face.[29]

ENDNOTES

[1] George Barna, Revolutionary Parenting (2007, Carol Stream), 37-38.

[2] George Barna, Revolutionary Parenting (2007, Carol Stream), xv.

[3] George Barna, Revolutionary Parenting (2007, Carol Stream), 24.

[4] George Barna, Revolutionary Parenting (2007, Carol Stream), 28-29.

[5] George Barna, Revolutionary Parenting (2007, Carol Stream), 33.

[6] George Barna, Revolutionary Parenting (2007, Carol Stream), 38.

[7] George Barna, Revolutionary Parenting (2007, Carol Stream), 42.

[8] George Barna, Revolutionary Parenting (2007, Carol Stream), 43.

[9] George Barna, Revolutionary Parenting (2007, Carol Stream), 45.

[10] George Barna, Revolutionary Parenting (2007, Carol Stream), 47.

[11] George Barna, Revolutionary Parenting (2007, Carol Stream), 49.

[12] George Barna, Revolutionary Parenting (2007, Carol Stream), 49.

[13] George Barna, Revolutionary Parenting (2007, Carol Stream), 52.

[14] George Barna, Revolutionary Parenting (2007, Carol Stream), 57.

[15] George Barna, Revolutionary Parenting (2007, Carol Stream), 56.

[16] George Barna, Revolutionary Parenting (2007, Carol Stream), 58.

[17] George Barna, Revolutionary Parenting (2007, Carol Stream), 64.

[18] George Barna, Revolutionary Parenting (2007, Carol Stream), 68.

[19] George Barna, Revolutionary Parenting (2007, Carol Stream), 69.

[20] George Barna, Revolutionary Parenting (2007, Carol Stream), 87.

[21] George Barna, Revolutionary Parenting (2007, Carol Stream), 75.

[22] George Barna, Revolutionary Parenting (2007, Carol Stream), 85.

[23] George Barna, Revolutionary Parenting (2007, Carol Stream), 82-83.

[24] George Barna, Revolutionary Parenting (2007, Carol Stream), 90.

[25] George Barna, Revolutionary Parenting (2007, Carol Stream), 91-92.

[26] George Barna, Revolutionary Parenting (2007, Carol Stream), 10.

[27] George Barna, Revolutionary Parenting (2007, Carol Stream), 118.

[28] George Barna, Revolutionary Parenting (2007, Carol Stream), 121.

[29] George Barna, Revolutionary Parenting (2007, Carol Stream), 129-130.

Spiritual Journeys & Small Groups

*I*t is said that, "It is relationships that wound you, and it is relationships that heal you." Functioning in community is God's primary plan for growth, healing, and vitality in the Body of Christ. For the benefits of community and connection, I encourage parents to work through this material in small groups. The purpose of small groups and sharing spiritual journeys* is to provide a place for believers to belong, be known, and be encouraged to live out their God-ordained destinies. Most of us are engaging this material with our children in mind. In light of this parents must understand that the single most important factor that determines whether our children will make sense of their own lives is if we as parents make sense of our own. In other words, children change and grow as parents change and grow.

Sharing our personal story, and hearing others share theirs, is a valuable part of the process of maturing as individuals and followers of Christ. Curt Thompson says this, "We live in a world that values knowing things. We tend to place a great deal of emphasis on the ways and the degree to which we *know* God (or know things *about* God) rather than to the degree we are *being known by* God. The Western mindset of *knowing things* often prevents us from the experience of being known, loving and being loved, which is in essence what living the Christian life *in community* is all about."[1] God deeply desires for us to not only know *about* Him, but also to *know Him*. Curt expounds further, "You cannot know God if you do not experience being known by Him. The degree to which you know God is directly reflected in your experience of being known by him. And the degree to which you are known by him will be reflected in the way in which you are known by other people. In short, your relationship with God is a direct reflection of the depth of your relationship with others."[2] Further, it's when we are known by God and others, that we can truly *know our own heart*.

Lives change when people share their story; something powerful happens when we share with others on a deeper level. The psychiatrist, Dan Siegel, explains what *telling your story* does to your brain, "an important part of how people change—not just their experiences, but also their brains—is through the process of telling their stories to an empathetic listener. When a person tells her story and is truly heard and understood, both she and the listener undergo actual changes in their brain circuitry. They feel a greater sense of emotional and relational connection, decreased anxiety, and greater awareness of and compassion for others' suffering."[3] One of the initial benefits of *sharing your story* is that it helps your brain make sense of your life and personal history. Another benefit is it helps you grow in trust in God and others. Some believers assume that even though they don't trust others—at least they trust God. The truth is—the way we trust others tends to reflect how much we really trust God.

As we choose to be more transparent and vulnerable, we often feel more connected to God and one another. Taking part in a small group and sharing our spiritual journey helps with the connection process. A healthy small group structure provides a place for believers to, not only be known, but to also belong. Whether perceived or not, relational connection is what we crave. It's what we are designed by God to experience.

As small group leaders and participants, it's important to keep in mind that for many people, the idea of "being known" is terrifying, and possibly a brand-new experience. This kind of vulnerability removes a sense of security and protection that *not being known* seemed to provide in the past. Furthermore, some believers have joined small groups in the past and chosen transparency only to experience additional wounding. Taking steps toward being known and connecting on a deeper level involves courage and a willingness to risk relationally. In order to assist and encourage one another in the process of *sharing our journey*, it's vital to keep your group atmosphere as "safe" as possible (See the small group guidelines.) May God grant you powerful breakthrough emotionally and relationally as you join together to spur one another on toward a transparent and vibrant Christian life!

a term coined by Lori Byrne, a Bethel Church pastor, for sharing our personal story and history with God

ENDNOTES

[1] Curt Thompson, M.D., Anatomy of the Soul (2007, Tyndale Publishers), 16.

[2] Curt Thompson, M.D., Anatomy of the Soul (2007, Tyndale Publishers), 24.

[3] Curt Thompson, M.D., Anatomy of the Soul (2007, Tyndale Publishers), xiv.

Spiritual Journey Guidelines

aring your Spiritual Journey is a way of getting to know one another on a deeper level. Share what you feel the Holy Spirit is leading you to share in a way that helps the group really get to know you. Below are some ideas for sharing:

- Describe your family's system of relating. How did your family members relate to each other? What kind of atmosphere was generally in your home?

- Were you a connected or disconnected family? Co-dependent and enmeshed, or was everyone doing their own thing and independent to the extreme? Were you an inter-dependent family with a healthy balance of trust and security while maintaining space for independence and developing individuality?

- Were there unspoken rules in your home? Such as: We don't talk about our feelings... We don't question authority... We keep our family life very "private" from outsiders ...

- How did your family handle conflict and problems?

- Were your parents more rule-driven or relationship-driven? Was there a high degree of love or a high degree of fear in your home? Did your parents motivate you out of guilt and fear, or love and connection?

- Were you over-controlled or under-guided? (i.e. too many boundaries or not enough?) Did your parents help you develop your gifts and talents, or did they leave you to develop yourself without their motivation and guidance?

- What was communication in your home like? Did your parents listen to you, or tell you what to think? Did you talk about feelings or only about rules and principles? Was the communication commonly peaceful or stormy? Where were there voids in communication?

- What are some of the most joyful and some of the most painful things you've experienced in your life? Be sure to focus on the joyful as well as the painful.

- How have you dealt with tragedy, pain, or abuse in your life?

- Describe your emotional and spiritual state now? Do you feel close to God and others, or distant to both? Do you feel you have to keep your guard up or are you comfortable and at ease with relationship and being transparent?

- As you think about your journey from childhood to adulthood, where do you see God's hand at work in your life? Give a few examples or testimonies.

Small Group Guidelines

TRANSPARENCY

Living in community involves sharing openly and honestly. Without transparency, it will be difficult to overcome issues and bond with others in a meaningful way. While vulnerability and transparency can be scary, they are foundational to personal and corporate breakthrough. Strongholds and areas of woundedness thrive on hiddenness and shame. Everyone has areas of weakness, struggle, and pain. It is important to resist the temptation to put up the front of "having it all together." Transparency creates trust and helps others who are dealing with the same issues to be transparent as well. Being transparent doesn't mean you have to share everything with everyone, but it is essential that you be willing to share as the Holy Spirit guides you.

CONFIDENTIALITY

Keep things confidential. Whatever is said in your small group *stays* in your small group (unless permission is given otherwise).

PRAYER

Make a commitment to pray consistently and earnestly for the members of your small group. It is powerful to have a network around you that is praying for your needs and those of your family. Prayer is one of the most profound and powerful ways to support each other. By the end of the year, you will be amazed at all the answers to prayer you will experience as a group.

JOURNAL

Bring a journal or place to write down prayer requests. This helps you to stay committed to praying. Tracking what God does keeps us aware of His power, goodness, and involvement in our lives.

BE CAREFUL OF GIVING UNSOLICITED ADVICE

While the small group time includes sharing stories and testimonies involving your own children, it is not a time for teaching and giving advice unless someone directly asks you. Advice is great in the right setting, but unrequested advice often seems overwhelming and offensive in a small group setting. Remaining teachable and slow to offense is a true sign of maturity, as ultimately small groups are about encouraging and learning from one another. Just be sensitive and attuned to others as you engage over sensitive topics.

EQUAL SHARING TIME

Each person should be mindful to keep his or her sharing within the agreed upon time allotment in order to hear from everyone. If you are given five minutes to introduce yourself—keep it to five minutes. Practice self-awareness, and be careful not to go on too long or dominate the group time with your own needs and testimonies. Make room for everyone to share.

TESTIMONY

Give good reports! Share testimonies of breakthrough in your personal or family life or ways God has encouraged or spoken to you. Think about what He is doing in your life that would encourage others and share it. Nothing is more powerful than a great testimony from someone you know well. It builds faith, fosters hope, and gives courage to those around you!

Recommended Resources

Do Hard Things: A Teenage Rebellion Against Low Expectations .... Alex Harris

Grooming the Next Generation for Success .... Dani Johnson

Guardians of Purity .... Julie Hiramine

One Million Arrows, Raising Your Children to Change the World .... Julie Ferwerda

Parenting from the Inside Out, How a Deeper Self-Understanding Can Help You Raise Children Who Thrive .... Daniel J. Siegel, M.D., and Mary Hartzell

Playstation Nation: Protect Your Child from Video Game Addiction .... Olivia & Kurt Bruner

Princess and the Kiss: A Story of God's Gift of Purity .... Jennie Bishop

Raising a Modern Day Knight .... Robert Lewis

Revolutionary Parenting: What the Research Shows Really Works .... George Barna

The 7 Habits of Highly Effective Families .... Stephen R. Covey

The Strong Willed Parent; Resolved Conflicts and Restored Relationships; The Angry Parent, Child, and Teen .... Mark Hamby
Life-Transforming Literature on CD or DVD, Lamplighter Ministries 1.888.246.7735

BOOKS FOR YOUR TEEN TO READ

Every Young Man's Battle: Strategies for Victory in the Real World of Sexual Temptation .... Stephen Arterburn & Fred Stoeker

Kissed the Girls and Made Them Cry: Why Women Loose When They Give In .... Lisa Bevere

When God Writes Your Love Story: The Ultimate Approach to Guy/Girl Relationships .... Eric Ludy & Leslie Ludy

WEBSITES

www.RaisingTomorrowsLeaders.net - order books (*Renaissance Kids*) in bulk and access other great resources for parenting and facilitating groups.

www.GenerationsOfVirtue.org - contains great books, DVDs and other materials regarding raising children of character

www.Tips4Moms.com

www.TheRebelution.com - website for Alex & Brett Harris

www.PureExcitement.com - Joe White's website which exists to encourage and challenge America's teenagers to sexual purity and commitment to Christ.